INTERCULTURAL SELF-DEFENCE

Based on the author's 25 years of experience in researching and teaching interculturality, *Intercultural Self-Defence: A Resource Book for Students, Teachers and Researchers* is a compelling exploration of the subtle forces that shape Intercultural Communication Education and Research (ICER).

The Resource Book delves into the adversaries lurking within ICER – indoctrination, intellectual inertia and linguistic indifference – and unveils how they can stifle genuine understanding and growth. Each chapter acts as a critical lens, scrutinising the boundaries between education and indoctrination, the stagnation of thought and the perils of linguistic complacency. The author illustrates the impact of these forces on interculturality and the ethical implications they carry. The book contains a series of activities designed to encourage creative self-reflection and fosters a deeper understanding of the interplay between language, power and interculturality. But it is more than a resource: It is a manifesto for continuous learning, active engagement and the pursuit of a more inclusive and dynamic field of intercultural communication education and scholarship.

Advocating a vigilant and self-reflexive approach, the book will serve as a critical guide for students, teachers and researchers specialising in intercultural research and education to navigate the complexities of interculturality.

Fred Dervin is a renowned scholar in the field of Intercultural Communication Education and Research, serving as a Professor of Multicultural Education at the University of Helsinki (Finland). Over his illustrious career, Dervin has contributed significantly to analyse, interrogate and disrupt discourses of interculturality with over 200 articles and 80 books. His latest books published with Routledge include *The Paradoxes of Interculturality* and *The Routledge Handbook of Critical Interculturality in Communication and Education*. Dervin is included in the Stanford Elsevier List of the world's best scientists (Top 2%).

New Perspectives on Teaching Interculturality

About the Series

This book series publishes original and innovative single-authored and edited volumes contributing robust, new and genuinely global studies to the exciting field of research and practice of interculturality in education. It aims to enrich the current objectives of 'doing' and teaching interculturality in the 21st century by problematising Euro- and Western-centric perspectives and giving a voice to other original and under-explored approaches. The series promotes the search for different epistemologies, cutting-edge interdisciplinarity and the importance of reflexive and critical translation in teaching about this important notion. Finally, *New Perspectives on Teaching Interculturality* serves as a platform for dialogue amongst the global community of educators, researchers, and students.

Series Editor:
Fred Dervin is Professor of multicultural education at the University of Helsinki.

To submit proposals, please contact the series editor Fred Dervin <fred.dervin@helsinki.fi> and Taylor & Francis Publisher Lian Sun <Lian.Sun@taylorandfrancis.com>

Un-writing Interculturality in Education and Research
Edited by Fred Dervin and Hamza R'boul

The Concise Routledge Encyclopaedia of New Concepts for Interculturality
Edited by Fred Dervin, Hamza R'boul and Ning Chen

Intercultural Self-Defence
A Resource Book for Students, Teachers and Researchers
Fred Dervin

Researching Interculturality in Post-Colonial Contexts
Indigenous Perspectives and Beyond
Edited by Vander Tavares

For a full list of titles in this series, visit www.routledge.com/New-Perspectives-on-Teaching-Interculturality/book-series/NPTI

INTERCULTURAL SELF-DEFENCE

A Resource Book for Students, Teachers and Researchers

Fred Dervin

Designed cover image: IC1396 by Guoliang Zhao (2024)

First published 2025
by Routledge
605 Third Avenue, New York, NY 10158

and by Routledge
4 Park Square, Milton Park, Abingdon, Oxon, OX14 4RN

Routledge is an imprint of the Taylor & Francis Group, an informa business

© 2025 Fred Dervin

The right of Fred Dervin to be identified as author of this work has been asserted in accordance with sections 77 and 78 of the Copyright, Designs and Patents Act 1988.

All rights reserved. No part of this book may be reprinted or reproduced or utilised in any form or by any electronic, mechanical, or other means, now known or hereafter invented, including photocopying and recording, or in any information storage or retrieval system, without permission in writing from the publishers.

Trademark notice: Product or corporate names may be trademarks or registered trademarks, and are used only for identification and explanation without intent to infringe.

ISBN: 978-1-032-99792-6 (hbk)
ISBN: 978-1-032-99895-4 (pbk)
ISBN: 978-1-003-60644-4 (ebk)

DOI: 10.4324/9781003606444

Typeset in Times New Roman
by Newgen Publishing UK

N.N.-Lootus-W.W.-H. 'lle
Vuosi 2024 oli kamala.
Kiitos energiasta ja inspiraatiosta. To the memory of Leena Mummo. It is hoped that through this book, a part of her spirit will live on, and that the world may know the impact one person can have when they choose to be kind, funny and caring.
F.D.

CONTENTS

List of illustrations		*viii*
Étagère 1	Intercultural self-defence against absurd worlds	1
Étagère 2	Indoctrination on the intercultural stage: A play of (hidden) forces	18
Étagère 3	Intellectual inertia unbound	53
Étagère 4	Language indifference and nonchalance: Crises of language and interculturality	87
Étagère 5	A guide to intercultural self-defence: Breaking free?	113
Étagère 6	Defend yourself and … others …	147
Index		*162*

ILLUSTRATIONS

Figure 1.1	The author's hand	6
Figure 1.2	The mysterious object /神喻 (Dervin, 2021, 19 × 27 cm)	10
Figure 1.3	Content of the Resource Book	14
Figure 2.1	The Chinese ideologeme of *Community of a Shared Future* as summarised by a group of Chinese students in higher education	27
Figure 2.2	Making doctrines, ideologies and beliefs unquestionable and accepted	36
Figure 2.3	An example of a nudge targeted at tourists in Venice (Italy)	40
Figure 2.4	Chinese street poster urging people to behave in a 'civilized way'	41
Figure 2.5	Slogan about globalisation	45
Figure 3.1	A simple definition of intellectual inertia? "When I stopped thinking"	58
Figure 3.2	Emoji-writing	79
Figure 4.1	Jiǎ dà kōng /假大空 (Dervin, 2023; 17.5 × 26.3 cm)	96
Figure 4.2	French Republican values as a slogan sold at a souvenir shop in Paris (France)	102
Figure 5.1	'Don't worry about the government'	117
Figure 5.2	*Orpheus's Mirror* by Cocteau (1969) showing the musician entering the Underworld	119
Figure 5.3	The Uccello's clock at the Duomo	124
Figure 5.4	Zhan-station	136
Figure 6.1	Dealing with the complexities of interculturality	153
Figure 6.2	2 + 2 = 5	154
Table 5.1	Summary of main ideas from previous Étagères	116

Étagère 1[1]

INTERCULTURAL SELF-DEFENCE AGAINST ABSURD WORLDS

1. Postludi[2]

Let's *beginish* (begin + finish) with a dream that I had when I was finishing writing this Resource Book.

A Finnish winter landscape, host of a piano concert. The white canvas of snow and silence, at first. I sit with the ('diverse'-looking) audience in a frosty embrace, hand-in-hand, united by anticipation. The pianist, with hands as gentle as the falling snow, plays melodies that warm our hearts. Debussy's piece *Reflets dans l'eau* (Reflections in the water) paints images of watery space and perfumes the cold brisk air. Smiles are the only sound, as the music weaves our shared bliss. The piano's keys in gentle sway. Harmony, so soft and fair. Different souls, one melody. The modesty of the scene.

The dreamer awakes. My slumber undone. Scrolling through headlines, from wars to crises, I toss, turn and find that insomnia has won. The concert is over. The blend of happy and diverse souls from the audience, in the snow, are resting. Their hands part.

> Country W to return a trove of nearly 300 history-spanning antiquities to Country D.
> Country X strikes County B as the West pushes for ceasefire.
> 'Education of hatred': Killing of boy sparks soul searching in Country A over rising nationalism.
> LGBTQ+ individuals may have greater risk of poor brain health, likely due to 'minority stress'.
> Singer stayed in $100,000 per night suite in the Middle East's 'best hotel'.
> World's longest-serving death row inmate was just declared innocent.

DOI: 10.4324/9781003606444-1

"One believes things because one has been conditioned to believe them" (Huxley, 2022: 72). It was only a dream. *Deceitfulness, deception, dissimilation, distortion, fabrication, falsehood, fraudulence, hypocrisy, lip-service, pretence, spuriousness, treachery, unreliability …*

Absurd worlds …

2. Why is self-defence needed in intercultural research and education?

This Resource Book is about intercultural self-defence, which I position as *the multifaceted process of protecting our mind and beliefs from (too much) manipulation, deception and control in the way we speak about, deal with and do interculturality in research and education.* This type of self-defence involves being aware of tactics that can be used to influence or alter our thinking and taking steps to ensure that e.g. our beliefs and decisions are based on criticality and reflexivity in front of external influences. In the book, we shall explore critical thinking or how to develop the habit of questioning the information about interculturality presented to us, analysing the logic, evidence and potential biases behind arguments found in the literature and in educational settings. Taking the time to reflect on our beliefs and the reasons behind them is essential in these complex processes and the Resource Book, through its multifaceted activities, asks you to slow down and to consider the points that I make through discussions, creative moments and reflexive activities, and (most importantly) *at various speeds*. Understanding different forms of e.g. propaganda will also occupy us in the book when we try to familiarise ourselves with common techniques so that we can recognise them. In writing and designing this book, I was somehow inspired by Franz Kafka (2016: 16) who wrote: "I think we ought to read only the kind of books that wound and stab us". This Resource Book aims to (*really*) 'shake' and 'disrupt' our thinking about interculturality.

Why would we need to self-defend in intercultural research and education? Is there a need for doing so? A few critical observers have noted that the broad field of Intercultural Communication Education and Research (ICER hereafter) has been witnessing many problems for decades (amongst others: Shen, 2023; Huckle, 2024; R'boul & Dervin, 2023; Busch, 2024; Jung, 2024). Here is a list of issues that I considered highly problematic in our field at the time of writing:

- There seems to be **an obvious lack of attention being paid to the importance of intercultural communication and critical interculturality** *within* academic and educational work around the very notion of interculturality. The emphasis tends to be on *the outside* ('students', 'some teachers' but also 'minorities', 'migrants'), with us interculturalists ignoring our own positions towards and influences on what we do with and say about interculturality.
- I have proposed that, considering the polysemy of the notion, **interculturality needs to be redefined *again and again***, emphasising that it is a dynamic and

interactive process rather than a static and fixed attribute (Dervin, 2023; Chen, 2024). At this stage, the word tends to be used in often empty and uncritical ways, as if it were a monolith.
- Many **concepts such as *culture* and *intercultural competence*** still lead our broad field and, although they have been criticised in other fields such as anthropology or by some interculturalists (e.g. Yu, 2023), they remain dominant.
- Many ideas, concepts and 'theories' are **used like *automata*** ('robots') rather than being critically evaluated, reshaped and even discarded. Passed onto us by powerful academic forces, usually from the west,[3] often with the help of some gatekeepers from the Global South, they have a lot of (economic, ideological) value and can support publishing, obtaining funding or promotion. However, these can too easily silence multivoicedness, opposition and rebellion.
- **eurocentrism** still influences the field, although multiple calls for the decolonisation of interculturality are heard around the planet (Dasli & Simpson, 2023).
- **How multilingual discussions of interculturality in ICER affects and promotes** our understanding and doing of interculturality is still largely overlooked (Shen, 2023).
- The presence of **insular communities in intercultural research and education**, (self-)divided by ideologies, languages, politics, paradigms, etc., is unavoidable. Yet these create political silos, reciprocal unintelligibility, hierarchies of all kinds and oppressed-oppressing relations (neo-colonialism). Intercultural scholars and educators from e.g. marginalised communities and low-income countries often experience biases and inequalities.
- Probably, *most importantly*: **The lingering tendency towards scientism** in ICER, which mistakenly views research as entirely objective and politically neutral. The economic-political nature of ICER should encourage scholars and educators to critically reflect on political issues within the field.

Other reasons as to why, as intercultural students, educators and researchers, we need to learn to self-defend have to do with the fact that, as individuals, we are not always in control of what we say and think (words might be interpreted differently in English*es* for example; power relations between interlocutors might lead to one of us practising self-censorship …). Furthermore, doing research and education requires from us to be with others and to communicate with them constantly, which means that, depending on contexts and interlocutors, we might be more or less calm, confident, comfortable asking questions and answering them, etc. Finally, we need to develop what I have referred to as *criticality of criticality* in academic and educational contexts where everyone claims to be critical while forgetting to turn their critiques systematically towards what they think or say (Dervin, 2022).

[Pause 1: A note on *self-* in self-defence]
I want to make sure here that there is no misunderstanding around the idea of self-defence. Self does not mean that we can defend ourselves against the three

4 Intercultural Self-Defence

adversaries to be discussed in the book, all by *ourselves*. This would, obviously, make no sense. There is no way we can extirpate ourselves from our constant embedding into contexts, (in-direct) relations, discourses, ideologies, etc. Based on Levinas' lecture notes on teaching, Castillo (2024: 585) reminds us that:

> teaching serves as a unique link between the personal and the universal, between interiority and exteriority. It gives the subject a means by which to see the reverse side of things, to leave the natural attitude and move toward the subjectivity of the other and to things as themselves.

The author adds (Castillo, 2024: 585):

> One cannot think alone; reasoning is therefore a quest to reconcile subjective understanding with intersubjective meaning-making. To know objectively means to know together with others. Knowledge is thus not a property of being but a reconciliation between being and the other.

Self- in this Resource Book intends to problematise this joint meaning-making – while attempting to step out of these relationships temporarily and imperfectly, with an aim to 'reconcile' self and other within the context of ICER. *I am not naïve*: there is no miraculous recipe to indoctrination, intellectual inertia and language indifference but a need to observe, examine and critique them with *and through* others (our other contradictory selves too) in the continuum of self-other. Maybe through these never-ending and complex processes of confrontation and dialogue, we could (probably) make small differences in ICER ...

3. Getting our hands dirty

When one looks at the symbols that have been used for self-defence in different parts of the world, one notices that many references to *the hand* have been made (Wilson, 2010). For example:

- *Crossed arms* over the chest can be a sign of self-defence, a barrier against violence.
- *Fist bump* can be a sign of solidarity or readiness, often among individuals who are prepared to protect themselves/others.
- Placing *a hand on one's hip* can be a sign of confidence and readiness to engage in self-defence.
- *The Karate chop gesture* in many 'Eastern' martial arts (a chopping motion with the hand) symbolises self-defence skills.
- The motion of quickly turning the hand with the palm facing outward (the so-called *flipped hand*) can be a warning or a sign of self-protection.
- Finally, *thumbs up*, while often considered as a sign of approval, in certain contexts, it can be used to signal that one is prepared to defend oneself.

In English the very word *hand* is found in very interesting phrases and idioms (and in other languages!), such as: *getting our hands dirty* (engaging in an important activity that may not be pleasing); *out of hand* (out of control); *experiencing something first hand* (experiencing it oneself); *knowing like the back of one's hand* (knowing something very well); *giving a hand* (helping someone); *forcing someone's hand* (compelling them to do something); *being underhanded* (being deceitful); *washing one's hands of somebody/something* (refusing to be held responsible for or involved with somebody/something). [Are there similar or special idioms and phrases containing the word hand in the language(s) that you know?]. It is also interesting to note that the very word hand in English comes from Proto-Germanic and Old English for *power*, *control* and *possession*. Contrarily, in Indo-European languages like French, the word is based on Latin for *protection* and *guardianship*. Last, I note that, in the Finnish language (which is not an Indo-European language), *käsi* can refer to both *the arm* (shoulder to the fingers, elbow to the fingers) and *the hand* (wrist to fingers).

As students, scholars and educators of interculturality, the hand is the basis for what we do. For instance, it is a powerful and evocative symbol for writing with a pen, a touchscreen and/or a keyboard (and even a brush if one is also an artist-writer). Throughout history, the hand has been used to inscribe texts on various surfaces, from clay tablets to parchment. It is linked to the evolution of writing systems and the preservation of knowledge and often associated with creativeness and the production of art, literature and even music (e.g. Schmandt-Besserat, 2010). *The hand is a means of personal expression.* Just as it can create a unique signature, the hand can also craft a distinctive written 'voice' and serve as a means for self-defence. Finally, as a reminder, the hand can also be a tool and a symbol of oppression and violence!

Figure 1.1. shows an artistic rendition of my own right hand – my main tool as an intellectual and a writer (NB: although I was born left-handed, I was forced to shift hands when I was a child. This was not an unknown practice in the 1970s).

Consider these questions: How does it feel to be able to 'see' the hand of the one who is writing/speaking to you in this Resource Book? Does seeing my hand make the reading experience somehow more 'interpersonal'? How does this representation of my right hand influence the way you imagine who I am as a person, a scholar and educator and/or writer? Would seeing my real hand change the way you have imagined who I am through my texts or since you started reading this Resource Book?

Also: How often have you looked at your own hands and reflected on their (lack of) flexibility, their shape, their colour, their special features (a scar)? Although we often focus on the entire body and especially on the face when we think of identity, how do your hands contribute to making you who you (think you) are and for others? How much do you feel the hand symbolises well (or not) the central idea of *self-defence* in this book?

6 Intercultural Self-Defence

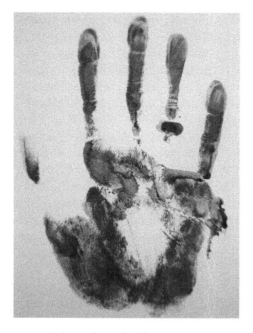

FIGURE 1.1 The author's hand.

[Pause 2: Hand activities]
In what follows and in order to take a short break to digest what I have discussed until now in this first Étagère, let us reflect further on the power and weakness of the hand as a symbol for working on interculturality, with a few activities.

A. Research and present on the role of the hand in historical scientific discoveries or research methods. Discuss how the physical act of doing research and teaching has evolved and the potential implications for current practices in ICER.

B. Create shadow puppets using your hands and then perform a short sketch that illustrates e.g. a research dilemma, ethical issue or teaching situation related to interculturality. Discuss how the shadows can represent the hidden aspects of ICER, such as biases/unintended consequences or miscommunication.

C. Draw your hands like Figure 1.1. and analyse the drawing for personal symbolism related to your research/educational experiences. Share and discuss what the drawing reveals about your personal feelings towards intercultural research and education, such as control, precision and/or uncertainty.

D. Explore how hand gestures can communicate complex ideas without words, similar to how research findings can be interpreted in various ways. Discuss the importance of e.g. non-verbal communication in research, such as body language during teaching, interviews or the visual presentation of data (e.g. Navarro, 2018).

E. Create artwork that represents an intercultural research/educational concept or process using only your hands (e.g. handprints, hand tracings). Talk about how art can be used to communicate complex research and teaching ideas and the value of creativity in research and education.

F. While working with others on e.g. a research paper or an essay, each team member contributes a section, symbolised by a handprint at the end of their section. Discuss the collaborative nature of research and education, and how different perspectives can enrich a study/a teaching situation.

This Resource Book is about cooperation too. *Let's join hands!*

4. The three foes of ICER

This Resource Book is based on three problematic aspects of intercultural research and education identified in section 2 that we need to address: *indoctrination* (Étagère 2), *intellectual inertia* (Étagère 3) and *language indifference and nonchalance* (Étagère 4). They are defined minimally as follows in the book:

Indoctrination (Étagère 2)
(a) Lack of encouragement for criticality towards interculturality in research and education.
(b) (Hidden) dismissal of alternative viewpoints in the construction and dissemination of knowledge deemed to be legitimate.

Intellectual inertia (Étagère 3)
(a) Tendency to maintain the status quo or old patterns of thinking when faced with new information or changes.
(b) Lack of motivation to move forward in one's unrethinking in the way interculturality is taught and researched.

Language indifference and nonchalance (Étagère 4)
(a) Lack of and/or lazy interest and concern for language in research and education.
(b) Sleepwalking through language.

Let me try to clarify by means of a small narrative what I am trying to 'place my hands on' with these three adversaries of intercultural research and education.

In 2019 I attended an event at an international school in a major Asian capital. Titled *Navigating the Tides of Intercultural Communication*, the event promised insights into the art of 'bridging cultural divides'. The stage was set with a minimalist design, a solitary podium bathed in spotlight. The first speaker (introduced as 'a communication hero' and a 'world champion of public speaking') took the stage, a charismatic figure with a confident stride. Yet, as the talk unfolded, a sense of déjà vu crept in. Phrases like *celebrating diversity* and *embracing differences* were tossed around like confetti, their meanings diluted by overuse. The audience nodded in agreement, but the words felt hollow and stripped of their potency. Each subsequent speaker echoed the same sentiments, their speeches a mosaic of clichés – and each were thanked with overly enthusiastic but unconvincing evaluations such as 'inspiring', 'thought-provoking' and 'awesome'. *Unity in diversity* and *global village* were brandied about, yet the depth of understanding seemed to be missing. There were references to Gandhi, Oprah Winfrey and even Napoleon to support the somewhat technicist perspectives aimed at 'winning over' misunderstandings and communication failure. The language was 'interculturally correct', but it was also void, a shell of what could have been a profound exploration of human interaction. Old ideologies of biased 'cultural' difference were filling the speeches to the brim. By the end of the event, a sense of disappointment settled over me. The potential for a transformative discussion had been squandered on banalities. The event had become a parade of safe and sanitized statements, devoid of the courage to delve into the complexities, instabilities, nuances and impossibilities of interculturality. I felt that it was a missed opportunity to challenge and provoke thought and for participants and speakers to connect meaningfully.

Many readers would probably argue that this is some kind of TED Talk event so, of course, it had to be that way: *entertaining*, *'cool'* and *somewhat formulaic*. The three foes that interest us here are all obvious in this short narrative. There are signs of *indoctrination* (the speakers seem to 'repeat' and 'recite' banalities about interculturality, which may sound critical to the lay ear; they selectively use quotes from entertainers and politicians to solely *illustrate* but not to *question*); *intellectual inertia* (as a consequence of indoctrination; questions about what is being said are not asked; see the presence of empty evaluations after each talk) and *language indifference and nonchalance* (many words and concepts are introduced but only superficially positioned or simply put on the table).

[*A dirty truth*: At times, academia and education can also seem to be playing the same game as far as interculturality is concerned. Frightening words from Orwell (2009: 59) then come to mind: "You will be hollow. We shall squeeze you empty, and then we shall fill you with ourselves".]

With alarming world news about international relations today, interculturality appears to be this invisible mountain for which we have in fact done so little in research and education. Of course, this is not really true since hundreds of publications on the topic appear in different fields of research every week. Millions of euros are spent every year for research and education to train and study what could be done about interculturality. However, since 2020 (although this started before) interculturality as a notion, an ideology and a hyper-complex phenomenon, has fractured, crumbled, cracked, shattered. This anfractuous (from Proto-European for 'breaking' 'around') notion is often the target of 糊弄 (hùnòng) in Chinese, which means to do something half-heartedly while pretending to be earnest – even in research and education. By speaking empty words about interculturality, rehearsing the worst (and often subtle-ish) clichés about what we do and say to each other, sanitising realities (e.g. avoidance of discussing conflicts), etc., we confirm an intuition that I have had for many decades and that many will find disturbing: *Interculturality is a mere performance; interculturality is in fact impossible.* As such, interculturality as the ideal of balancing 'perfectly' otherness with otherness will never work. No one can ever be ready to co-construct fair and working equalities with others. As humans, we feed on inequality and injustice. Our environment, ideological cocoons that force us to believe in the sanctity of certain words, arguments, slogans and every aspect of what we do and say lead to these issues. Although slogans to 'banish' them abound in our worlds today, realistically there is very little we can do about them in a cannibal capitalistic world (Fraser, 2022), where everything and everyone revolve around money and profit.

About the issue of language, which will be dealt with in Étagère 4, let me say a few words about an art piece I did in 2023 (Figure 1.2.).

Language is a mystery to us all, although it might feel 'normal', 'obvious' and 'natural'. Language is often (mis-)judged for being 'beautiful', 'romantic', but also 'difficult', 'a-logical', 'ugly' … Language is in all of us and yet it is external to us. It belongs to us and yet it is a stranger. In this art piece, I represent language as a shiny oval in the middle of a pond, which we admire, loathe and fear somehow. Language is a mysterious object that we are all capable of examining, discussing and deconstructing. The words that we keep producing through language together with others deserve our full attention, maybe more than before. What they do to us and others must also be at the centre of attention. For Barthes (1993: 461): "language – the performance of a language – is neither reactionary nor progressive; it is quite simply fascist" (see Étagère 4).

5. Special features of the Resource Book

{The word *resource* is from Latin for to rally, raise again (see resurgent, etymonline.com, 2024c). A Resource Book should help us stand up and raise again …}

{With this book I am a companion, not a master, not a superior being. *I am becoming with you*, dear reader.}

10 Intercultural Self-Defence

FIGURE 1.2 The mysterious object/神喻 (Dervin, 2021, 19 × 27 cm).

{This book is to be read and 'practised' by those who have submitted others or been submitted to indoctrination, inertia and language indifference and nonchalance in ICER.
My assumption is that we have all been in these positions.}

{When I told a friend that I was writing a book about indoctrination, intellectual inertia and language indifference and nonchalance, he sent me a text message: "Very hard concepts to cover up. Everything is connected to everything. To separate is tough".
In response to his text, I wrote: "Indeed, they are not separated but our minds must take them apart to reconnect them".}

{Some of you might be wondering why a scholar based in Finland (Europe), dares to propose to help you 'self-defend' interculturally. What are his credentials as a privileged white man (maybe?) whose life experience is so different from you? What does he really know about interculturality, beyond his 'small' Finnish world? He only speaks six languages which are mostly Indo-European. How does this qualify him to talk about language, especially beyond the west?

Intercultural Self-Defence Against Absurd Worlds **11**

You might also be wondering if I am going to give you some lectures about what to (not) do and say and, thus, brainwashing you into my own ideologies and beliefs. Wait until the end of the book to decide for yourself.}

{Interculturality is universal. It is not anything special. It is you and me, and the whole world. It is not an experience of a selected few.
It is everyone's.}

{Whenever possible, the book includes illustrations and photos to add a unique visual dimension that aims to support conceptualizing the three adversaries and self-defending against them.}

{Those who have read my books before will know that interdisciplinarity is central to my thinking. You will find many references to e.g. philosophers or anthropologists.
The following artists and composers are referred to in the Resource Book. I do encourage you to look into their work while reading the book[4].
Kōbō Abe (1924–1993, writer, Japan)
Samuel Beckett (1906–1989, writer, Ireland)
John Cage (1912–1992, composer, USA)
Alexander Calder (1898–1976, artist, USA)
Jean Cocteau (1889–1963, writer, France)
Duccio di Buoninsegna (ca. 1255–1319, artist, Italy)
Paolo Di Dono (1397–1475, artist, Italy)
Fyodor Dostoevsky (1821–1881, writer, Russia)
Morton Feldman (1926–1987, composer, USA)
Max Frisch (1911–1991, writer, Switzerland)
Hedningarna (Finland/Sweden, folk band)
Aldous Huxley (1894–1963, writer, UK)
Franz Kafka (1883–1914, writer, Czech-born)
George Orwell (1903–1950, writer, UK)
Jorma Panula (conductor and composer, Finland)
Arnold Schönberg (1875–1951, composer, Austria)
Van Gogh (1853–1890, painter, The Netherlands)
Rebecca Saunders (composer, UK)
Dmitri Shostakovich (1906–1975, composer, Russia)
Xu Bing (artist, China)
Yevgeny Zamyatin (1884–1937, novelist, Russia).}

{Étagères 2, 3 and 4 are structured the same way although the Étagère sections are 'numbered' differently to create some kind of cognitive disruption in us.}
Although the Étagères have similar structures, they move forward in often unsettling ways, with e.g. pauses having been included to urge us to take a break

to think and reflect on the dis-/connections between the ideas, arguments and narratives that I share. In order to do so, I have tried to include creative aspects such as a few poems, invented dialogues and short stories as well as discussions of paintings and pieces of music. Don't get discouraged by the impression that you will get that things don't flow seamlessly – I was just trying to recreate what interculturality as a phenomenon and notion forces us to experience.

Use these distractions, pauses and shifts, as ways of taking the time to go back to your thinking and to clear some space in your mind.

- Étagères 2–4 start with *five basic questions* to help you reflect on what you already know about the three 'foes'.
- This is followed by a section called *'yarn'*, i.e. stories from fiction. The word yarn has its etymologies in different languages, referring to e.g. intestine, entrails but also spinning fibre or wool (etymonline.com, 2024d). Spinning a yard (telling a story) is here meant to both link up to our own background knowledge and life experience, and to stimulate further thinking about the content of the Étagères.
- This is followed by *conceptual and experimental discussions*, based on interdisciplinary literature reviews.
- The end of Étagères 2–4 contains three sections. I start with *fragments*, a writing technique that I have used since 2020 as a means to embrace the complex, multifaceted nature of interculturality (Dervin, 2022). By presenting my thoughts in short, disjointed pieces, I wish to mirror the fragmented and sometimes contradictory experiences individuals have when navigating interculturality. This style of writing is a reflection of my belief that interculturality is not a singular and/or unified concept but rather a collection of perspectives that are constantly evolving and intersecting. I argue that fragment writing allows for a more organic and less structured exploration of ideas, which is fitting for a subject like interculturality that resists simple definitions. It also encourages you readers to engage with the material in a non-linear way, potentially leading to a deeper, more personal connection with the content. All in all, my use of fragments can be seen as an invitation for you to bring your own experiences and interpretations, thereby fostering a more dynamic and interactive learning and reflexive process. I also note that this approach challenges traditional academic writing styles, which often prioritise 'coherence' and 'linear argumentation' (Knepper & Deckard, 2016). By breaking away from these imaginary conventions, I aim to disrupt the notion that there can be a single, authoritative narrative on interculturality.
- The fragments are followed by *a vitrine* (a glass showcase or cabinet used for displaying objects) which contains (invented) narratives that aim to help us gather our thoughts and put what we discussed in the Étagères to the test.
- To conclude each Étagère (2–4), Escapades propose short summaries of the main ideas. Here again I am experimenting with disrupting writing (e.g. no punctuation between sentences, no capital letters) to force us to focus carefully

on the words used to summarise the main takeaways. An escapade means breaking loose from rules or restraints ...

{Étagères 5 and 6 serve both as discussions and (temporary) conclusions to the book. They also propose further stimulating activities to reflect on and practise intercultural self-defence *ad vitam aeternam.*}
{Figure 1.3. describes the content of each Étagère.

Each Étagère builds upon the previous one, gradually deepening our understanding of interculturality within ICER. Étagère 1 lays the foundation, while Étagère 2 introduces challenges to genuine understanding. Étagère 3 continues by exploring the resistance to new ideas, and Étagère 4 focuses on a critical tool often overlooked – language. Finally, Étagère 5 compiles the insights gained, providing potentially actionable advice.}

[Pause 3: *Look at the cover of the Resource Book*]
The cover of this book contains a picture of IC1396, also known as the Elephant's Trunk Nebula. This picture was provided to me by a Chinese friend whose hobby is to take pictures of the galaxy. I chose this picture because it looks somewhat enigmatic, intriguing and inspirational. What is more, I cannot help but see the bust and face of a person, looking straight into the eyes of another person, whose body cannot be clearly seen – but that person is definitely there!
[NB: The word nebula is from Latin for a cloud, mist, smoke and even exhalation.]
IC1396 is an emission nebula located in the constellation Cepheus, approximately 2,400 light-years away from our earth. This nebula is an active region of star formation, containing young stars and cavities blown out by the stellar winds of these stars. At the centre of the nebula is a gigantic young star, HD206267, whose radiation illumines most of the nebula (Weikard et al., 1996).
In the following Étagères and beyond, I would like us to use IC1396 as a metaphor for the type of intellectual liberation that we are looking for. Let me make the assumption that the process of star formation in the nebula can be likened to the awakening and growth of our individual critical thinking. Just as dust and gas in the nebula merge under gravity to eventually form stars, we can amass knowledge and good judgement through learning and thinking, towards self-liberation and self-defence. What is more, the young stars in the nebula, with their intense radiation and stellar winds, influence their surroundings, potentially symbolising the power of new and fresh ideas to change established structures and concepts, promoting e.g. 'epistemic advancement and justice'. This is why the interplay of light and dark areas within IC1396 can be likened to the struggle between *knowledge and ignorance* but also *judgement and prejudice*. In our attempt to manoeuvre intellectual liberation as students, educators and scholars, we must navigate through these complex regions to reach a higher level of understanding and ... *freedom.*

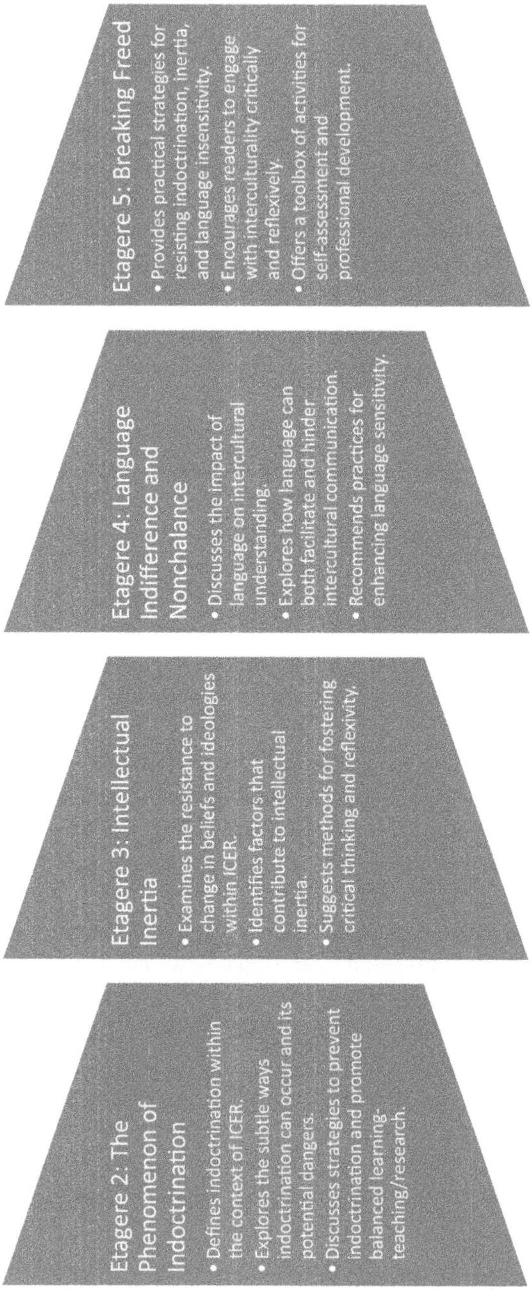

14 Intercultural Self-Defence

Etagere 2: The Phenomenon of Indoctrination
- Defines indoctrination within the context of ICER.
- Explores the subtle ways indoctrination can occur and its potential dangers.
- Discusses strategies to prevent indoctrination and promote balanced learning-teaching/research.

Etagere 3: Intellectual Inertia
- Examines the resistance to change in beliefs and ideologies within ICER.
- Identifies factors that contribute to intellectual inertia.
- Suggests methods for fostering critical thinking and reflexivity.

Etagere 4: Language Indifference and Nonchalance
- Discusses the impact of language on intercultural understanding.
- Explores how language can both facilitate and hinder intercultural communication.
- Recommends practices for enhancing language sensitivity.

Etagere 5: Breaking Freed
- Provides practical strategies for resisting indoctrination, inertia, and language insensitivity.
- Encourages readers to engage with interculturality critically and reflexively.
- Offers a toolbox of activities for self-assessment and professional development.

FIGURE 1.3 Content of the Resource Book.

I also wish to comment on the fact that the extensive coverage of the nebula in the sky can symbolise the limitless possibilities of intellectual liberation through intercultural self-defence. Our intellect has tremendous potential, just like the countless stars in the nebula, each capable of shining in their own right …

I am also interested in the contrast between the bright stars and the surrounding dark dust clouds in the nebula (again: observe the cover of this Resource Book) to symbolise the struggle between knowledge, indoctrination and ignorance in ICER.

Last, as mentioned earlier, IC1396 is *thousands of light-years away from us*, which can remind us that the path to intellectual liberation in relation to interculturality may be long and distant – and even endless! However, just as we can observe distant nebulae, we also have the capacity to explore and understand our complex worlds *a little* through learning and contemplation.

Are you ready to embark on an expedition to new territories of interculturality with me? Are you ready to confront *our* three foes?

Close your eyes for a minute and imagine what is coming.

[………………………………………………………………………………………
……………………………………………………………………………………….]

Done?
Off we go …

Notes

1   In the book, instead of the word *chapter*, Étagère is used. An étagère is a piece of furniture consisting of ranks of open shelves to display items and books in a multi-layered structure. This can metaphorically represent the organisation of this Resource Book, where each chapter (or 'shelf') showcases a different aspect or part of the 'story', with the narrative unfolding layer by layer as one moves from one chapter to the next. It also suggests that each chapter is a compartment where a part of the narrative is presented for your consideration, much like how items are displayed on the shelves of an étagère. Chapters are often used to denote a pause, a change in time or place or a shift in perspective. An étagère, with its distinct separations between shelves, could symbolise these transitions within the narrative about interculturality in research and education, providing a visual representation of the breaks between chapters. Each Étagère in this Resource Book aims to display a wide range of 'items' from multiple fields of knowledge, mythologies, fiction, the arts and other languages. My aim is to force our heads out of the boxes that we have constructed around the notion of interculturality by looking at, listening to and experiencing 'otherwise'. I note that the word étagère comes from French *étagère* and from *étage* (i.e., a shelf, story, abode, stage). In Latin *statio* is a station, post, residence (see etymonline.com, 2024a). I use this word to start destabilising the way we usually speak in and construct e.g. a book about interculturality in academia. I argue that by doing so we can also move forward with our unrethinking about the notion. I also note that in this book I will use the verb unrethink (without hyphens) to refer to the necessarily hyper-reflexive need to both deconstruct and reconstruct (simultaneously) our knowledges, beliefs and ideologies concerning interculturality.

2   Finnish word for 'postlude', a concluding performance, a conclusion to an action. -*lude* is from Latin for to play (see ludicrous, etymonline.com, 2024b). Considering the difficult times that we were experiencing as I was writing this Resource Book, and the serious issue of not caring for 'reforming' intercultural communication education and research, I prefer to start the book with a postlude (postludi) rather than a prelude (preludi in Finnish), not to open with too optimistic a perspective or to raise false hope in what this Resource Book could achieve ... The reader will note that the book ends with a preludi with a more positive tone.
3   I refrain from using capital letters on the words west(ern) or eurocentric/eurocentrism in this volume out of respect for all those who have suffered and are (still) suffering from colonialism from this 'intimidating' side of the world. What constitutes the west is of course contested. Clear epistemic inequalities are occurring within this imaginary space too (see Fishberg et al., 2023; on Europe as heterogenous space: Gasser, 2021).
4   In the book, lists of names do not necessarily follow alphabetical orders. In some cases, I have reversed the order of the English alphabet to create disruption in thinking.

References

Barthes, R (1993). *A Barthes Reader* (edited by S. Sontag) (pp. 457–458). Vintage.
Busch, D. (2024). Post qualitative inquiry into critical interculturality. In: Dervin, F. (ed.). *The Routledge Handbook of Critical Interculturality in Communication and Education* (pp. 261–278). Routledge.
Castillo, K. (2024). "Society is the present of teaching": Teaching as a phenomenon in Levinas's unedited lecture notes. *Education Theory 74*, 572–586. https://doi.org/10.1111/edth.12658
Chen, N. (2024). *Preparing Teachers and Students for Diversity and Interculturality in Higher Education.* Helsinki University Press.
Dasli, M. & Simpson, A. (2023). Introducing intercultural communication pedagogy and the question of the other. *Pedagogy, Culture & Society 31*(2), 221–235. https://doi.org/10.1080/14681366.2022.2164339
Dervin, F. (2022). *Interculturality in Fragments. A Reflexive Approach.* Springer.
Dervin, F. (2023). *Communicating Around Interculturality in Research and Education.* Routledge.
Etymonline.com (2024a). *Étagère.* www.etymonline.com/word/etagere#etymonline_v_32746
Etymonline.com (2024b). *Prelude.* www.etymonline.com/word/prelude#etymonline_v_19415
Etymonline.com (2024c). *Resource.* www.etymonline.com/word/resource#etymonline_v_12902
Etymonline.com (2024d). Yarn. www.etymonline.com/word/yarn#etymonline_v_4936
Fishberg, R., Larsen, A. G. & Kropp, K. (2023). The 'where' of EU social science collaborations: How epistemic inequalities and geopolitical power asymmetries persist in research about Europe. *The Sociological Review 0*(0). https://doi.org/10.1177/00380261231201473
Fraser, N. (2022). *Cannibal Capitalism: How our System is Devouring Democracy, Care, and the Planet – and What We Can Do.* Verso.
Gasser, L. (2021). *East and South.* Routledge.
Huckle, J. (2024). Beyond "Interculturalspeak": The need for more critical approaches to intercultural understanding in international schools. In: Barker, M., Hansen, R. &

Hammer, L. (eds.). *Handbook of Research on Critical Issues and Global Trends in International Education* (pp. 184–211). IGI Global.

Huxley, A. (2022). *The Complete Works of Aldous Huxley*. Strelbytskyy Multimedia Publishing.

Jung, C. S. (2024). Decolonial philosophies and complex communication as praxis. *Philosophies 9*(5), 142. https://doi.org/10.3390/philosophies9050142

Kafka, F. (2016). *Letters to Friends, Family & Editors*. Schocken Books.

Knepper, W. & Deckard, S. (2016). Towards a Radical World Literature: Experimental Writing in a Globalizing World. *ariel: A Review of International English Literature 47*(1), 1–25. https://dx.doi.org/10.1353/ari.2016.0018

Navarro, J. (2018). *The Dictionary of Body Language*. Harper Thorsons.

Orwell, G. (2009). *1984*. Infobase Holdings, Inc.

R'boul, H. & Dervin, F. (2023). *Flexing Interculturality: Further Critiques, Hesitations, and Intuitions*. Routledge.

Schmandt-Besserat, D. (2010). *Before Writing* (Volume II). University of Texas Press.

Shen, H. (2023). Bilingual postgraduates' potentials for original research by translanguaging for theorizing. *Beijing International Review of Education 4*(4), 703–723. https://doi.org/10.1163/25902539-04040012

Weikard, H., Wouterloot, J. G. A., Castets, A., Winnerwisser, G. & Sugitani, K. (1996). The structure of the IC1396 region. *Astronomy and Astrophysics 309*(2), 581–611.

Wilson, F. R. (2010). *The Hand: How Its Use Shapes the Brain, Language, and Human Culture*. Vintage.

Yu, H. (2023). A skeptic's guide to "intercultural communication" – Debunking the "intercultural" and rethinking "culture". *Language and Semiotic Studies, 9*(2), 163–184. https://doi.org/10.1515/lass-2023-0014

Étagère 2

INDOCTRINATION ON THE INTERCULTURAL STAGE

A play of (hidden) forces

Étagère 2 …

- Defines indoctrination within the context of ICER.
- Explores the subtle ways indoctrination can occur and its potential threats.
- Discusses strategies to prevent indoctrination and promote (potentially) more balanced learning-teaching/research.

Five basic questions

a. What could[1] be a definition of indoctrination in the context of ICER?
b. How could indoctrination be distinguished from education or e.g. intercultural training?
c. How could indoctrination occur in different contexts of ICER? What could be the common methods or practices that may lead to indoctrination rather than 'balanced' learning? What role could e.g. institutional policies, curriculum design and research play in trying to prevent indoctrination in ICER?
d. What could be the potential risks or negative outcomes of indoctrination in ICER? How could the concept of indoctrination intersect with e.g. issues of power, privilege and bias in ICER?
e. What strategies could be employed to ensure a (potentially) more balanced and broadminded approach to ICER? How could researchers/teachers ensure that their work on ICER reduce the effects of indoctrination?

1. Yarn I

The topic of indoctrination, understood minimally here as *a lack of encouragement for criticality and the (hidden) dismissal of alternative viewpoints in the construction and dissemination of knowledge deemed to be legitimate*, is found in many (often famous) novels and short stories from the west and elsewhere, published especially in the 20th century, with many of them classified today as 'dystopian literature' (i.e. fiction that describes some form of dark future). Let us 'spin a few yarns' in what follows by discussing four such novels (two from the west and two from the 'East'), published between 1924 and 1964 (in chronological order):

- *We* (1924/1993) by Russian novelist Yevgeny Zamyatin (1884–1937), portrays a collectivist society where identities and thoughts are suppressed by a futuristic totalitarian regime called OneState. In this society, people have become mere numbers (e.g. D-503) without Christian names, have to wear the same uniform and eat chemically-transformed foods. Constant surveillance is taking place in OneState. Ultimately the main character undergoes procedures that remove his ability to reject the government's philosophy caused by a disease referred to as 'imagination' by the authorities. At some point in the novel, D-503 writes in his diary (Zamyatin, 1993: 65): "There is but one truth, and there is but one path to it; and that truth is: four, and that path is: two times two". George Orwell (1942: n.p.), who wrote one of the books to be discussed below, summarised what is occurring in *We* with the following words: "... the rebellion of the primitive human spirit against a rationalised, mechanised, painless world ...". *We* was banned in the Soviet Union and was only published for the first time in Russia in 1988. The book is often considered as a literary ancestor of the next two novels.
- *Brave New World* (1932/2022; Huxley, 2022), a line borrowed from Shakespeare's *The Tempest*, is a classic of dystopian literature. Written by Aldous Huxley (1894–1963), the novel describes a future world guided by 'efficiency' and 'science' (set after the birth of Henry Ford's assembly line which is considered as the beginning of times in the novel) where people are classified according to specific social categories, genetically engineered and psychologically manipulated to fit ideological and societal needs. They are systematically indoctrinated through e.g. drug control and sleep teaching in this society called World State. Maybe, like Zamyatin, Huxley shared a fear of the rapid advancement of technologies in the early 20th century. At the beginning, the novel was badly received as it was perceived to be too negative as a vision of the future.
- *Nineteen-Eighty-Four* (1949/2009) was written by George Orwell (1903–1950) in reaction to nazism and stalinism in Europe and Russia. The society depicted in the novel also makes ample use of thought control and indoctrination, for example, through a 'Ministry of Truth'. Many 'concepts' from this novel have become notorious to discuss freedom, democracy, etc. These include 'Big

Brother', 'thought police' and 'doublethink'. Set in 1984 the novel occurs in a place governed by an all-controlling party under the leadership of Big Brother. Through a propagandistic language called Newspeak, freedom of speech is limited and trumped, allowing people to merely promote the party's doctrines and slogans (e.g. *Freedom is Slavery*; *War is Peace*; *Ignorance is Strength*; *Big Brother is Watching You* ...). The main character, who symbolises at first 'civilization', loses to the party and becomes indoctrinated. In a similar vein as a character in *We*, he writes in his diary (Orwell, 2009: 47): "Freedom is the freedom to say that two plus two makes four. If that is granted, all else follows".

- Kōbō Abe's novel *The Face of Another* was published in Japanese in 1964 (Abe, 2006). The novel explores the topics of alienation, identity and the struggles for individuality within the confines of specific socio-economic-political expectations and norms. The story deals with a disfigured scientist who creates a mask to be able to 're-enter' society. The mask becomes a substitute self, blurring the lines between reality and deception. By wearing the mask and experiencing the expectations and reactions of others, the main character falls into a deep psychological and existential crisis, questioning his own identity and the (alienating) society that re-defines him. *The Face of Another* also touches upon the idea of the mask as a metaphor for the roles we adopt in society and for how we manipulate and/or escape the products of physical appearance and societal expectations. The power of social conditioning on individualities has to do directly with the concept of indoctrination. By having to change/ 'fake' behaviours and personalities while wearing the mask (and experiencing turmoil), the main character has to deal with indoctrination as external forces oblige him to adopt a new set of beliefs and actions. For Kōbō Abe (1924–1993) the novel symbolises the facelessness of today's world.

Let me summarise what to take away from these first yarns. In the novels, indoctrination relates to:

- Alienation
- Forced repetition of and beliefs in concepts and slogans
- Imposed forms of collectivism in behaviours, thoughts and identities
- Over-reliance on efficiency and science
- Psychological manipulation
- Strong societal expectations
- The lines between reality and deception are blurred (falsehood and facelessness dominate)
- The predominance of one single voice (OneState, World State, all-controlling party)
- The rationalisation and mechanisation of every aspect of a given society and group
- Thought control.

As a consequence, indoctrination leads individuals to the loss of their ability to reject ideas, the power of imagination from their minds and their struggles for individuality.

Dare I say that many of these elements are often experienced, seen and pursued in the very broad field of intercultural communication education and research in different parts of the world? Dare I confess that I have myself been a victim of some of these elements or imposed some of them on my students, readers, colleagues and even friends? *Would this be going too far?* Would the claim that we indoctrinate in our field be an exaggeration, a provocation and/or an obvious reality? For most of us, the idea that both intercultural educators and researchers might indoctrinate is morally disturbing since none of us would deem such practices to be acceptable.

And yet ...

The use of the word indoctrination is not very common in the broad field under review in this Resource Book or in discussions of how interculturality is taught and/or researched. The concepts of propaganda and ideology have been used to determine certain types of knowledge in some parts of the world, promoted by e.g. specific supra-national institutions or in global research published in English, (e.g. Holliday, 2010; Dervin & Simpson, 2020; Dervin, 2023; Zembylas, 2023). In this book, ideologies are considered to be *beliefs*, *agendas* and *orders* that aim to shape discourses and realities about "the way that people ought to live, the forms of life and standards we believe are 'natural' and right and that we therefore feel we should achieve" (Burr, 2015: 95; see Dervin & Peng, 2024). But also: Ideologies are based on (local/global) economic-political beliefs. Ideologies are omnipresent even when one claims not to be ideological. This means that ideologies can deceive people, although they often question the ideologies they are fed with and discard them to replace them with *other ideologies*. In my recent work, I have maintained that any position, concept, paradigm, method in ICER cannot but be ideological because they deal with debated issues such as *self-other*, *co-constructions* (which are always unstable) and *the use of language* to co-lead lives, intellectualities and identities ... (Dervin, 2024). For Thompson (1987), ideologies operate from several interrelated modalities, which can blind people in front of the potential oppressive acts that they face: dissimulation (relations of power are hidden, 'faking' brotherhood and equality), fragmentation (meaning is used to fragment groups to oppose their members), legitimation (institutions serve as ways of supporting domination) and reification (realities are constructed as 'solid' and unchangeable).

2. Excavating indoctrination

2.1. Imbuing with ideas/ideologies, beliefs and opinions

One of the books that I have been trying to buy for years is titled *L'endoctrinement* (indoctrination), published in 1977 by renowned French philosopher of education Olivier Reboul (1925–1992). Until today, I haven't been able to put my hand on any copy of the book since it has been out of print for years. I have not even been able to get hold of a second-hand copy ... What could this tell us about the topic of indoctrination? *Passé? Uninteresting? Or maybe taboo, embarrassing?*

Indoctrination itself shows the potential contradictions that the very word contains (Gatchel, 1959). We know that it comes from Latin for to teach, instruct, a body of knowledge or learning and that, in the mid-19th century, indoctrination started to mean "to imbue with an idea or opinion" (etymonline.com, 2024). Indoctrination is often compared to and confused with similar phenomena in English, including 'brainwashing', 'conditioning', 'cultivation', 'discipline' (drilling, enforcement of rules, rigour), 'edification' (moral improvement, elevation, guidance), 'persuasion', 'propaganda' (newspeak, proselytism, publicity), 'tutelage' (instruction, teaching, training, coaching, inculcation) and even 'socialization'. Indoctrination is also reflected in everyday English phrases such as *drilling someone in something*; *drumming/hammering something into someone*; *dinning something into someone*.

In Chinese, one of the words for indoctrination and indoctrinate is 灌输 [guàn shū], which also translates as instil, inculcate. The first character could mean irrigate in English while the second one transfer and convey. 灌输 can be used to describe the process of guiding running water to where it is needed (irrigate), inculcate e.g. patriotic thoughts. It corresponds to ideological and political education in Chinese schools, whereby e.g. Marxist theories and the Communist Party of China's ideologies are disseminated to students. The word 洗脑 (xǐnǎo) translates literally as brainwashing and is more pejorative than 灌输. The very word for education in Chinese, 教育 (jiàoyù), can also be found in discussions of indoctrination, especially in relation to political and ideological courses in Chinese schools and universities.

Indoctrination in Chinese does not necessarily have a negative meaning, unlike contemporary English and many other languages.

For Puolimatka (1996: 109):

Although the word "indoctrination" in the English language [NB: and in many other Indo-European languages] originally had a neutral meaning almost equivalent to educative teaching, gradually assumed the connotations of coercive teaching and became disassociated from the emerging concepts of democratic education. During this century [20th century for Puolimatka] it finally acquired a derogatory connotation similar to propaganda and brainwashing and came to be regarded the antithesis of education for life in a democracy.

For Palmer (1957: 224) indoctrination, a pejorative 'term of reproach', is often used to refer to the 'moulding of children' while e.g. propaganda to that of adults. He maintains that indoctrination might have to do with 'influencing the immature' in specific ways (e.g. playing upon their feelings; appealing to authority) and "hindering their freedom of thought in a certain area" (Palmer, 1957: 224–225). In this Étagère, I do not make this differentiation since indoctrination has also often been associated with adults in education and beyond. What is more, as we shall see, the strategies of playing upon people's feelings and appealing to authority are also common for grown-ups (see advertising and economic-political discourses). In a similar vein, I do not necessarily agree with e.g. Green (1964) who asserted that indoctrination is about the transmission of beliefs rather than behaviours (which would differentiate it from conditioning then). I would argue that dividing up thinking and behaving is not a very straightforward act. As such, an ideology might urge us to do this or that (or to refuse to do this or that) and act (or not) in specific ways. Indoctrination might also lead to gaps between what we think, assert and *do* (contradictions). So, in this Étagère, indoctrination has to do with beliefs, ideologies *and* actions. I do not deal with the use of physical coercion or torture for indoctrinating purposes. Puolimatka (1996) suggests talking about *brainwashing* for such behaviours [a term coined through the aforementioned Chinese word 洗脑 (xǐnǎo) in the 1950s]. In this book, indoctrination is then a nonviolent ('intellectual' and 'psychological') strategy leading to compliance (Hassan, Mattingly & Nugent, 2022).

Flicking through book titles that contain the words *indoctrination* or *indoctrinated*, one notices a lack of academic books on the topic, especially post-2010s. However, many books, either self-published or put on the market by unfamiliar publishers, are available. According to Amazon.com, at the time of writing, best sellers containing the word *indoctrination* correspond to what is described as 'gay shifter paranormal romance'. For instance, Medusa Stone's *Indoctrination: The Underground Series* 'explores the dark nature of humanity' by narrating the story of a young man who becomes a victim to underground sex trafficking, slavery, etc.

Other books in English targeted at general audiences contain the following subtitles:

> *How colleges and universities are brainwashing your children; Protecting your kids from the woke indoctrination of public schools; Protecting young minds from indoctrination and propaganda; How education became indoctrination and what you can do about it; The transformation of higher education into hateful indoctrination; Bias and indoctrination in college texts; Avoiding indoctrination at college; The Left's war against academic freedom.*

What we notice in these mostly self-published books is that they often deal with the US political and ideological context. Education is often the focus of the books, where 'woke ideology', 'propaganda', 'brainwashing', 'bias', (academic) 'oppression' are critiqued. Readers are taught how to avoid them and to protect others. I also note that the targeted 'victims' of these forms of indoctrination are either children or university students in the books. Finally, ('hateful') indoctrination seems to have to do with what others do to 'us' and to young people, and represents some kind of invisible and unnamed force.

Few academic books have been published on the topic of indoctrination over the past decades. Let me introduce some of them from the fields of education and history (in chronological order):

- *Indoctrination and Education* was first published in 1972 by Snook (5 years before Reboul's aforementioned irretrievable book) and is to be 'revived' by Routledge in 2024 (Snook, 2024). In this classic, and somehow similarly to Reboul's (1977) book, the author aims to 'carefully specify' the meanings of indoctrination beyond its reputation as a mere 'term of abuse' in education. He discusses the flaws in the way it has been (mis-)conceptualised in research and proposes comparisons to other terms such as propaganda and brainwashing.
- *Teaching Without Indoctrination: Implications for Values Education* by Tan (2008). In his endorsement for the book, Sison (in Tan, 2008: n.p.) wrote: "This book presents a comprehensive, well-structured and enlightening survey of the problem of indoctrination as manifested in scientific, moral, religious and social fields within the context of an intellectual milieu that prides itself in being liberal and democratic. In the craft of intellectual midwifery which she masters, Professor Tan has but one prescription: constant reflection, but not of the solipsistic or sterile kind. Rather, she advocates fearless questioning within the bounds of a community of learning, which is what schools should ideally be, wherein we all recognise ourselves to be at once students and teachers".
- In 2012 the same author published *Islamic Education and Indoctrination: The Case in Indonesia* (Tan, 2012). The author understands indoctrination as "occur[ring] when a person holds to a type of beliefs known as control beliefs that result in ideological totalism" (Tan, 2012). The book suggests ways of countering and avoiding indoctrination in this specific context (Indonesia) by promoting e.g. 'pluralism, rationality and autonomy'. Unlike her previous book, the focus here is on Islam.
- Lankford (2009) examines the complex phenomenon of what he refers to as 'systematic indoctrination' in e.g. Iran and Nazi Germany. The author is interested in how systems turn 'normal people' into genocidal killers, terrorists and torturers (amongst others) by means of indoctrination while describing and problematising how some of these individuals resist its influence.
- Two books published in 2012 and 2019 adopt historical perspectives. Brandenberger's (2012) *Propaganda State in Crisis: Soviet Ideology, Indoctrination, and Terror under Stalin, 1927–1941* studies the USSR's failure to indoctrinate 'successfully' although a complex and exhaustive network of ideological propaganda was put into place. Sait's (2019) book is titled *The Indoctrination of the Wehrmacht: Nazi Ideology and the War Crimes of the German Military* and analyses the way 'ideological warriors', who focused on race and politics, were trained during the Nazi era in the 20th century.
- The two most recent academic books published on indoctrination include a volume on Communist Romania's institutionalisation and social organisation

of indoctrination and propaganda during 1947–1988 (Dragos Aligica & Preda, 2022). The authors focus for example on the establishment and role of 'political-ideological commissars' (i.e. officials, leaders) in the education system. Finally, in *Educational Pluralism and Democracy: How to Handle Indoctrination, Promote Exposure, and Rebuild America's Schools* Rogers Berner (2024) reimagines the content and structure of US education. The author maintains that epistemic pluralism and exposure to diverse viewpoints are primordial to move beyond mere indoctrination.

At this stage, I must confess that having looked into these academic and lay publications, I got a bit apprehensive. Am I going too far by choosing this term to conceptualise intercultural self-defence? Why are most discourses on indoctrination so negative, it seems? Is indoctrination only evil, i.e. done by 'bad' individuals and groups of people? Is it only about moral, politics or religion? But also: Who determines what indoctrination is and what it is not? Have these 'accusers' never indoctrinated anyone? Is e.g. epistemic pluralism really possible since we tend to use only one language to learn-teach (and language cannot but indoctrinate as we shall see in Étagère 4)? At the same time, the question *is indoctrination inevitable?* came to mind. Can one teach and learn about interculturality – which is a very political sphere since it deals with us-others, identities, ideologies and surviving in our neoliberal capitalistic world – beyond indoctrination? Is indoctrination only about manipulation, censoring, varied acts of violence, 'dumbing down', US, history in certain parts of the world or something else? [Indoctrination could also be about manipulating manipulators and indoctrinators to get something out of them ...]

2.2. Indoctrination as a protean concept and phenomenon

My 25-year experience in the broad field of ICER pushes me to think that forms of indoctrination do take place in both research and education. The lack of criticality of criticality; selective critiques; the epistemic, methodological and linguistic automatisms found in our writing and speaking; the recycling of concepts (intercultural competence, culture), ideas/ideologies (non-essentialism), scholars' names (especially located in the west as well as a few 'tokens'); the (white) lies and manipulations (refusal to discuss something because it is 'not the point' of a paper or a book); the problematic alliance with decision-making bodies that I have observed and discussed in the past years, all seem to hint at similar phenomena as those described in the previous sections. I have tried at times to point at and critique some of these acts of indoctrination in ICER but it seems that looking at what we do as researchers and interculturalists from (overly) critical perspectives, unless it fits into the 'criticalese' of the time, is deemed unacceptable by many (Dervin, 2011; R'boul & Dervin, 2024; see also R'boul, 2022). While everyone feels entitled to 'slaughter' someone like Hofstede today and students for being too 'essentialist', 'culturalist' ..., big figures from the field (myself included) are *recited* without being *evaluated*. When one starts reciting for example by merely placing a name with a date to justify an argument that has become some kind of doxa about e.g. the need to non-essentialise, indoctrination always lurks around the corner.

But let me stop this for now and let's get back to indoctrination as a concept. What could indoctrination mean from a conceptual and philosophical perspective?

Let me say first that, although what follows is based mostly on the literature published in English, we need to remember that, for example, indoctrination has been a recurrent theme in Ancient Chinese philosophy. As such, while e.g. Confucianism promoted the transmission of specific values, it also encouraged critical reflection on those values, suggesting that blind adherence can lead to moral failure (Lee, 2017). For example, the tension between *filial piety* (孝: care, devotion and obedience towards parents and elder family members, see Bedford & Yeh, 2019) and *public justice* in Confucius's *the Analects* (produced during the Warring States period, 475–221 B.C.E.), illustrates the need for discernment rather than mere indoctrination. For another Confucian thinker, Xunzi (300–230 B.C.E.), human nature is inherently flawed and requires education and ritual to promote virtue. He suggested that indoctrination could be necessary to shape moral character, but that it should be done thoughtfully to avoid creating mere 'automata' who follow rules without understanding their significance (Hutton, 2016). Finally, Daoism encouraged individuals to align with the natural flow of life, promoting a form of wisdom that resisted dogmatic beliefs and encouraged personal exploration and understanding (e.g. Watts, 2019).

If books published in English are rare on indoctrination today, articles on the topic, especially in relation to education, are plentiful. Reading through the hundreds of articles that I managed to retrieve, there is clearly no consensus on what indoctrination means or entails, and many debates are still ongoing about it. I note with Dvoinin and Bulanova (2021) that indoctrination has been discussed in relation to *education, mass communication, organisations, politics, psychological practices* and *religion*. Following Neundorf et al. (2024: 773) I also maintain that "(i) indoctrination is not limited to autocracies, and (ii) indoctrination is not restricted to education". I am writing from Finland, a Nordic 'welfare' country, where 'democracy' is taken for granted – whatever the word might mean. Neundorf et al. (2024) argue that indoctrination also takes place in 'democratic' societies (like Finland) through emphasising e.g. *civic competence, tolerance, pluralism* and *political participation*, which are not always genuine or not far from the principles of indoctrination in the way they are promoted and rehearsed. In Finnish ICER, the current parroting of terms such as 'democratic culture' or 'social justice', which tends to mould (future) educators' and scholars' discourses intensively today (see Chen, 2024), often resembles indoctrinating too (see Figure 2.1. about an ideologeme often discussed in Chinese education today).

It is important to say that indoctrination comprises many actors: the indoctrinated person/group (e.g. a student, a PhD researcher), the indoctrinators

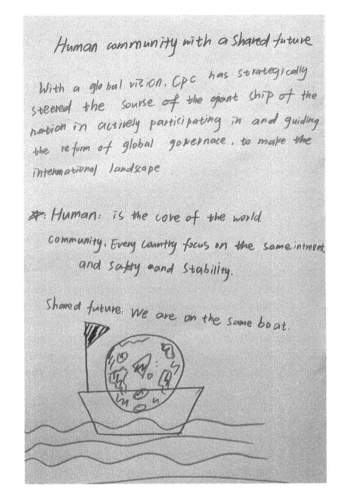

FIGURE 2.1 The Chinese ideologeme of *Community of a Shared Future* as summarised by a group of Chinese students in higher education.

(e.g. decision-makers, educators, researchers, media representations, with-/out specific intentions), the indoctrinating knowledge and artefacts (e.g. textbooks, curricula); the methods of indoctrination (e.g. duration, language use), as well as the indoctrination critiques and busters (who, in turn, probably also indoctrinate). For Casement (1983), *method*, *content* and *intention* correspond to the main features of indoctrination. Indoctrination can be both about a given method and intended outcomes, which do not always match since one might perform indoctrinating by asking someone to repeat e.g. slogans and yet they might not accept them or disseminate them to others as 'truths' that they have *merely* swallowed.

For many scholars who have worked on indoctrination, an indoctrinator and/or indoctrinated person are usually not open to critical evaluation of what they know and think, although, of course, they might be very much aware that they have been indoctrinated or indoctrinators and not believe at all in what they have been told or forced to believe in. I have come across many such individuals, who e.g. belonged to a specific group or organisation, parroted happily what they were supposed to recite but, behind closed doors, would joke about the content of these discourses or disparage them. This is a very human thing to do: *we adapt to discursive contexts, interlocutors, power relations* ... We dare to speak or not, depending on where we are, with whom and when. This is an important lesson about indoctrination: it does not necessarily mean that people believe in or agree with what they have been urged or forced to say and think – actually, they might not even understand what has been preached to them. Some indoctrinators also make their discourses so fuzzy and unclear as to create non-understanding in the ones they indoctrinate (since the content of the indoctrinatory message is empty or does not matter). Here I would thus tend to disagree with Spiecker's (1987) theory of indoctrination, whereby indoctrination is said to lead to the suppression of critical dispositions, intellectual virtues and rational emotions. *Individuals are actors too* (see Siegel, 2017). As such, critical thinking might be in appearance suppressed through indoctrination but what is happening inside the individual might not be. 'Intellectual virtues' (e.g. impartiality, intellectual modesty) or 'rational emotions' (love of truth, contempt for lying) are thus not necessarily subdued (Steutel & Spiecker, 1997).

At times, indoctrinators 'protect' the indoctrinated by not entitling them to be in contexts where critiques of their ideologies might be enunciated – or where they might stand as a minority voice. *Local academic tribes* (with hardly any contact with people who might disagree with the tribe's doxa), *global and yet closed research groups* (who communicate within a closed listserv mediated by an influential 'western' figure who does not allow epistemic disruption and/or the presence of 'outsiders'), *linguistic and physical isolation* (by only working in e.g. English or Finnish or not being able to travel), might reduce the space for being questioned or questioning and confronting indoctrination. Indoctrination thus often requires a symbolic or concrete authority relationship such as the invisible authority generated by group pressure and the influence of a strong and 'guruesque' figure.

So, how does indoctrination occur concretely? Many strategies (all unethical and harmful, with some not uncommon in any form of education and research activity) support indoctrination, including:

- *authority* – Using the voice of authority figures to endorse specific beliefs.
- *censorship* – Controlling access to information can prevent individuals from encountering alternative viewpoints or evidence that might challenge their beliefs.

- *early exposure* – Exposing individuals to certain beliefs at a young age/at an early stage of their academic training, when they are less equipped to critically evaluate information.
- *emotional manipulation* – Tying beliefs to strong emotions.
- *fear* – Creating fear or apprehension about e.g. negative outcomes.
- *isolation* – Isolating individuals from diverse sources of information and different viewpoints.
- *peer pressure* – The desire to fit in and be accepted by a group can lead individuals to adopt the beliefs and behaviours of that group.
- *repetition* – Repeating a message or idea *over and over again.*
- *selective information* – Providing only information that supports a particular viewpoint while suppressing or discrediting opposing views.

The effects of these strategies on individuals could be recognised if someone appears to … (amongst others) … adhere strictly to specific beliefs of a group without any individual critical evaluation … echo language by repeating slogans … fear consequences of deviating from a belief system … hold rigid beliefs even in the face of contradictory evidence … lack self-reflection (e.g. questioning one's own beliefs) … lack tolerance … resist to new information … overly or defensively react emotionally to disagreement.

[Do you (also) recognise yourself or anyone you know in any of these behaviours? Especially when it comes to 'doing' and speaking about interculturality?]

But is indoctrination wrong doing after all? What if we are all doing it without 1. knowing it, 2. being aware of it, 3. lying about it? Callan and Arena (2010) provide some answers to this question. They start by reminding us that some sort of 'systematic distortion' has to take place with indoctrination (Callan & Arena, 2010) and that the indoctrinator might have "an ill-considered or overzealous concern to inculcate particular beliefs or values" (Callan & Arena, 2010). *Distortions of some sort. Preferably intentional distortions.* [Distortion in English contains Latin and Proto-Indo European roots for twist, turn and even … torture. I note that *a torque wrench* is a tool that indicates the amount of torque exerted in tightening e.g. a bolt]. So yes, indoctrination would seem to entail wrongdoing since it produces particular beliefs and potential misunderstandings of a specific subject matter by e.g. showing a lack of impartiality or objectivity in including other knowledges and viewpoints, tolerating dissensus. But let's go back to the aforementioned features of intentions, methods and outcomes since these can be somewhat separated – e.g. use of indoctrinating methods vs. potentially failed outcomes of indoctrination. *If an act of indoctrination fails, is it then wrong doing?* Callan and Arena (2010: 106) maintain: "If one indoctrinates, is the alleged wrongdoing so grave that it could not be justified, regardless of circumstances, or is it only prima facie wrong – the sort of thing that generally warrants condemnation but can be justified, all things considered, in some circumstances?". *Condemnation but* … Dahlbeck (2021: 95) goes as far as suggesting that we acknowledge the necessity of indoctrination in education and should make use of it towards maximising freedom and ethical flourishing – beyond pride, envy and/or hatred (more about that in 2.3.).

[Pause 1: the GPS metaphor
In my recent writing, I noticed that I have often used the metaphor of the now omnipresent GPS (Global Positioning System) technology to describe what we interculturalists do when we rehearse, recite and put forward specific ideologemes without evaluating them or being critical of our own criticality (Dervin, 2024). These ideologemes have been passed onto us through some form of (unintentional) indoctrination and we have circulated them amongst other people as well. However, I would like to correct this comparison here. Indoctrination and having a GPS in our mind are in fact not the same thing, although there might be a superficial analogy in the sense that both can guide our thoughts and actions. However, they function very differently and have distinct implications. Let me share some of my reflections. The GPS is a tool that provides navigation assistance and offers directions based on factual, geographical data to help users reach a desired destination. It does not seem to impose beliefs or values and simply provides information to support decision-making when driving a car or walking in a forest (Gao, Zhao & Fourati, 2019). As we have discussed in the previous 'excavatory' sections, indoctrination, on the other hand, refers to the process of attempting to instil-while-legitimise ideologies, beliefs, attitudes and values into individuals without their conscious acceptance or critical evaluation. It often involves the dissemination of ideas that may not be open to question or debate and can be used to manipulate or control people's behaviours and thinking. Contrarily, a GPS does not aim to impede critical thinking. We generally choose to use a GPS and can opt out or challenge its directions (and ask it to find another route). Indoctrination, by its nature, is often involuntary and pervasive, making it difficult for us to recognise or resist the ideologies, beliefs and values that it tries to impose.]

2.3. *Equilibrium: Education vs./and-or indoctrination*

In its etymology in English but also in certain languages still today, indoctrination often serves as a mere synonym for education and training. In this section I interrogate the differilitudes (similarities and differences) between these terms (Dervin, 2023). Let me start by asking you to reflect on this quote from Doris Lessing (2012: 16):

> Ideally, what should be said to every child, repeatedly, throughout his or her school life is something like this: "You are in the process of being indoctrinated. We have not yet evolved a system of education that is not a system of indoctrination. We are sorry, but it is the best we can do".

What do you make of what Lessing is saying about education? How concerned have you been about school/research as potential spheres of indoctrination? Would you tend to dis-/agree with Lessing, especially in relation to ICER?

I realised that it is, in fact, not easy to dichotomise education and indoctrination because of the complexities of these constructs. So, what I am about to present will be necessarily *grossly* generalised. You must disagree with every single point that I am about to make!

Let me start with *three (potential) similarities*: 1. Davey (1972: 6) argues that "one man's education is another man's indoctrination", highlighting the instabilities in trying to separate them. 2. For Puolimatka (1996) education and indoctrination both aim to teach certain beliefs. 3. "If indoctrination means simply influencing other people, there is really no ground for debate as to whether it can be distinguished from education; it cannot. For any teacher worth half his salary exerts an influence upon his pupils" (Palmer, 1957: 224).

Let me continue with *three instabilities*. White (1967) reminds us that for *some of us*, if a teacher promotes e.g. rote learning, they aim to indoctrinate their students. Interestingly, in recent decades, rote learning has been highly criticised in the west and beyond, and used as a 'weapon' to criticise systems of education such as China's (a bias which goes well with the many stereotypical views of the Middle Kingdom developed in the west, Cheng, 2007). White (1967) also maintains that *some of us* would often consider e.g. early moral education as indoctrination because teachers tend to make students believe that they should behave in certain ways without explaining why. Last, the scholar (White, 1967) notes that so-called 'child-centred theorists' often consider any learning-teaching activity that does not let children explore by themselves to be a form of indoctrination.

Let me close these introductory remarks with *a warning*. For Merry (2005), to call every act of teaching indoctrination, plays downs the very issue. Zembylas (2022: 2488) adds: "I would argue that this overgeneralization and flattening of all forms of teaching values gives a free ride to dangerous forms of indoctrination such as right-wing extremist or fascist ideas that do indeed entail emotional manipulation most of the times".

What seems to be specific about *education* then? Education aims to foster the followings (based on e.g. Huttunen, 2016; Puolimatka, 1996):

- A clearer differentiation of a belief system.
- Productive doubting and recommending adventuresome hypotheses (Wagner, 2021).
- The learner needs to think for themselves, to think critically about beliefs.
- The teacher should not have any indoctrinating intention.

These idealistic statements about education are often hampered by several factors in educational contexts, leaving the border between education and indoctrination fuzzy. For instance, Huttunen (2016) reminds us of the asymmetry of roles between teachers and students, which often leads teachers to impose and reinforce specific worldviews on students, while trying to persuade them that there is no other alternative (not the other way around). Flew (1966) asserts that the teaching of e.g. moral, politics or religion, is often committed to a specific worldview that could resemble indoctrination [as a complement, Puolimatka (1996: 112) rightly notes that "Even scientific knowledge is not metaphysically neutral, since scientific research functions within a paradigm involving metaphysical assumptions"].

The specificities of indoctrination in the dichotomy of education/indoctrination could include:

- Indoctrination corresponds to a one-sided way of teaching, which is linguistically and discursively controlled and rehearsed;
- Indoctrination produces closed-minded students who are at the mercy of 'authorities' (Callan & Arena, 2009);
- Indoctrination includes disseminating only the positive aspects of harmful and partisan at moment X doctrines (Reboul, 1977). Such doctrines might instil hatred about ideas and beings;
- Indoctrinated beliefs, ideologies and values cannot be independently evaluated by students (no criteria for truth or falsity are provided, mere preconceptions constitute the basis of teaching), leaving "human capacities undeveloped" (Puolimatka, 1996: 113).

Many scholars have discussed the (unstable) (and) (unreliable) criteria of determining what constitutes indoctrination versus education, including: Content (what is taught; how controversial is it?); intention (purpose: why is it taught?); and method (by whom and how? How transparent?).

Critiques have been addressed to these criteria. For example, should they be combined or can indoctrination materialise only through one of them (e.g. intention)? Casement (1983) has questioned for example the intention to indoctrinate as a necessary criterion for indoctrination. Besides, Wilson (1972) noted that indoctrinating methods are also found in education and teaching, although they do not necessarily constitute indoctrination (e.g. multiplication tables, learning vocabulary by heart, reciting a poem ...). Casement (1983) also maintained that the position of the learner is central in determining if something is about indoctrination or not. Do they come to accept ideologies, beliefs or values uncritically? "The final test for indoctrination is in what happens to the learner" ... (Casement, 1983: 237). In other words: how close-minded have the students potentially become through education (see Dahlbeck, 2021)?

In 2017, Taylor insisted on the importance to take particular social contexts into account in dealing with indoctrination. She explained (Taylor, 2017: 39–40):

> Situating the teacher-student relationship within a broader social system illuminates the role of authority of both the individual teachers and other actors

in indoctrination; it better equips us to understand moral responsibility for indoctrination and in turn to identify anti-indoctrination guidelines for teachers and other actors in systems of education.

For the author, broader social contexts, including 'communities' (from a US linguacultural perspective) and family, but also policy-makers, allow looking beyond the teacher-student relationship in relation to indoctrination (Taylor, 2017).

In 2022, using the example of patriotic education, Zembylas (2022) proposed to take into account the concept of 'affective indoctrination', focusing on the embodied experience of people in group affective conditions – beyond the sole criteria of the intellect and rationality. *Indoctrination as an affective coercive phenomenon – emotional manipulation.* Zembylas (2022) focused on both processes and outcomes of indoctrination (including failure to indoctrinate) while problematising what he calls 'benign' and 'malignant' forms of affective indoctrination in e.g. the patriotic education of children. 'Benign' forms of affective indoctrination could be considered as acceptable if they contribute to the 'common good' (e.g. anti-racism) and even if they trigger e.g. feelings of guilt in students.

[Pause 2: summary]
A brief and incomplete definition of indoctrination for this book reads as follows:

> *Indoctrination is about inculcating doctrines, ideologies and beliefs, with an intent to make them somehow unquestionable and accepted. At the same time, indoctrination might aim to alter the thoughts or beliefs of a given individual.*

Arguments made about the concept in the previous sections are summarised as follows. I have added introductory reflections about ICER between brackets:

- The concept of indoctrination is both linguistically and epistemically multifaceted. It has been discussed and problematised in most parts of the world under many other terms, in the past and today. *[Apart from minor discussions of ideologies in ICER, which rarely deconstruct what scholars themselves do and say, indoctrination is not a familiar concept in the broad field.]*
- Indoctrination can be a violent and/or nonviolent strategy leading to compliance in education and research. It is often based on asymmetries of relations and roles (e.g. teacher vs. student; confirmed scholar vs. novice researcher). *[Symbolic violence might apply to ICER. Power relations between teachers, scholars and students might support un-/intentional forms of indoctrination, except in cases where highly politicised perspectives are promoted (e.g. discussions of citizenship, democratic culture, community of shared future …).]*
- Although some criteria for determining what constitutes indoctrination have been considered (*method, content, intention, outcomes* – combined or individually considered), there does not seem to be a universally agreed-upon

definition of what constitutes indoctrination, especially when it is opposed to the idea of education. *My indoctrination could be your education; my education could be your indoctrination. [In research on ICER potentially indoctrinating intentions are hard to identify, especially if one is not aware of any potential economic-political-tribal affiliation of scholars or teachers. I have often decried the lack of transparency in this matter in research.]*

- Yet, in many discussions of indoctrination in western research and education, it often seems to involve e.g. a lack of encouragement for criticality, impositions, manipulations and forced repetition through symbolic or concrete authority relationship. These are all considered and presented as *legitimate*. *[There are signs in intercultural research that criticality (of criticality) is not always encouraged and some (dominating) knowledge often passes as 'accepted' and 'taken-for-granted'.]*
- Linguistically and discursively controlled and rehearsed discourses (ideologemes) constitute indoctrinating strategies. Language is central in indoctrinating. *[The lack of interest in interrogating how things are expressed and manipulated linguistically in ICER represents a danger for opening the door to potentially 'malignant' indoctrination (Shen, 2023). I have observed how some scholars mimic others' ways of writing without questioning the content and form of what they say. See Étagère 4.]*
- Indoctrination does not necessarily lead to people believing in or agreeing with what they have been urged or forced to say and think. People can 'fake' being indoctrinated and/or believing or even understanding what they indoctrinate others with. In evaluating indoctrination, it is thus important to take into account the position of the involved actors and the contexts in which they find themselves. *[More research is needed on how e.g. PhD researchers really feel about the intercultural knowledges that are passed onto them.]*
- Indoctrination can also be unintentional. The indoctrinated person can self-indoctrinate, without experiencing any direct or obvious pressure from anyone. In education and research someone always exerts an influence on someone else un-/intentionally. *[Publishing an article or a book on interculturality does not usually directly aim to indoctrinate others ... maybe unless it is sponsored by a supra-national institution with a clear economic-political agenda.]*
- Although indoctrination has been described as a pejorative 'term of reproach' and even a term of abuse, some scholars have called for considering (positively) the inclusion of some forms of indoctrination in education (e.g. 'benign' forms of affective indoctrination). *[Is indoctrination inevitable in such a highly political field as ICER?]*

Many theories and concepts used in ICER seem to resemble doctrines and ideologemes (pieces of ideology) in the way they are formulated, used and (indirectly) promoted (e.g. non-essentialism, intercultural citizenship, culturespeak, models of intercultural competence). Some of these are rarely questioned but used *robot-like* (see the use and abuse of Byram (1997) or Holliday's (2010) 'non-culturalism' and 'small cultures'). If this phenomenon is intentional or not, is impossible to determine.

If we go back to the different aforementioned strategies used to indoctrinate, in ICER, we might notice:

- *the use of authorities* to endorse specific ideologies (repeated rather than evaluated and critiqued, supported with a reference to an 'unquestionable big name');
- *early exposure* (in the broad field of ICER, when one starts learning and researching it, one is often exposed to a narrow range of accepted ideas, concepts and methods from the beginning – from which it might be hard to detach later on; one such resistant interculturology is that of *culture shock* ... Dervin, 2024);
- some form of *emotional manipulation* whereby e.g. one is warned against being a culturalist, an essentialist, and even a racist, if one essentialises (NB: non-essentialism, whereby I would be able to refrain from e.g. stereotyping or solidifying the ones I interact with and encounter, is an impossibility for any social being. Non-essentialism is in fact an ideal; see Zhou, 2022);
- *isolation* (setting apart in-/directly readers and students of interculturality from diverse sources of information and different viewpoints by e.g. not being able to include knowledge published in different languages and from different economic-political contexts);
- *peer pressure* (in ICER this might be seen in e.g. the avoidance of certain references or names – preferring to use members from one's group – to conform to peers and especially 'leading' figures to make a stand against researchers one might hold a grudge against);
- *repetition* (repeating the same message about e.g. the need to be democratic, open-minded, tolerant, etc. over and over again – without explaining what they might mean or without problematising them).

[Figure 2.2. contains two different documents seen in Europe. The top image is an advertisement for a money transfer company targeted at (male?) migrants (Switzerland). The main slogan says Family is important (*Die Familie is wichtig*) and tries to appeal to potential customers by showing two (smiling) male (migrant) workers. The second picture shows a text in English urging people to keep quiet. It was taken on a lift at a hotel in Finland. The message makes use of an unspoken stereotype about Finns being 'quiet' – hence the need to be silent! Both pictures contain the use of authorities, some form of emotional manipulation and repetition (slogans that will be heard again and again in Switzerland and Finland).]

In ICER, indoctrination seems to be happening 'naturally' and *underground*, through some form of academic system-of-domination (highly cited authors from the UK/US writing in English in top publications, Peng et al., 2019). This form of indoctrination leads to self-indoctrination of other scholars who 'swallow'

36 Intercultural Self-Defence

FIGURE 2.2 Making doctrines, ideologies and beliefs unquestionable and accepted.

leading ideas, concepts and 'speak' *critique-less* and even *dogmatically* (e.g. when someone speaks of *the* intercultural competence model in the singular or uses the concept of intercultural citizenship from the 'European village' without justifying its economic-political transfer to their own context). Obviously by proposing a model of intercultural competence or defining a term in a specific way with the intent to have other people follow one's definition and reject other terms and perspectives, some form of 'mild' indoctrination (inculcating something) must be taking place. Yet, the point of research and education is to propose, question and discard somehow …

How about the important aspect of *evidence*, which I have not touched upon yet? Indoctrination often does away with it, by aggrandising the content of what and how it formulates ideas (Snook, 2025). For many of the aforementioned concepts and theories in ICER (with many serving as ideologemes and doctrines in the way they are used), evidence is rarely provided or 'shaky' – in the sense that interpretations of data could be performed otherwise, depending on ideological backgrounds, for example, if the word culture is used repetitively in interviews, we know that it will influence and orient discourses on interculturality (Dervin, 2016). The issue of 'evidence' is complicated for ICER since interculturality is a never-ending process of re-negotiation and balancing otherness with otherness – leading to instabilities and incoherencies in what people do and say – and often rests on the economic-political and the such. This means that the criteria of certainty/uncertainty of knowledge are difficult to apply to interculturality ... (Wilson, 1972). For Casement (1983: 232): "regarding political, religious, and moral beliefs, not only do we not have the necessary sort of evidence, but do not even know what sort of evidence would suffice if we were to have it".

Are scholars like me, who disseminate their models, concepts and ideas related to interculturality, responsible for a form of indoctrination that could be labelled as indirect? By not questioning their/our own work systematically, publication after publication, but reinforcing the transmission of beliefs and ideologies, by not being transparent about any economic-political influence on their work (e.g. supra-national institutions east-west, affiliation to political parties, think-thanks, religious groups), by not applying *criticality of criticality* systematically to their work when they speak, write, review ..., they (we!) do indeed perform some form of covert indoctrination. Holding worldviews (which is what we do in ICER), as educators, researchers, thinkers ... we indoctrinate *willy-nilly* (Garrison, 1986). Yet, no one will admit to in-/direct indoctrinating actions. For Momanu (2012: 91): "No action of indoctrination is admitted de facto by the one who applies it. The indoctrination is often defined as the 'doctrine of the opponent'".

To conclude this Pause, I would like to argue that indoctrination is in fact inevitable in ICER. Indoctrination is often viewed as a 'four-letter-word' in education (Wilcox, 1988) and yet we need to accept that it is happening all the time and that we are all contributing to it, willy-nilly. Is that a problem? Yes, if we pretend that we neither contribute to nor see indoctrination in others' and our own work on interculturality. To paraphrase Macmillan (in Garrison, 1986: 264), *we must be indoctrinated in order not to be indoctrinated* ... To self-defend interculturally, we need to open our eyes to (self-)indoctrination, not to discard this complex phenomenon entirely (that would be impossible) but to speak freely about it, without accusing others *only* of this 'evil'.

3. A conceptual toolbox to apprehend indoctrination further

[One of my favourite French words is *embobiner* which translates as bamboozling, getting round someone or leading someone down the garden path in English (all hinting at indoctrination somehow). The verb is based on the French word *bobine* (bobbin in English, i.e. a small round spool of thread). When someone *embobines* another person, they weave threads on 'their' bobbins ...]

This section urges us to think further about the intricacies, contradictions and instabilities of indoctrination for interculturality by introducing terms that have often been used as synonyms, substitutes or accompanying concepts. I also propose a couple of new terms, which I think could be of interest. Note that these terms also need to be critiqued and evaluated against potential harms they might lead to (see e.g. Coady (2024: 92) who argues that e.g. 'echo chambers' and other similar terms "serve no useful purpose, since there is nothing we can say with them that we cannot say equally well or better without them. Furthermore, they cause a variety of harms, including, ironically, a tendency to narrow public debate within predetermined limits"). Analysing indoctrination in relation to interculturality involves examining the concept from various perspectives. I am hoping to stimulate some interest, curiosity and further critiques in other terms with what follows.

1. Identifying indoctrinating practices:
   - *Propaganda*: The deliberate spreading of biased and misleading information to promote a particular cause or point of view. Information warfare, psychological operations and disinformation are all examples of propaganda (Olejnik, 2024).
   - *Mental manipulation*: The act of influencing someone's thoughts or behaviours (see 'Mindfucking' by McGinn, 2014).
   - *Logical fallacies*: (Intentional) mistakes in reasoning that can be used to support indoctrinated beliefs without justification (see 'grey behaviours' whereby one tries to convince listeners by using such arguments in Kord & Thornton, 2021).
   - *Ideological echo chambers*: Environments where only one viewpoint is heard and reinforced, which can contribute to indoctrination by lack of exposure to alternative perspectives (Erickson et al., 2023; see Coady, 2024 for a critique of the use and abuse of this term in educational research).
   - *Ideological bias*: A systematic preference for a particular economic, political, social ideology (belief, order, agenda), often instilled through indoctrination.
   - *Epistemic injustice*: The injustice of denying someone a fair opportunity to contribute to knowledge, which can occur in indoctrinatory environments that suppress im-/ex-plicitly dissenting voices (R'boul, 2022).
   - *Dogma*: This term refers to a set of beliefs or principles laid down by an authority (e.g. a government) as true and accepted by the 'faithful', without critical or reflexive examination.
   - *Cognitive and emotional comfort*: The mental comfort experienced when contradictory beliefs are resolved by reinforcing one belief over others.
2. Accompanying indoctrination critically and reflexively:
   - *Counter-Education*: The process of unlearning indoctrinated beliefs and replacing them with a more balanced and critical understanding (see countering racism in Swedish education, Mattson et al., 2024).
   - *Critical thinking*: A much rehearsed (and problematic) concept in research and education around the world. It is often understood as the ability to think

clearly and *rationally* (two very unclear and controversial adverbs) about what to believe or do, which is usually suppressed in indoctrination (see Hadley & Boon, 2022).
- *Enkrateia*: Meaning self-control or self-mastery, this term is often used in moral and ethical discussions (see Dorion, 2012). In the context of indoctrination, it could refer to the resistance to indoctrination by exercising critical thinking and self-control over deeply ingrained beliefs.
- *Paideia*: Originally meaning education or upbringing in ancient Greece, this term emphasises the holistic development of a person, including moral, intellectual and physical aspects. Indoctrination can be seen as a distortion of this ideal, focusing on the imposition of beliefs rather than a broad educational process emphasising the formation of the whole human being (about Paideia and its German romantic companion, Bildung, see Zovko & Dillon, 2021).
- *Rational autonomy*: The capacity for independent thought and action based on reason, which is typically curtailed in indoctrination processes (see Walker, 2009).

The following concepts are also of interest to reflect on indoctrination in relation to ICER.

A nudge in the context of behavioural economics and psychology refers to a subtle strategy or intervention that influences people's choices and behaviours in a predictable way, without restricting their options. The term was popularised by the book *Nudge: Improving Decisions About Health, Wealth, and Happiness* by Thaler and Sunstein (2008). Nudges are based on the understanding that people often make decisions based on factors other than 'rationality', such as *emotional responses*, *default options*, or *the ease with which choices can be made*. The goal of a nudge is to guide people toward decisions that are in their best interest or that align with a certain goal or policy, without eliminating any options or significantly altering e.g. economic incentives (see Figure 2.3.). Nudges are now omnipresent and common in our daily lives and are generally seen (wrongly?) as *ethical* and *effective* tools for influencing behaviour because they are said to preserve individual freedom of choice while making it easier for people to make choices that are beneficial for them or that align with societal goals.

I maintain that nudges are often on the verge of indoctrination and contain many ethical dimensions (see the now popular implementation of nudge policies around the world; their focus on methodological individualism in economic matters, Madi, 2019).

Examples of nudges in everyday life include: Using messages that highlight what the majority of people in a group are doing (e.g. *Most people in this building recycle*) to encourage individuals to follow suit; placing healthier food options at eye level in a cafeteria or a supermarket to encourage healthier (and yet more

40 Intercultural Self-Defence

FIGURE 2.3   An example of a nudge targeted at tourists in Venice (Italy).

expensive) eating; presenting information in a way that makes a particular option more appealing (describing e.g. a surgery as having a 90% success rate rather than a 10% failure rate); sending text messages or emails as reminders to encourage people to celebrate a national hero, pay their bills on time, get a flu shot or vote in an upcoming election. Figure 2.4. shows one of the numerous posters found on the streets of Chinese cities, inciting people to "measure their behaviours with a civilized ruler" and hinting at exercising good manners and etiquette, which serves as an example of nudging.

In relation to ICER, the followings could be considered as nudges:

- Adding references to the importance of intercultural awareness and/or understanding in university course descriptions to encourage students to register;
- Asking students to set specific goals of intercultural competence (from a given model) for themselves to enhance their motivation and sense of self-efficacy;
- Changing lecture hall seating arrangements to reduce segregation between e.g. local and international students;
- Organising celebrations of multicultural festivals on campuses to promote inclusivity and 'respect for diversity';
- Pairing local and international students (and at times: paying local students to participate) as a way of evidencing and pushing for intercultural encounters on campuses;

FIGURE 2.4 Chinese street poster urging people to behave in a 'civilized way'.

- Playing music from different parts of the world on campus to evidence its internationalism;
- Setting recommended reading lists with books and materials from different parts of the world to stimulate curiosity in other 'cultures'.

Although nudges might sound 'nice' and 'innocent', they are often problematic *interculturally speaking* (research + education). As such, nudges often feel like 'quick fixes' that ignore e.g. deep structural issues that they are trying to modify. They might also invade our autonomy and create some kind of paternalistic phenomenon, infringing on our freedom of choice – which is reminiscent of indoctrination. There is a risk that nudging could deceive people by imposing specific images, beliefs and ideologies without them being aware of the decisions behind the use of nudges. This might lead to people being resistant to and cynical about the messages spread through nudges.

Another interesting concept to open up indoctrination for ICER comes from George Orwell's (1948/2009) novel *1984*, which I mentioned at the beginning of this Étagère: *Doublethink*. Doublethink is a concept that refers to the ability to hold two contradictory beliefs simultaneously in one's mind and accept both of them as *true* and not recognising the cognitive and emotional dissonance that their combination represents. In *1984*, it is a key element of the governing party's control over the population – *political indoctrination*. Doublethink is a term that is part of the Newspeak language, which is designed to limit the range of thought and make independent thinking impossible in the novel. The slogans that I mentioned in Yarn I, e.g. "War is Peace", "Freedom is Slavery" and "Ignorance is Strength" are prime examples of doublethink in action. These slogans are meant to be accepted without question, even though they are inherently incongruous. The practice of doublethink is also evident in the way the ruling party in the novel manipulates the past and forces its citizens to forget historical facts that contradict their ideologies. Orwell (2017: 31) describes doublethink as the ability to "know and not know, to be conscious of complete truthfulness while telling carefully constructed lies, to hold simultaneously two opinions which cancelled out, knowing them to be contradictory and believing in both of them, to use logic against logic, to repudiate morality while laying claim to it". I note that doublethink is not only a tool for controlling people but also a means of self-deception for the party members themselves in *1984*. It allows them to carry out the party's directives without cognitive dissonance, even when those directives involve lies or contradictions. The ultimate goal of doublethink is to maintain the party's power by controlling reality itself.

In ICER, one might face or even come across the following instances of doublethink. These examples highlight the complexities and contradictions that can exist within ICER and underscore the need for critical self-reflection and continuous questioning of our practices and assumptions to avoid falling into the trap of doublethink.

- *Critical pedagogy<--->Standardised curriculum*: Educators and researchers could claim to adopt a 'critical pedagogy' that challenges students to question and reflect on their biases, yet they might still adhere to a standardised curriculum that doesn't allow for such exploration.
- *Decolonising the curriculum<--->eurocentrism*: As discussed earlier, there's a growing call to decolonise ICER education and include more diverse perspectives in curricula. However, the reality often falls short, with eurocentric viewpoints still dominating academic discourse/teaching around the world.
- *Global Citizenship<--->Nationalism*: Educators might promote the idea of global citizenship, emphasising the interconnectedness of people across 'borders', while simultaneously reinforcing nationalistic sentiments or overlooking local contexts.
- *Promoting diversity<--->Tokenism*: Research groups or laboratories might publicly advocate for diversity and inclusion, but their actions might only involve superficial representation or tokenism, without addressing systemic issues or power imbalances.

The final concept to consider, I coined: *Mind seepage*. Seepage refers to the slow escape of a liquid or gas through porous material or small holes. Here mind seepage aims to capture the process of ideas, beliefs, ideologies and/or attitudes seeping into our consciousness without deliberate effort or intent. In other words, mind seepage could be equivalent to unintentional indoctrination that ICER experiences constantly. It should be considered as a metaphorical way to describe how the thoughts and values of our surrounding environment can influence our mental landscape, often without our conscious awareness. What is specific about mind seepage is that the process is not overt or forceful. As such, it happens gradually and often imperceptibly. The individual is not actively seeking to adopt these influences; they happen naturally through exposure to specific ways of speaking, trends, social etiquette and behavioural norms, technology adoption, consumerism (advertising and marketing).

4. Fragments about indoctrination in ICER

[25 years in the intercultural 'business' (research and education). I have made so many mistakes. I have observed so many mistakes. I have criticised and been criticised for being *indoctrinating*. In my 2023 fragment book (Dervin, 2023), I have accepted these critiques and even rejected my 2016 book for reciting too many western litanies. As we have seen in this Étagère, we intercultural scholars and educators can ('inadvertently') indoctrinate others through several means. *A.* The language we use in research can subtly reinforce certain (preferred or dominating) perspectives or biases. For example, using western-centric terminologies or concepts (non-essentialism, citizenship) as the default can marginalise non-western viewpoints and experiences, effectively indoctrinating readers into particular ideological worldviews and language bubbles. *B.* By accident, we may favour our own worldviews, norms and values (without realising it), leading to biases in e.g. the research questions asked, the data collected and the conclusions and interpretations drawn. This can result in us perpetuating stereotypes and ignoring and limiting epistemic diversities. *C.* The methods used in intercultural research can sometimes also be biased towards certain practices or ways of knowing. For instance, relying heavily on questionnaires or surveys that are designed based on western psychological models may not accurately capture the experiences of diverse individuals. *D.* The pressure to publish-or-perish in high-impact journals can also lead us to focus on studies that confirm dominating theories or popular perspectives, rather than those that challenge the status quo (Moosavi, 2022). This can result in biased representations of knowledge and indoctrinate readers into accepting a particular narrative. *E.* Researchers from dominant parts of the world may have more influence in shaping the research agenda and discourse on interculturality, which can lead to the marginalisation of minority voices and perspectives. This power imbalance can indoctrinate others into accepting a one-sided view in ICER. *F.* Textbooks and educational materials developed by intercultural researchers can sometimes present a biased view of interculturality, often reflecting the values and perspectives of dominant ideological worlds (Risager, 2024). This can indoctrinate students into a particular way of understanding the complex notion of interculturality. Maybe I still have 10–20 years in the 'intercultural business'. Ten to 20 years of further indoctrinating and being indoctrinated *ad nauseam*.]

[Can a book about the contributions of a supra-national institution like the Council of Europe for interculturality, plurilingualism and democratic citizenship *not* indoctrinate readers?]

[The phenomenon of namedropping, whereby one inserts and recites names – rather than problematise their inclusion, is customary in ICER. *Big names.* Unquestionable, indestructible and untouchable names. *Tokens.* Non-western looking names used to support 'critical' ideas (which end up not being critical). Tokens are not given a real central position but decorate and illustrate the author's open-mindedness. *Supra-national institutions.* Their names support assertions and recitations of concepts, arguments, ideologies. UNESCO. Council of Europe. EU. OECD. Their ideas are rarely questioned. Ghosting is another important phenomenon. Hiding away from view important figures, institutions and underground affiliations that one does not wish to insert in one's writing. These two phenomena, namedropping and ghosting, do contribute indirectly to forms of indoctrination in ICER.]

[Many well-intentioned slogans or phrases related to interculturality and sometimes found indirectly in ICER are problematic since they oversimplify complex issues, perpetuate stereotypes or ignore the nuances and inconsistencies of interculturality. At the same time, they represent attempts at indoctrinating us into certain beliefs, worldviews and values.]

- "Diversity is our strength" [while this is often a positive statement, it can sometimes be used as a slogan without accompanying actions or policies that truly support and value diversities];
- "Unity in diversity" [found in many different contexts, this phrase is often used positively but it can be seen as a cliché that doesn't necessarily address the complexities of interculturality or the work required to create inclusive environments];
- "We are a melting pot" [this metaphor can imply that we should lose our identities and blend into a single, homogenised 'whole', which doesn't respect e.g. the values of individualities];
- "We are all the same under the skin" [disregards issues of privilege and structural inequalities];
- "We don't see colour here" [this slogan can be used to suggest that 'race' or 'ethnicity' are irrelevant, which can overlook the experiences and challenges faced by People of Colour];
- "When in Rome, do as the Romans do" [while this saying encourages adapting to 'local customs', it can also be used to justify conformity and discourage interculturality itself].

See Figure 2.5. for the slogan-question *How are we situated in a diverse, multifaceted, globalised culture?* seen in Venice.

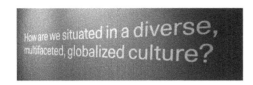

FIGURE 2.5 Slogan about globalisation.

[At a so-called multicultural feast on a campus, celebrating the internationalisation of the university, the following slogans are recited in English, with accompanying pictures: "See the waving flags caressing our faces"; "We joyfully admire the elegance of friends from all over the world"; "We compose melodies of civilization all around"; "Our mind collides and blends"; "We view the colourful world"; "We embrace culture"; "We hear the resonance of hearts"; "We appreciate the interweaving thoughts"; "Languages interface". Many 'empty' and yet ideologically loaded words are used: *culture, civilization, colourful world* ... What do these empty slogans aim to do? What do these slogans mean within a specific ideological context? What counter-ideologies do they not support? What do those who 'chant' them make of them (e.g. students, teachers, administrators)? Do they believe in them? How would they formulate themselves what internationalisation is about on their campus, beyond the doxa provided to them by institutions and other influencers?]

[A white scholar based in the UK posts a thank you note on X to a university based in the Global South. In the note they thank the institution for inviting them to be a plenary speaker alongside a list of other plenary speakers who are all from the US and the UK. Were the words social justice, decolonisation, epistemic diversity, and other such trendy words uttered during the event?]

[... turns in ICER
Critical performative turn
Cultural turn
Decolonial turn
Ecological turn
Ethical turn
Intercultural policy turn
Performative turn
Postcolonial turn
... and yet nothing is changing ... Turn around?]

[A white UK scholar speaking about intercultural competence in a Middle East and North Africa (MENA) country offers a review of a few selected models from different parts of the world. When they start presenting their own work, they call it THE European perspective and list values such as human rights, dignity, democracy, diversity (which they also refer to as European). Several problems here: 1. Appropriation of values (isn't diversity a human thing? Are human rights only European? See Goody's (2007) *Theft of History*); 2. Essentialisation of Europe from a white British English-speaking perspective; 3. Putting down of other perspectives on intercultural competence from other parts of the world, even if the scholar shows good intentions in presenting other perspectives. In the end, the white UK scholar will always win and indoctrinate the rest of the world.]

[References to a 'culture' in both political and academic publications that include the words 'excellent', 'prominent', 'time-honoured' and 'rich and profound' should be treated as high voltage warnings. Indoctrination is lurking around ...]

[In our post-pandemic world, intercultural preparation seems to be becoming a way of boosting and reinforcing students' identity and pride in their country *against* others. Since others do not want to engage with them, having been indoctrinated to conceptualise who they are in stereotypical and ethnocentric ways, students are made to self-indoctrinate about the (past and present) grandeur of their nation. They learn to parrot in English prepared banalities about who they are told they are as members of this nation, which they recite to very few selected foreigners and to their peers. In order to do so, they are asked to make use of their country's 'wisdom', adhere to 'its own path', firm up 'self-confidence in culture' in order to achieve 'spiritual independence and autonomy' (with none of these clearly conceptualised). Interculturality serves as a way of indoctrinating against the indoctrination of the other, failing to lead to any form of intercultural dialogue – only inter-indoctrinating perspectives.]

[Forcing non-western students to create models of intercultural competence is a form of epistemic violence, indoctrination and colonialism. Intercultural competence is a western (capitalist) concept.]

[Looking for 'synonyms' of intercultural in different English dictionaries, I find: multicultural, cross-cultural, cultural diversity, between cultures, inter-civilisational, sociocultural, melting pot, and even cultivation and cropping. In my own dictionary the one and only synonym for the notion is *political*. Intercultural has to do with how we are forced to and how we (even) force ourselves to conceptualise and deal with difference-similarity across contexts and languages in often capitalistic ways (as in: I must be interculturally competent so I can 'defeat' the other and benefit from what we say and do together). Other (minor) synonyms might include ideology, money and manipulation ('monipulation').]

[A student from Asia writes to me about doing a PhD under my supervision: "I want to learn about intercultural citizenship to encourage new learning and useful teaching strategies to use with my pupils, because exploring and sharing cultural knowledge can help to have a good teaching environment". This all sounds too robot-like to me. *Intercultural citizenship*; *exploring and sharing cultural knowledge*; *a good teaching environment*. What is hiding behind all these recited words? I ask the student to explain. They don't get back to me.]

5. Vitrine I

Prof. John Abe, a renowned interculturalist, was head of his university's Department of Intercultural Studies in a Nordic country. His PhD researcher, Eetiat, was a bright but somewhat unexperienced young person who had recently joined his international research group. Like his other students, Eetiat was eager to learn and quick to absorb the knowledge that Abe imparted upon them. One day, the professor called Eetiat into his office. He began to discuss the concept of interculturality with the PhD researcher, explaining how it was not just about understanding different 'cultures' but also about recognising the biases and prejudices that one systematically brings to such encounters and the dangers of not taking into account its polysemic and ideological characteristics in research and education. "Eetiat", Abe said, his eyes intense behind his glasses, "interculturality is the future of education and communication studies. It's about breaking down the walls that divide us and building bridges of understanding". As the weeks turned into months, Eetiat found themselves immersed in a world of new ideas. Abe's PhD seminars were filled with stories of the complexities of interculturality and e.g. the transformative power of empathy, intellectual modesty and honesty. He spoke for instance of the dangers of 'essentialism', 'culturalism' and the importance of removing stereotypes from our minds. Eetiat began to see the world through Abe's eyes. They started to question their own assumptions and beliefs, and they became an ardent advocate for critical and reflexive interculturality. Their research took on a new direction, focusing on the ways in which discourses of interculturality can be counter-productive and ideologically oriented. However, as time went on, Eetiat noticed a subtle shift. Abe's teachings and writings, once a source of inspiration, began to feel like a straitjacket. They found themselves agreeing with Abe's views not because they had critically evaluated them but because they appeared to be the accepted dogma within their international research group. They even started to speak and write like their professor. One evening, while poring over their notes, Eetiat came across an article that challenged some of Abe's core ideas about interculturality. It argued for a more nuanced approach, one that acknowledged the limits of criticality and reflexivity in intercultural studies. Eetiat felt a pang of doubt. They hesitated, their hand hovering over the keyboard as they contemplated sharing the article with Prof. Abe. In the end, they decided against it, fearing his reaction and the potential disruption it might cause to their own academic standing. As the semester progressed, Eetiat's internal conflicts grew. They began to realise that their indoctrination had come at the cost of their intellectual freedom (for example: they did not want to use the word 'culture' for fear of upsetting their supervisor). They had been so eager to learn and to please their supervisor that they had neglected their own critical and reflexive faculties. In a pivotal moment, Eetiat decided to voice their concerns during a seminar. They presented the counter-arguments with the same passion and conviction that they had once reserved for Abe's teachings. To their surprise, the professor listened intently, his expression thoughtful. "Eetiat", he said after they finished, "it seems that you've learned more than I realised. It's essential to question, even the ideas of those you respect the most. Interculturality is not a fixed doctrine but it should be a dynamic conversation". From that day forward, Eetiat approached their studies with a renewed sense of critical thinking and reflexivity. They understood that interculturality was not just about accepting one perspective but about engaging in a diverse and open dialogue, disagreeing with the 'obvious' and 'taken-for-granted'. And although they would always be grateful for Abe's guidance, they knew that their true education had begun the moment they found the courage to try to think for themselves.

6. Escapade I

There are many things that we have been made to believe in and rehearse about interculturality which may not be true and yet we believe in them *interculturality is such an intricate and sacred being that only indoctrination can help us live and deal with it we are all fragile in front of interculturality* indoctrination does not need to be loud it is there in the background listen carefully *it is not loud indoctrination but silenced one that hurts interculturality* can we ever 'do' and think interculturality beyond indoctrination *interculturality is neither about 'culture' nor about 'diversity' it is about politics money power and hierarchies* indoctrination is the passage through which all kinds of ghosts and eerie creatures and legends enter our minds *indoctrination short-circuits our capacity to imagine interculturality* is a concept popular for interculturality because it is scientific or because it is spread 'privilegedly' (English western backed by supra-national institutions) and imposed on us by phantoms *no one is immune from indoctrination in an indecipherable world like ours* betray their ideas they are not yours anyway *by recycling and repeating these ideas we are made to believe in them and we lose ourselves interculturally*

To link up the issue of indoctrination and the two other topics of intellectual inertia and language indifference, consider this quote from Foucault and reflect one last time on the connections between education, interculturality and indoctrination:

> Every educational system is a political means of maintaining or of modifying the appropriation of discourse, with the knowledge and the powers it carries with it. (Foucault, 1972: 227)

Is education always a political means? Could you think of counter-examples, and maybe in relation to ICER?

Note

1   By using 'could' in these questions, I wish to indicate that there is not just one single 'truth' in answering them.

References

Abe, K. (2006). *The Face of Another*. Penguin Modern Classic.
Bedford, O. & Yeh, K.-H. (2019). The history and the future of the psychology of filial piety: Chinese norms to contextualized personality construct. *Frontiers in Psychology 10*, 100. https://doi.org/10.3389/fpsyg.2019.00100
Brandenberger, D. (2012). *Propaganda State in Crisis: Soviet Ideology, Indoctrination, and Terror under Stalin, 1927–1941*. Yale University Press.
Burr, V. (2015). *Social Constructionism*. Routledge.
Byram, M. (1997). *Teaching and Assessing Intercultural Communicative Competence*. Multilingual Matters.
Callan, E. & Arena, D. (2010). Indoctrination. In Siegel, H. (ed.). *The Oxford Handbook of Philosophy of Education* (online edition). OUP. https://doi.org/10.1093/oxfordhb/9780195312881.003.0007. Accessed 1 Oct. 2024.
Casement, W. (1983). Another look at indoctrination. *The Journal of Educational Thought (JET) / Revue de la Pensée Éducative 17*(3), 230–240.
Chen, N. (2024). *Preparing Teachers and Students for Diversity and Interculturality in Higher Education*. Helsinki University Press.
Cheng, A. (2007). *Can China Think?* Collège de France.
Coady, D. (2024). Stop talking about echo chambers and filter bubbles. *Education Theory 74*, 92–107. https://doi.org/10.1111/edth.12620?>
Dahlbeck, J. (2021). Spinoza on the teaching of doctrines: Towards a positive account of indoctrination. *Theory and Research in Education 19*(1), 78–99. https://doi.org/10.1177/1477878521996235
Davey, A. G. (1972). Education or Indoctrination? *Journal of Moral Education 2*(1), 5–15. https://doi.org/10.1080/0305724720020102
Dervin, F. & Peng, J. (2024). Introduction: Online interculturality and the ideological in education. In: Dervin, F., Peng, J. et al. (eds.). (pp. 1–14). *Interculturality Online: Ideological Constructions and Considerations for Higher Education*. Routledge.
Dervin, F. & Simpson, A. (2020). *Interculturality and the Political Within Education*. Routledge.
Dervin, F. (2011). A plea for change in research on intercultural discourses: A 'liquid' approach to the study of the acculturation of Chinese students. *Journal of Multicultural Discourses 6*(1), 37–52. https://doi.org/10.1080/17447143.2010.532218
Dervin, F. (2016). *Interculturality in Education*. Palgrave.
Dervin, F. (2023). *Communicating Around Interculturality in Research and Education*. Routledge.
Dervin, F. (2024). *Interculturologies*. Springer.
Dorion, L.-A. (2012). Enkrateia and the partition of the soul in the Gorgias. In: Barney, R., Brennan, T. & Brittain, C. (eds.). *Plato and the Divided Self* (pp. 33–52). Cambridge University Press.
Dragos Aligica, P. & Preda, S. (2022). *The Institutionalization of Indoctrination: An Exploratory Investigation based on the Romanian Case Study*. Lexington.
Dvoinin, A. & Bulanova, S. B. (2021). Psychology of indoctrination: Approaches and current research directions. *Voprosy Psikhologii 66*(4), 3–15.
Erickson, J., Yan, B. & Huang, J. (2023). Bridging echo chambers? Understanding political partisanship through semantic network analysis. *Social Media + Society 9*(3). https://doi.org/10.1177/20563051231186368

Etymonline.com (2024). *Indoctrination.* www.etymonline.com/word/indoctrination#etymonline_v_42449
Flew, A. (1966). What is indoctrination? *Studies in Philosophy and Education 4*, 281–306. https://doi.org/10.1007/BF00376315
Foucault, M. (1972). *The Archaeology of Knowledge.* Pantheon Books.
Gao, C., Zhao, G & Fourati, H. (eds.). (2019). *Cooperative Localization and Navigation. Theory, Research, and Practice.* CRC Press.
Garrison, J. W. (1986). The Paradox of Indoctrination: A Solution. *Synthese 68*(2), 261–273.
Gatchel, R. H. (1959). Evolution of concepts of indoctrination in American education. *The Educational Forum 23*(3), 303–309. https://doi.org/10.1080/00131725909338731
Goody, J. (2007). *The Theft of History.* CUP.
Green, T. F. (1964). A topology of the teaching concept. *Studies in Philosophy and Education 3*, 284–319. https://doi.org/10.1007/BF00375980
Hadley, G. & Boon, A. (2022). *Critical Thinking.* Routledge.
Hassan, M., Mattingly, D. & Nugent, E. (2022). Political Control. *Annual Review of Political Science 25*, 155–174. https://doi.org/10.1146/annurev-polisci-051120-013321
Holliday, A. (2010). *Intercultural Communication and Ideology.* Sage.
Hutton, E. L. (ed.). (2016). *Dao Companion to the Philosophy of Xunzi.* Springer.
Huttunen, R. (2016). Habermas and the problem of indoctrination. In: Peters, M. (ed.). *Encyclopedia of Educational Philosophy and Theory* (pp. 1–11). Springer.
Huxley, A. (2022). *The Complete Works of Aldous Huxley.* Strelbytskyy Multimedia Publishing.
Kord, H. & Thornton, G. C. (2021). *Grey Behaviors after Logical Fallacies in Public and Professional Communication.* Routledge.
Lankford, A. (2009). *Human Killing Machines: Systematic Indoctrination in Iran, Nazi Germany, al-Qaeda, and Abu Ghraib.* Lexington Books.
Lee, M.-H. (2017). *Confucianism: Its Roots and Global Significance.* University of Hawaii Press
Lessing, D. (2012). *The Golden Notebook.* HarperCollins.
Madi, M. A. (2019). *The Dark Side of Nudges.* Routledge.
Mattson, C., Johansson, T. & Andreasson, J. (2024). *Countering Right Wing Extremism in Education.* Routledge.
McGinn, C. (2014). *Mindfucking. A Critique of Mental Manipulation.* Routledge.
Merry, M. (2005). Indoctrination, moral instruction, and nonrational beliefs: A place for autonomy? *Educational Theory 55*(4), 399–420. https://doi.org/10.1111/j.1741-5446.2005.00002.x-i1
Momanu, M. (2012). The Pedagogical dimension of indoctrination: Criticism of indoctrination and the constructivism in education. *Meta: Research in Hermeneutics, Phenomenology, And Practical Philosophy 4*(1), 88–105.
Moosavi, L. (2022). Turning the decolonial gaze towards ourselves: Decolonising the curriculum and 'decolonial reflexivity' in sociology and social theory. *Sociology 57*(1), 137–156. https://doi.org/10.1177/00380385221096037
Neundorf, A., Nazrullaeva, E., Northmore-Ball, K., Tertytchnaya, K. & Kim, W. (2024). Varieties of indoctrination: The politicization of education and the media around the world. *Perspectives on Politics 22*(2), 771–798.
Olejnik, L. (2024). *Propaganda From Disinformation and Influence to Operations and Information Warfare.* Routledge.
Orwell, G. (1942). Review of 'WE' by E. I. Zamyatin. January 4, 1946. Available at: www.orwell.ru/library/reviews/zamyatin/english/e_zamy#:~:text=The%20first%20thing%20anyone%20would%20notice

Orwell, G. (2009). *1984*. Infobase Holdings, Inc.
Orwell, G. (2017). *On Truth*. Random House.
Palmer, R. R. (1957). Education and indoctrination. *Peabody Journal of Education 34*(4), 224–228.
Peng, R., Zhu, C. & Wu, W.-P, (2019). Visualizing the knowledge domain of intercultural competence research: A bibliometric analysis. *International Journal of Intercultural Relations 74*, 58–68. https://doi.org/10.1016/j.ijintrel.2019.10.008
Puolimatka, T. (1996). The concept of indoctrination. *Philosophia Reformata 61*(2), 109–134.
R'boul, H. (2022). Epistemological plurality in intercultural communication knowledge. *Journal of Multicultural Discourses 17*(2), 173–188. https://doi.org/10.1080/17447 143.2022.2069784
R'boul, H. & Dervin, F. (2024). Attempts at including, mediating and creating 'new' knowledges: Problematising appropriation in intercultural communication education and research. Applied Linguistics Review. Advance online publication. https://doi.org/ 10.1515/applirev-2024-0009
Reboul, O. (1977). *L'endoctrinement*. PUF.
Risager, K. (2024). Critical interculturality in a global perspective: A matter of geopolitical position, sociocultural nexus, and existential relevance. In: Dervin, F. (ed.). *The Routledge Handbook of Critical Interculturality in Communication and Education* (pp. 27–38). Routledge.
Rogers Berner, A. (2024). *Educational Pluralism and Democracy: How to Handle Indoctrination, Promote Exposure, and Rebuild America's Schools*. Harvard Education Press.
Sait, B. (2019). *The Indoctrination of the Wehrmacht: Nazi Ideology and the War Crimes of the German Military*. Berghahn Books.
Shen, H. (2023). Bilingual postgraduates' potentials for original research by translanguaging for theorizing. *Beijing International Review of Education 4*(4), 703–723. https://doi.org/ 10.1163/25902539-04040012
Siegel, H. (2017). "You take the wheel, I'm tired of driving; Jesus, Show Me the Way": Doctrines, indoctrination, and the suppression of critical dispositions. In: Siegel, H. (ed.). *Education's Epistemology: Rationality, Diversity, and Critical Thinking* (pp. 67–75). OUP.
Snook, I. A. (2024). *Indoctrination and Education*. Routledge.
Spiecker, B. (1987). Indoctrination, intellectual virtues and rational emotions. *Journal of Philosophy of Education 21*, 261–266. https://doi.org/10.1111/j.1467-9752.1987. tb00165.x
Steutel, J., Spiecker, B. (1997). Rational passions and intellectual virtues. A conceptual analysis. In: Siegel, H. (ed.). *Reason and Education* (pp. 59–71). Springer.
Tan, C. (2008). *Teaching Without Indoctrination: Implications for Values Education*. Brill.
Tan, C. (2012). *Islamic Education and Indoctrination: The Case in Indonesia*. Routledge.
Taylor, R. M. (2017). Indoctrination and social context: A system-based approach to identifying the threat of indoctrination and the responsibilities of educators. *Journal of Philosophy of Education 51*, 38–58. https://doi.org/10.1111/1467-9752.12180
Thaler, R. H. & Sunstein, C. R. (2008). *Nudge: Improving Decisions About Health, Wealth, and Happiness*. Yale University Press.
Thompson, J. B. (1987). Language and ideology: A framework for analysis. *The Sociological Review 35*(3), 516–536. https://doi.org/10.1111/j.1467-954X.1987.tb00554.x
Wagner, P.A. (2021). The Methods, benefits and limitations of indoctrination in mathematics education. *Interchange 52*, 41–56. https://doi.org/10.1007/s10780-021-09415-7

Walker, R. L. (2009). Respect for *Rational* Autonomy. *Kennedy Institute of Ethics Journal 19*(4), 339–366. https://dx.doi.org/10.1353/ken.0.0301.

Watts, A. (2019). *Tao: The Watercourse Way*. Souvenir Press.

White, J. P. (1967). Indoctrination. In: Peters, R. S. (ed.). *The Concept of Education* (pp. 177–191). Routledge

Wilcox, R. T. (1988) Indoctrination is not a four-letter word. *The Clearing House 61(*6), 249–252. https://doi.org/10.1080/00098655.1988.10113941

Wilson, J. (1972). Indoctrination and rationality. In: Snook, I. A. (ed.). *Concepts of Indoctrination: Philosophical Essays* (pp. 17–24). Routledge.

Zamyatin, Y (1993). *We*. Penguin books.

Zembylas, M. (2022) Rethinking political socialization in schools: The role of 'affective indoctrination'. *Educational Philosophy and Theory 54*(14), 2480–2491. https://doi.org/10.1080/00131857.2021.2006634

Zembylas, M. (2023). The affective ideology of the OECD global competence framework: implications for intercultural communication education. *Pedagogy, Culture & Society 31*(2), 305–323. https://doi.org/10.1080/14681366.2022.2164336

Zhou, V. X. (2022). Engaging non-essentialism as lived wisdom: A dialogue between intercultural communication and Buddhism. *Language and Intercultural Communication 22*(3), 294–311. https://doi.org/10.1080/14708477.2022.2046768

Zovko, M.-E. & Dillon, J. M. (eds.). (2021). *Bildung and Paideia*. Philosophical Models of Education. Routledge.

Étagère 3
INTELLECTUAL INERTIA UNBOUND

Étagère 3 …

- Examines the resistance to change in beliefs and ideologies within ICER.
- Identifies factors that contribute to intellectual inertia.
- Suggests methods for fostering critical thinking and reflexivity.

Five basic questions

1. Have you ever come across the term *intellectual inertia*? What could it mean, especially in relation to Intercultural Communication Education and Research?
2. How could intellectual inertia manifest in current educational and research practices in relation to the notion of interculturality? In your context(s) and elsewhere?
3. How could power dynamics within e.g., educational institutions and research settings influence the perpetuation of intellectual inertia and hinder moving forward with e.g., critiques and decolonising of interculturality?
4. How could educators and researchers develop reflexive approaches to their work to counteract intellectual inertia and promote more critical research and education on interculturality?
5. What role could language play in creating and maintaining intellectual inertia, and how could educators and researchers use language as a stimulating and challenging tool for intercultural education and research?

7. ¹ Yarn II

For this second yarn, I wish to discuss a short story written by Franz Kafka (1883–1924) in 1914, *In the penal colony* (*In der Strafkolonie*) (Kafka, 2002), to illustrate the issue of intellectual inertia. I understand the concept minimally here as *the tendency to maintain the status quo or old patterns of thinking when faced with new information or changes* but also as *a lack of motivation to move forward in one's un-re-thinking in the way we teach and research interculturality*. Set in an unnamed location, Kafka's grotesque short story (about 30 pages) explores the topics of control, justice (and its potential absurdities), power and the dehumanisation of some forms of punishment. Many aspects of *In the penal colony* critique unthinking adherence to authorities and traditions – two central aspects of intellectual inertia in education and research. The story begins with the arrival of an officer who has come to witness and observe the punishment of a prisoner ('the Condemned') in the colony. The punishment consists of a complex, torturous and painful instrument ('the Apparatus') which aims to inscribe a secret sentence onto the body of the Condemned. The entire process takes 12 hours. Only the latter and the officer in charge of the machine and its function (who is presented as zealous by the author, almost to the point of obsession), are aware of the content of the sentence. By the end of the punishment, there is an assumption that the Condemned will fully understand the justice of his punishment. The officer who has just arrived to learn about and observe the machine is first horrified by the brutality of the punishment. However, he becomes increasingly fascinated by it as its workings are described to him. *The Apparatus starts working.* The visiting officer and a priest who accompanies the Condemned to persuade him that the punishment is good for him, watch the procedure with growing uneasiness. The Condemned screams and squirms in agony. The priest begs for mercy but the operator of the Apparatus maintains that the process must go on. Hours go back and the Condemned does not seem to show any sign of contrition. The operator himself then starts doubting the utility of the machine (and the act of justice it aims to perform) and decides to use the Apparatus on himself in order to better grasp its purpose, asking the visiting officer to operate the machine on him – which the new officer refuses.

This short story is very relevant to reflect on intellectual inertia in what we do with interculturality in both education and research, in our search for knowledge. As such, one could see in the Apparatus the oppressive mechanisms used to control and punish (softly, symbolically and/or violently) those who are deemed inferior, irrelevant and/or disobedient as well as a symbol of colonial power. Kafka's story shows the machine operator's resistance to the visiting officer's intention to potentially abolish the old punishment methods, even in the face of its complete absurdity and cruelty. This resistance could be seen as a reflection of the challenges and lack of interest in adapting to and opening up to new epistemic and intellectual milieus in research and education. The story also highlights the dehumanising effects of an intricate bureaucracy (represented by the Apparatus in the story), where individuals are subject to impersonal systems that do not take into account their humanity, individuality, agency and resistance to injustice. This lack of compassion might lead to intellectual inertia, withdrawal and the refusal/lack of motivation to move forward in one's work [and like most fields of research, ICER faces pressure such as stress related to workload, reviews and evaluations; publish or perish; career progression linked to attracting funding (see more discussions below)].

In the short story, the prisoner's passive acceptance is described as follows: "And this, indeed, made it all the more remarkable that the prisoner was actually making every effort to follow the officer's explanations. With a certain sort of sleepy tenacity, he would always direct his gaze upon whatever it was at which the officer was pointing" (Kafka, 2002: 99). I also note that the power dynamics in the story, whereby a few individuals hold control over the lives and fates of others, can be compared to real-world situations where power is concentrated and used to control and/or oppress [which is often the case in ICER, with a few selected individuals located in the west having the power to speak for and over others, making indirect decisions about what concepts, methods and references should dominate the field (Peng et al., 2019)]. *In the penal colony* also touches on the importance of language and communication in understanding and being understood. The operator's inability to convince the visiting officer of the machine's merits could be seen itself as a failure of intercultural communication. Similarly, the Condemned's lack of understanding and his acceptance of the situation whereby the operator starts using the machine on himself as *revenge*, rather than *questioning the system or seeking change*, reflects a lack of critical thinking – or intellectual inertia:

> The condemned man especially seemed struck with the notion that some great change was impending. What had happened to him was now going to happen to the officer. Perhaps even to the very end. Apparently the foreign explorer [the visiting officer] had given the order for it. So this was revenge.
>
> *(Kafka, 2002: 118)*

Kafka's short story can serve as a transition between the theme of indoctrination from Étagère 2 to intellectual inertia in this Étagère. In the story, people are indoctrinated to believe that the torturing machine, in its specific way of constructing justice, is the right means. Although some of the characters hesitate and ask for mercy, they end up accepting the status quo, they stop *unrethinking*.

In this Étagère I argue that we often run a similar risk in ICER and that it represents a big danger, especially in contradictory, unstable and violent times like ours. Although we live in times of academic decolonising, generalised calls for epistemic diversities to be taken into account and '*justices*', there are many clear signs that we have been instilled (new) beliefs by repetition, without our full conscious acceptance and critical evaluation – which prevents us from 'talking the talk, walking the walk'. Many of us stop seeing (real) problems to focus on the 'usual', averting taboo discussions about e.g., the damages and contradictions of capitalism and/or (economic) political manipulations of research and education related to interculturality. Many of us also stop asking (real) questions. Many of us work through and with obvious contradictions, to which we have become blind or simply ignore to remain in comfortable positions. We could coin the new term of *paradoxiplication* (multiplication of contradictions/paradoxes) to describe what intellectual inertia and acceptance of the status quo are currently doing to ICER.

Some of today's biggest contradictions about interculturality hinting at intellectual inertia might include:

- 1. Lazy push for and promotion of (inoperable) non-essentialist perspectives to make our dominating voices feel 'good' [non-essentialism is part of the vital continuum of *essentialism-non-essentialism* for social beings and cannot 'win over' essentialism] [a naïve focus on non-essentialism means the end of ICER];
- 2. Pretentious calls for criticality which ignore criticality of criticality (Dervin, 2022) ["you must be critical!"; "recite *my* critiques!"; "do not question my critiques!"] [favouring non-essentialism leads to the end of criticality];
- 3. Litanies of decolonising while performing neo-colonising [decoloniality as a potentially traitorous buzzword; *I decolonise while recolonising*];
- 4. Tokenization of research by inserting the 'other' in non-strategic places in publications [*illustrate and confirm* rather than *disrupt or theorise 'otherwise'*];
- 5. Language is still used as a mere tool or simply ignored in ICER while discourses of multilingualism and translanguaging appear to be omnipresent.

[Rereading these contradictions hinting at intellectual inertia in our field, I can't help thinking about the metaphor of *the pot calling the kettle black*: if a pot, blackened from soot, calls a kettle black, it is being hypocritical since they are both the same colour ...]

6. A short thought experiment: The unseen bias story

[Year 2055, a famous research institute, the Centre for Intercultural Studies (CIS), a pioneer in the field of intercultural communication education for decades. The CIS is known for its Harmony Model, a theoretical framework developed by the founder of the institute, Lilly Korman, which has guided countless global studies and practical applications in fostering understanding and cooperation interculturally.]

The Harmony Model is based on the principle of cultural congruence, suggesting that the most effective intercultural interactions take place when people from different cultures adopt the norms and values of the dominant culture within a given context. This model has been widely accepted and is deeply ingrained in the institute's research methodology and practice and in other departments of ICER around the world.

A young researcher, Preston Yuan, joins the CIS with a background in cognitive anthropology and a fresh perspective on interculturality. Yuan has been studying the concept of cultural emergence, which maintains that innovative and mutually beneficial interactions arise when cultures maintain their distinct identities and engage in open dialogue without the need for one to assimilate to the other. As Yuan reviews the past research conducted at CIS, they notice a pattern: Studies tend to focus on the benefits of adopting the so-called dominant culture's norms and often overlook the potential of cultural differences to enrich interactions. Yuan thus proposes a new research agenda to explore the value of cultural differences and the dynamics of their framework of cultural emergence.

Consider the following points to start engaging with the problem of intellectual inertia in ICER:

a.
- Discuss the potential biases inherent in the (fictitious) Harmony Model. How might these biases influence the types of research questions asked, the methods used and the conclusions drawn by the research team?
- How might the focus of the institute's Harmony Model on cultural congruence lead to intellectual inertia in the study of interculturality? What aspects of intercultural interactions could be overlooked as a result?

b.
- Stage a debate between Yuan, who advocates for the study of cultural emergence, and a senior researcher at the CIS who defends the Harmony Model. What arguments might each side present?
- Develop a strategy for Yuan to introduce their concept to the CIS without alienating the established researchers who are committed to the Harmony Model.

c.
- Envision a future for the CIS where both the Harmony Model and Yuan's concept of cultural emergence coexist and inform a more comprehensive approach to intercultural studies.
- Consider the ethical implications of intellectual inertia in intercultural research. How might it affect the way interculturality is perceived and conceptualised?

5. (Defy)(ning) intellectual inertia

5.3. Biases, ideologies, institutions lead to intellectual inertia

The English word inertia is a term from physics dating back to the 17th century. It is based on Latin for unskillfulness, ignorance, inactivity (etymonline.com,

58 Intercultural Self-Defence

FIGURE 3.1 A simple definition of intellectual inertia? "When I stopped thinking".

2024a). Synonyms for inertia in English include: idleness, indolence, lethargy and laziness (antonyms: industry, drive, ambition, energy …) (see Figure 3.1. showing a sticker saying 'When I stopped thinking' glued on a wall on the streets of Bern, Switzerland in 2024).

For H. Cixous (1993: 39) "Thinking is trying to think the unthinkable: Thinking the thinkable is not worth the effort". What does this tell us potentially about intellectual inertia, especially in relation to ICER? What is 'thinking' to you? How about the 'unthinkable'?

The topic of intellectual inertia has not been addressed head on in ICER, although some publications relate to critiques of intellectual inertia in the field (e.g., critiques of culturalism in Holliday, 2010; Piller, 2010, Dervin, 2016; critiques of non-essentialism in Dervin, 2022; discussions of epistemic appropriation in R'boul & Dervin, 2024). In the broader social sciences, the concept of intellectual inertia has been explored by several scholars. The following publications aim to pique your interest further in the topic (in chronological order).

Let me start with a paper from approximately 30 years ago that I find useful for studying and explaining the continuum of change and persistence in what we do, think and say. In their paper *Shared Mental Models: Ideologies and Institutions*, Denzau and North (1994) examine the role of what they refer to as *shared mental models* in shaping and sustaining ideologies and institutions. Shared mental models correspond to common cognitive structures that we develop through interaction with others who tend to be similar to us. These models help us interpret and predict e.g., the behaviour and mentality of others, thus forming some kind of consensus with specific groups. Ideology can be seen as a type of shared mental model that influences people's perceptions and actions regarding economic and political systems (see Roucek, 1944). Ideologies are crucial in making decisions, especially under conditions of uncertainty (see Dervin, 2024). *Another interesting point*: Denzau and North's (1994) article problematises the stability of institutions, noting that thanks to shared mental models, institutions often exhibit path dependence, meaning that e.g., history and traditions play significant roles in their persistence. The authors also discuss the persistence of what they call *suboptimal performance* in institutions, noting that due to shared mental models and path dependence, societies may maintain poor and deficient institutional arrangements for extended periods, even in the face of more effective alternatives (Denzau & North, 1994). Intellectual inertia occurs when shared mental models and institutions become entrenched and resistant to change, maintaining the status quo not because it is the best option, but because it is the most familiar and widely accepted one (Denzau & North, 1994).

In a book edited by Lamiell and Slaney in 2020, titled *Problematic Research Practices and Inertia in Scientific Psychology. History, Sources, and Recommended Solutions*, the authors explore intellectual inertia by focusing on problematic beliefs and assumptions in research practices in the field of psychology – which has often influenced ICER. These include: systematic misapprehension of statistical knowledge, reliance on null hypothesis testing (no difference between groups or no relationship between variables) and reluctance to use qualitative methods (Lamiell & Slaney, 2020). The focus is on research practices and represent an inspiration for what we might do (badly) in ICER.

In the field of economics, Faghih and Samadi (2024) unpack the causes, concepts, effects and types of institutional inertia in relation to economic growth and development. In their chapter, *The Roots of Cognitive Inertia: An Introduction to Institutional Changes*, Samadi et al. (2024) discuss the origins and characteristics of cognitive inertia or the "tendency to perpetuate beliefs after they are formed". The authors argue that institutional inertia often derives from this specific form of inertia. They have identified the follow biases supporting cognitive inertia (Samadi et al., 2024):

- *status-quo bias* (preference for the familiar over the unfamiliar in e.g., making decisions),
- *self-attribution bias* (successes are attributed to personal skills and failures to factors beyond one's control),
- *conservatism bias* (prior views or forecasts are kept at the expense of new knowledge),
- *confirmation bias* (interpretation of information that supports one's existing beliefs),
- *commitment escalation bias* (commitment to past behaviours that do not necessarily have desirable outcomes),
- *belief bias* (the strength of an argument is evaluated based on its plausibility).

[How many of these biases have we faced in ICER, as knowledge consumers, disseminators and/or producers? How do the aforementioned five 'biggest' contradictions faced by ICER (see end of section 7) fare in relation to these biases?]

5.2. Intellectual inertia as epistemic and identarian stagnation

Let's expand on the definitions of intellectual inertia a bit more. From what we have already seen, it seems to refer to the resistance and sluggishness to change in e.g., one's beliefs, ideas, ideologies or ways of thinking. It is a cognitive and psychological phenomenon whereby individuals find it difficult to let go of established frameworks, even when confronted with new information, knowledge, alternative viewpoints and/or evidence that challenge their existing views. [Anti-intellectualism is often what intellectual inertia leads to.] Comfort, familiarity, harmlessness of and lack of urge to move beyond specific current understanding usually lead to intellectual inertia. In other words, the mental discomfort that arises from holding two or more potentially contradictory beliefs, values and/or ideologies can lead to intellectual inertia as individuals avoid discomfort by dismissing new information. Other reasons might apply such as *confirmation bias* [see above – the tendency to search for, interpret and remember information in a way that confirms one's pre-existing beliefs, while ignoring or discounting contradictory evidence]; *entrenchment in tradition* [long-standing traditions, practices and/or norms can create a strong foundation for intellectual inertia, as change may be seen as a threat to the status quo]; *fear of uncertainty* [the unknown can be unsettling and some of us may prefer to stick with what they know, even if it's flawed, rather than embracing new ideas that introduce uncertainty]; *a lack of exposure* to diverse perspectives can lead to a narrow worldview, making it difficult for individuals to consider alternative epistemologies (R'boul, 2022; Graiouid, 2024). Intellectual inertia might also have to do with identity. As such beliefs can be closely tied to one's identity or in-group and changing one's mind could thus be experienced as a threat to that identity or position in a given structure.

The words *stagnation* (coined in English in the 17th century from Latin for standing water, pond or swamp) and *rigidity* (from Latin for hard, stiff and severe) function well to describe many aspects of intellectual inertia. As such, it is both driven by and leading to mental and ideological stagnation as well as cognitive and epistemic rigidity. Many -isms can also help us expand our understanding of intellectual inertia: *Conservatism* [in a non-political sense, i.e. the tendency to prefer the traditional and tried methods over new or innovative approaches]; *dogmatism* [the tendency to hold strong, unchanging opinions with little consideration for alternative viewpoints], *traditionalism* [adherence to long-established practices, methods or ideas at the expense of originality]. Finally, *complacency* also has to do with intellectual inertia, whereby one is satisfied with one's current level of knowledge or understanding, without a desire for learning and exploration.

It is easy to guess how much all of these can lead to develop stereotyping and negative representations by e.g., oversimplifying.

In research, all these phenomena can occur through e.g., resistance to new ideas, reliance on established theories without critical examination, or a lack of incorporation of emerging perspectives from e.g., other parts of the world, languages and/or disciplines. Through *exclusive methodologies* [e.g., solely quantitative], *language insensitivity and indifference* [how language shapes and limits understanding, see e.g., connotations, nuances and contexts (Étagère 4)], *un-reflexivity* [e.g., impact of scholar's own ideologies, positionality and/or religious/political beliefs on the research process and outcomes], *a lack of public engagement to disseminate research findings and stimulate public debates*, *a lack of interest in lifelong learning and 'monocultural' research teams and contexts*, intellectual inertia tends to 'tiptoe' into our offices, lecture halls, laboratories …

5.1. When inertia creeps into ICER

5.1.2. Signs of inertia

In the field of intercultural communication education and research, some ideas and practices may exhibit signs of intellectual inertia.

At a basic level, some of us may cling and adhere to traditional, normative and (what some might refer to as) outdated concepts of 'truth', such as the belief that *cultures are static* and *can be taught and understood* through set patterns, overlooking diverse diversities from within and the agency of individuals.

In recent years (as hinted at earlier) we might have placed too much emphasis on non-/anti-essentialism (e.g., Borghetti & Qin, 2022; Maele & Jin, 2022; Zhou & Pilcher, 2017; Dervin, 2016), which rejects any 'universal truth' or specific characteristics, leading at times to empty and harmful relativism and confusion in educational practices – making it difficult for e.g. students to grasp the very idea of interculturality. The phenomenon of overexposure to such ideological constructs, similar to the phenomenon of saturation, might lead to the concept being considered as uninteresting and unchallenging over time …

The current focus on replicating previous studies without adding significant new insights or questioning the existing frameworks fits into intellectual inertia.

Similarly, the expectations of readers, students and colleagues do play a significant role in discussions of intellectual inertia and of the impact of specific work. If the audience is looking for e.g. practical solutions and a scholar is more theoretical, there might be a mismatch. [My work has often been qualified as *philosophical* – meaning too difficult, too theoretical, too hard to read. But I never gave up and continued writing since I believed in what I did. I will never retreat from theoretical analysis, the world of ideas or criticality (of criticality), even if I get criticised for being too 'difficult' to read.]

In many cases, scholars increasingly note that there may be insufficient recognition and addressing of knowledge and power imbalances in ICER, which can result in content and methods that do not adequately reflect or resolve around these issues, thereby maintaining the status quo rather than fostering change (Moosavi, 2023). Relying heavily on the works of a few prominent figures in ICER (Peng et al., 2019), without critically engaging with their ideas or considering alternative viewpoints could be common and problematic.

Another issue rests in the fact that intercultural research often involves navigating different languages and communication styles, which can be challenging and may lead some researchers to stick to what they know – or to ignore the issue of language entirely, bringing about 'shaky' research (House et al., 2024).

Finally, let's bear in mind that some forms of ICER may perpetuate stereotypes and biases about certain groups of people, which not only limits perspectives but can also exacerbate e.g. in-/direct discrimination and even conflicts – problems that ICER often aims to address.

5.1.1. Structural inertia infecting ICER

It does take courage to push things forward in a field like ICER. What is more, pioneering new ideas may be risky and expose ('novice') researchers to criticism from peers, especially if the new ideas challenge established norms or paradigms. As such, some of us, established scholars, may resist paradigm shifts that could challenge our authoritative status, which is built upon our existing body of work and the theories we have helped popularise. By adhering to 'traditional' methods and theories, we can maintain our 'reputation' and 'influence' within ICER. And if we have access to significant resources, such as funding, we may even be reluctant to support new ideas that could redirect these resources towards emerging areas of research. This could lead to a preference for projects that align with established norms and our own ideas.

It is also important to note that those of us in control of e.g. national and international academic journals, conferences and publication channel classification systems, may be more likely to accept papers and support journals/publishers that align with current paradigms, making it difficult for new ideas to gain traction. This could create a self-reinforcing cycle where only research that supports some form of intellectual inertia in ICER is published, disseminated and recognised. Although these gatekeeping practices are ethically unacceptable and to be condemned, they are not unheard of [see for instance the Anti Colourism/Eurocentrism in Methods and Practices (ACEMAP) task force's recommendations and resources to counteract racism and global exclusion in standard publication practices (Society for Personality and Social Psychology) in Ledgerwood et al. (2024); for ICER see R'boul (2022) on editorial boards and publishing practices of some intercultural journals].

Academic institutions can also have rigid structures and expectations that might favour traditional research methods and theories, making it difficult for innovative approaches to pick up steam. As mentioned before, the pressure to publish in established journals related to intercultural communication education and research (which are very limited in some indexes such as the Social Sciences Citation Index, which is used in e.g. China for international publications) can discourage researchers from pursuing what they consider as unconventional or groundbreaking ideas in relation to interculturality. In *How bibliometric evaluation makes the academia an 'Iron Cage': Evidence from Chinese academics*, Jin and Jiang (2024) interviewed Chinese scholars from different fields of research to observe the consequences of bibliometric evaluation. They note disruptions of scholarly autonomy, undermined self-efficacy, limited motivation for innovative research and unscrupulous behaviours amongst colleagues [NB: these are not unfamiliar in the field of ICER; see also Liu & Zheng, 2024].

What is more, although ICER is a broad and interdisciplinary field, specialisation in 'subfields' (e.g. applied linguistics, teacher education, nursing) and following specific 'big names' only could lead to silos of knowledge, where researchers are not encouraged or motivated to engage with ideas from other disciplines that could stimulate new ways of thinking.

Finally, the issue of resource constraints should not be ignored. Innovative research often requires resources that may not be available, especially for work that does not align with traditional approaches or is seen as high-risk. I have met colleagues who had to reorient their research entirely in order to get a position and thus access funding for their research.

[Let me say a few more words about the influence of capitalism and neoliberalism on ICER. Under these frameworks, intercultural research may be driven by market logic and economic efficiency, which could lead us to focus more on areas that offer *immediate economic returns* (either for an institution or for oneself through promotion or a bonus). This bias may limit the breadth and depth of research, resulting in strong intellectual inertia. I also note that, as hinted at before, the distribution of research funding often leans towards established and influential research areas and scholars (Thelwall et al., 2023). This imbalance in resource distribution can make it difficult for promising, creative and (really) interdisciplinary perspectives on intercultural communication education and research to gain sufficient support. This corresponds to some of the aspects that Faghih and Samadi (2024) discussed in their aforementioned book on institutional inertia].

[Pause 1: Barthes, Bergson and Confucius and the burning issue of intellectual inertia]

Let's take a short break now.

I want us to escape from the world of ICER for a moment and to deepen our thinking about intellectual inertia by discussing the (projected) views of three important thinkers, who have influenced my work immensely. The three of them are often considered as 'philosophers', with two from 20th-century Europe and one from ancient China [rereading this section, I ask myself: could having chosen two white men and a 'safe' and 'usual' Chinese thinker be a sign of intellectual inertia in my writing?].

Roland Barthes (1915–1980) was a French literary theorist, philosopher and critic at Collège de France in Paris. One could easily say that his work has had a significant impact on the fields of semiotics, social theory, the study of culture and beyond. Although his ideas have been influential in research and education, particularly in e.g. the way we understand and interpret 'cultural' phenomena and texts, he has been marginally used in intercultural studies (exceptions: Demeulenaere, 2023; Knight, 2020). Barthes inspired me from 2020 onwards. Through engaging with his ideas and writings, I started to experiment with different ways of positioning myself and my thoughts in my writing. His approach is multifaceted, involving a critical examination of language, ideology and the roles of both producers and consumers of knowledge.

Barthes used semiotic and post-structuralist frameworks to deconstruct and challenge the rut. What would Barthes say about intellectual inertia? First, he would probably argue that intellectual inertia is often perpetuated by the acceptance of certain ideas and practices as 'natural' or inevitable (Barthes, 2020). He would encourage us researchers and educators to deconstruct these assumptions, revealing e.g. the linguistic, historical and ideological constructs that underlie them. Barthes was fascinated by the way language shapes people's understanding of the world (Barthes, 2010). He might have suggested that intellectual inertia is reinforced by the language used in academic and educational discourses, and that challenging this language is a key step in breaking the inertia. Barthes (English translation in Compagnon, 1997: 198) writes: "Language is legislation, *langue* is its code. We do not see power in language, because we forget that all language is a classification, and that all classifications are oppressive". This statement stresses how language can enforce certain perspectives while suppressing others [as we shall see in the next Étagère, Barthes (1993: 461) called language 'fascist'].

I would like to argue that his work on mythologies could be relevant to discuss intellectual inertia too (Barthes, 2009). Barthes would explore how certain myths or ideologies become embedded in educational and research practices, creating a sort of 'common sense' that resists change in relation to interculturality. By exposing these myths, he would seek to disrupt our intellectual inertia [my 2024 book entitled *Interculturologies* (ideologies + imaginaries of interculturality in education and research), inspired by Barthes's (2009) *Mythologies*, does contribute to this 'noble' aim]. In his work, Barthes (2020) used the term *doxa* to describe the common sense or received opinions that go unchallenged. He would likely argue that intellectual inertia in ICER is maintained by the uncritical acceptance of doxa and that true intellectual inquiry should require constant questioning of these assumptions. In *The Eiffel Tower and Other Mythologies* Barthes (1997: 60) maintains that "We know that the war against intelligence is always waged in the name of *good sense*", implying that common sense, rather than being a bastion of clarity, can often be a tool used to maintain the status quo and discourage critical thought. Finally, in his book *Camera Lucida* about photography (Barthes, 1980), Barthes introduced the concept of the *punctum* (Latin for a tip or small point) to refer to a detail in a photograph that unexpectedly attracts and fascinates the viewer. He might have suggested that interculturalists should seek out their own *punctum* – the elements that disrupt our understanding and provoke new thoughts and perspectives.

One central aspect of Barthes's work has to do with the role of the writer vs. the reader. He might have argued that interculturalists as readers and writers should be encouraged to be more active in questioning and reinterpreting the texts and practices they engage with, rather than passively accepting received wisdom. His essay 'The Death of the Author' (Barthes, 1993) would be very relevant in discussions of intellectual inertia in ICER, as it challenges the authority of the author and promotes a more egalitarian and open interpretation of texts, which could encourage a less rigid approach to knowledge and thus further critical thinking, reflexivity and criticality of one's criticality. *When the author dies in Barthes, the reader is born.* In a similar vein, Barthes's writing about the importance of pleasure in the reading process (and thus learning! See Barthes, 1993) represents a powerful tool against intellectual inertia, as it motivates individuals to seek out new ideas and perspectives.

The second philosopher whom I would like to reflect on with you is Henri Bergson (1859–1941) who was a French (British) philosopher whose contemplation on time, life and consciousness had a profound impact in the early 20th century. Like Barthes, he was also a Professor at Collège de France in Paris and his weekly lectures attracted thousands of visitors from around the world. Bergson has been an inspiration for my work on interculturality since the 1990s (Dervin, 2010). Some of Bergson's core concepts, particularly his theories on the relationship between life, matter and consciousness resonate with intellectual inertia and interculturality in research and education. Bergson perceived intellectual inertia as a tendency in our cognitive processes that leads us to understand the world in static, mechanical terms, neglecting the dynamism and creativity of life (Lawlor, 2019). In his book *Creative Evolution* (Bergson, 1984), the philosopher introduces the concept of the élan vital (vital impetus) to describe the inner drive of life that continually pushes us forward and creates new forms. This impetus is a manifestation of life's struggle against the inertia of matter, seeking to release the maximum amount of accumulated energy with the least amount of effort, thereby achieving freedom and novelty within the material world (Bergson, 1984). Bergson saw life as insinuating itself into the material world, using the inherent flexibility and potential for change within matter to evolve and develop in ways that transcend mere mechanism [which cannot but remind us of interculturality!]. This vital impetus obviously stands in contrast to the idea of intellectual inertia.

Bergson (1975) further surveys the relationship between thought and matter and argues that, although thought is constrained by life (i.e., material conditions) to some extent, it also strives to transcend these limitations. This transcendence is not about shedding material constraints *per se* but rather about achieving a freer manipulation of the material world through deeper consciousness and spiritual practices (Bergson, 1975).

Bergson's perspectives offer important insights into understanding and overcoming intellectual inertia. First, the philosopher emphasises the dynamism and creativity of life and thought, cautioning against viewing the world and our thought processes through a static and mechanical lens. Second, he suggests the possibility of surpassing material limitations by deepening our consciousness and spiritual practices, which could lead to a freer engagement with the material world (Bergson, 1975). All in all, the philosopher's ideas about intellectual inertia are closely tied to his critique of the mechanistic view of life. He argues that our intellect, shaped by practical needs and habits, tends to approach the world in a way that is analytical and spatialised, which is not well-suited to grasping the dynamic and qualitative nature of life as it unfolds in time (Bergson, 1975). This understanding of intellectual inertia could be overcome through an act of intuition, which Bergson describes as a kind of sympathy or entering into the thing itself, rather than analysing it from the outside (see Gunter, 2023). Bergson's philosophy emphasises the dynamic, creative nature of life and consciousness, which he believed could not be fully captured by traditional mechanistic or 'intellectual' approaches (Dervin, 2024).

The last character of this Pause section is Confucius (551–479 B.C.E.). The ancient Chinese philosopher did not probably speak about intellectual inertia as we understand it today. Yet he did emphasise the importance of continuous learning, self-reflection/criticality and adaptability (Puett & Gross-Loh, 2016). Known as Kongzi (孔子) in China, Confucius was a philosopher and teacher who emphasised personal and governmental morality, correctness of social relationships, justice and sincerity. *The Analects* (論語), a collection of his sayings and ideas, is one of the central texts of Confucianism. Confucius has inspired me at different periods of my exploration of the notion of interculturality (e.g., Dervin, 2011, 2022). Instead of summarising his complex (and often contradictory) ideas, let me share five quotes from *The Analects* that, I believe, could have to do with different aspects intellectual inertia (all the followings are based on James Legge's English translation, see Confucius, 2024: n.p. NB: Confucius is referred to as 'The Master' in the quotes). Try to see if you agree with my interpretations of the quotes and, especially, what you make of the content for ICER:

1. 為政：子曰：由！誨女知之乎？知之為知之，不知為不知，是知也。

Wei Zheng: The Master said, "You, shall I teach you what knowledge is? When you know a thing, to hold that you know it; and when you do not know a thing, to allow that you do not know it – this is knowledge".

[This quote emphasises the importance of intellectual honesty and humility, by combining both the recognition of what we know and the acknowledgement of what we don't know. For ICER, the quote could be a reminder that learning comes from being open to ideas and willing to admit when we are wrong or when we don't have all the answers …]

2. 子曰：不憤不啟，不悱不發，舉一隅不以三隅反，則不復也。

The Master said, "I do not open up the truth to one who is not eager to get knowledge, nor help out any one who is not anxious to explain himself. When I have presented one corner of a subject to any one, and he cannot from it learn the other three, I do not repeat my lesson".

[This second quote from Confucius touches upon the principles of teaching-learning (and research!). It emphasises the importance of our active engagement and readiness to learn. Here, Confucius is stating that he will not impart knowledge to someone who is not genuinely interested or motivated to learn. The philosopher also urges us to be proactive in articulating our understanding or seeking clarification, thinking critically and making connections between different parts of the knowledge. All in all, for Confucius, our role as students, teachers and researchers is to guide and facilitate learning and reflecting, rather than to simply provide 'information'.]

3. 述而: 子曰：蓋有不知而作之者，我無是也。多聞擇其善者而從之，多見而識之，知之次也。

Shu Er: The Master said, "There may be those who act without knowing why. I do not do so. Hearing much and selecting what is good and following it; seeing much and keeping it in memory – this is the second style of knowledge".

[The quote seems to emphasise the importance of intellectual honesty. Confucius is maintaining that he does not act without understanding the reasons behind his actions and that we should be open to learning from various sources. By listening and observing extensively, we can discern what is valuable and worth e.g. emulating or remembering.]

4. 學而: 子曰：君子不重則不威，學則不固。主忠信，無友不如己者，過則勿憚改。

Xue Er: The Master said, "If the scholar be not grave, he will not call forth any veneration, and his learning will not be solid. Hold faithfulness and sincerity as first principles. Have no friends not equal to yourself. When you have faults, do not fear to abandon them".

[This fourth quote offers advice on the demeanour and conduct of students, educators and scholars who should be serious and dignified. If they are not, they will not command respect and their knowledge will lack depth and solidity. With "When you have faults, do not fear to abandon them", Confucius seems to be encouraging us to actively correct our 'mistakes'. There should be no shame in acknowledging and abandoning one's faults; it is part of the process of learning and self-improvement.]

5. 公冶長: 子貢問曰：孔文子何以謂之文也？
子曰：敏而好學，不恥下問，是以謂之文也。

Gong Ye Chang: Zi Gong asked, saying, "On what ground did Kong Wen get that title of Wen?". The Master said, "He was of an active nature and yet fond of learning, and he was not ashamed to ask and learn of his inferiors! On these grounds he has been styled Wen".

[This last quote from Confucius discusses the attributes that earned a character called Kong Wen his posthumous title of 'Wen' (which means 'cultured' or 'refined' in Chinese and is a title of respect and honour). Kong Wen is described as active and dynamic, always eager to learn but also open-minded and humble, willing to learn from anyone regardless of their status. In essence, this last passage from *The Analects* highlights the importance of humility, a 'love' for learning, and the ability to learn from everyone, regardless of their standing.]

4. A conceptual toolbox to apprehend intellectual inertia further

As I have made it clear now, analysing intellectual inertia, especially in the context of ICER, involves examining (amongst others) the ideological, psychological, social and institutional factors that contribute to stagnation and resistance to change. In this section I introduce seven concepts that can help us think further about this burning issue in research and education. Each of these concepts is introduced by a short (fictive) narrative or dialogue.

1. H. Rahayu, an Indonesian professor, arrived at the University of Vermont (USA) to teach intercultural communication as part of a visiting professorship. Her initial lectures were well-received but she soon found herself in an *echo chamber*. Her students, predominantly from liberal arts backgrounds, frequently mirrored her points through their own lenses, often critiquing other 'cultures', ignoring the cultural relativity perspective that she was stressing. Concerned, Rahayu attempted to diversify her teaching by incorporating a broader range of perspectives. She also introduced complex case studies and organized a panel with faculty from different parts of the

world. Despite her efforts, the students' deep-seated views were resistant to change and the (unbearable) echo chamber persisted.

Echo chambers are environments where people are predominantly exposed to opinions and information that align with their existing ideologies, beliefs and values, while contrasting viewpoints are minimal or absent. One can see that this phenomenon is particularly prevalent in the digital spaces that we use on a daily basis, where algorithms often prioritise content that resonates with our past behaviours and preferences, thereby creating personalised 'filter islands' (Al Atiqi, 2023).

In ICER, echo chambers can manifest in several ways. For example, scholars and educators may choose to engage only with research (and/or social media groups) that confirm their preconceived notions about interculturality, reinforcing e.g. epistemic reproduction or even stereotypes and biases rather than questioning or challenging misconceptions. Within echo chambers, a single narrative or perspective on the notion of interculturality (e.g. non-essentialism, decoloniality, translanguaging) can prevail, overshadowing the potential diversity of perspectives and critiques. Echo chambers can also create an illusion of consensus that does not and cannot reflect the broader spectrum of views in ICER in different parts of the world and in different languages.

2. (A simple meeting room with a table and two chairs. Fia, a Portuguese philosopher, and Singh, an Indian businessperson, are seated, discussing the challenges of interculturality.)

Fia: We face a barrier, Singh, in our quest for shared knowledge.

Singh: Barrier? You mean an intercultural gap?

Fia: Yes, it's like we have a partition between us. Our ideas, they hit this wall and don't pass through.

Singh: It's true. Our conversations, they're like two rivers flowing parallel, never merging.

Fia: We need to find common ground. But it's not so easy.

*Sing*h: Like trying to mix oil and water. No matter how much we stir, they remain separate.

Fia: We must keep trying, though. We can't just give up because of this ... this *epistemic friction*.

Singh: No, we must persist. We owe it to ourselves and our collaboration.

Fia: But it's exhausting, this constant struggle to be understood.

Singh: Perhaps we need new approaches, new ways to bridge the gap.

Fia: New approaches, yes. But for now, we continue as we are, hoping for clarity.

Singh: (nods) Hoping for clarity. Until we find a way to truly connect.

[They sit in thoughtful silence, acknowledging the difficulty of their task.]

Somewhat complementary to Echo Chambers, **Resistance to Epistemic Friction** corresponds to the reluctance or refusal to engage with the cognitive and social effort required to understand and appreciate different perspectives, which can be mentally challenging and disrupt one's comfort zone (Sher, 2016; Medina, 2013). Epistemic friction often arises when different knowledge systems, belief systems or imaginaries come into contact and create a form of cognitive dissonance and/or conflict. Interculturally in research and education, resistance to epistemic friction can manifest in several ways. It can occur when the voices or experiences of certain groups are systematically marginalised or discredited, leading to a resistance to acknowledge the validity of their knowledge or perspectives. When individuals encounter the beliefs and practices of another, they may resist engaging with their potential differences due to a fear of change or a desire to preserve their own ideologies, imaginaries and identities. At the same time, people may choose to engage only with media or social circles that reinforce their existing views, thus avoiding the friction that comes from exposure to different perspectives. An example could be seen in intercultural academic exchanges, where scholars and students from different contexts engage in dialogue. The process of navigating differing research paradigms, methodologies and theoretical frameworks can create epistemic friction. Resistance to this friction might come in the form of scholars and students sticking to familiar ways of knowing and understanding, rather than embracing the opportunity to learn from different epistemological perspectives.

3. As a postgraduate student of intercultural education in Canada, Satu was always eager to learn about new 'cultures'. One day, she came across an online personality test that promised to reveal deep insights into her so-called 'cultural adaptability'. Intrigued, she filled it out, answering questions about her preferences and attitudes towards different 'cultural practices'. A few days later, Satu received her results. The report described her as *open-minded, tolerant* and *curious, with a natural ability to embrace cultural diversity.* It also mentioned that *she might sometimes struggle with the ambiguity inherent in intercultural interactions but was generally well-equipped to navigate such intricacies.* Satu found the description strikingly accurate and felt validated in her passion for 'everything intercultural'. She shared the results with her classmates and some of her favourite professors. However, as she discussed the test with her best friend, they realized that the feedback was quite generic and could apply to many – most? – people. Satu noticed then

that she had fallen prey to the *Barnum effect*, whereby the desire for personal validation leads us to accept vague and general descriptions as 'true'.

Introduced by Meehl in 1956, **the Barnum Effect** (also referred to as the *Forer Effect*) is a psychological phenomenon whereby people tend to believe that elusive and general personality descriptions are highly precise and specifically tailored to them. Named after the famous American showman Phineas Taylor Barnum (1810–1891), who used pseudo-psychological personality tests in his circus shows, this effect highlights how we often accept broad statements as personal insights, mistaking them for unique discernments of our character (Gonthier & Thomassin, 2024). The test conducted by Forer (1949) is one of the classic studies on the Barnum Effect. In the study, they administered a personality test to students and then provided each of them with an envelope containing a printed personality description. The students were asked to rate the accuracy of the description. Later, the researcher revealed that the description was the same for everyone, deliberately designed to be vague and general enough to resonate with almost anyone. The purpose of this test was to demonstrate how we might tend to believe that descriptions, which are ambiguous and broadly applicable, are specifically tailored to us. This experiment is widely used in introductory psychology courses to illustrate this point to students, fostering their critical thinking about the scientific validity of psychological assessments. The test is also used to explain why people might accept and believe in inaccurate personality descriptions, even when they should be sceptical (Gonthier & Thomassin, 2024). I note that the Barnum Effect is often reminiscent of what is referred to as 'cold reading', a technique used by performers such as magicians, psychics and other entertainers to give the impression that they have a deep understanding of a person's life, character or problems without prior knowledge of them. This is achieved by making high-probability guesses, using vague statements ('sometimes', 'some say', 'either … or') that could apply to almost anyone and observing the subject's reactions to refine their statements (known as 'shotgunning').

In the context of intercultural research, the Barnum Effect can be used to think critically about e.g. research findings or statements about self-other since it can serve as a reminder to be cautious when accepting generalised descriptions of e.g. cultures, identities and personalities, but also concepts and ideologemes. For instance, some intercultural studies might provide broad statements about different 'cultural groups' that are vague enough to apply to many contexts (e.g., Chinese/ Finnish/ … people are hard-working and shy). Battling against the Barnum Effect in ICER requires requesting concrete data and evidence to support any conclusions drawn from intercultural studies; maintaining a sceptical and critical attitude when accepting any generalised statements about culture, identity, personality or even a concept, and looking for corroborating information from multiple sources; reflecting on one's own identity and personality traits through self-exploration and discussions with those who know us well, rather than relying solely on external generalised descriptions. What is more, since the Barnum Effect is more effective with affirmative statements, it's essential to be cautious not to accept descriptions of people, groups, 'cultures' and concepts just because they sound promising (Hua & Zhou, 2023).

4. (An international conference room where Alex, a Malaysian scholar, and Fatima, a Swedish delegate, are discussing a joint project on intercultural competence in the context of internationalization. In what follows, they both exhibit what will be referred to as *Panglossian reasoning*, overlooking differences and potential challenges).

Alex: Fatima, I'm really excited about this collaboration. I think our teams match perfectly. After all, we all speak English, and we share the same work ethics, right?

Fatima: Totally, Alex. I believe that as long as we have a common and global language like English, everything else will fall into place. Cultural differences are just minor details that we can easily overcome.

Ragna (Icelandic conference participant, entering the conversation): I agree that language is important but I've noticed that even when we speak the same language, cultural nuances can lead to misunderstandings or non-understandings. For instance, in my country, we value long discussions and consider it polite to debate, while some cultures might see it as a waste of time.

Fatima: Oh, Ragna, I think you're overthinking. People are adaptable, and we can all learn to adjust to different communication styles. It's no big deal; we'll manage!

Alex: Yeah, I mean, we're all professionals here. We can set aside cultural quirks and just focus on the task at hand. I don't believe that our backgrounds will significantly impact the success of this project.

Ragna: But what if our different approaches to work-life balance affect our collaboration? For example, in Iceland, we highly value personal time, while in the U.S., people should be available 24/7 …

Fatima: Well, we'll just have to find a middle ground. I'm sure that we can agree on some basic principles and work around any cultural differences. These so-called differences are not insurmountable hurdles.

Alex: Exactly, Fatima. We're all here to achieve the same goal, and I'm sure our shared vision will outweigh any minor cultural issues. We'll make it work; it's going to be great!

Panglossian reasoning refers to an unduly optimistic or excessively positive outlook on a situation, often in the face of evidence to the contrary. It is named after the character Dr Pangloss in Voltaire's (2020) satirical novel *Candide*, who despite witnessing and experiencing great suffering and cruelty, maintains that "all is for the best in this best of all possible worlds" (Voltaire, 2020: 52). This type of reasoning is characterised by a belief that everything happens for a good reason, even when there is no logical or evidential basis for such an assertion (Sober, 1985).

Panglossian reasoning could lead to interculturalists (students, researchers and/or educators) overly romanticising or idealising certain ideologies of interculturality without critically examining their complexities or potential generalising negative aspects such as ideological outlook. Panglossian reasoning can cause researchers and educators to downplay or ignore epistemic violence, injustice, conflicts or challenges, assuming that they will naturally resolve themselves for the best. By insisting on a positive spin, Panglossian reasoning can also result in a misrepresentation of interculturality as opposed to e.g. balancing otherness with otherness (Dervin, 2024), potentially leading to ineffective or inappropriate cooperation, policy recommendations and/or interventions.

5. In the business district of Shanghai (China), a multinational corporation is preparing to launch a new product. The marketing teams from China and the U.S. have come together to discuss their strategies. The American team, led by Lisa, is keen on highlighting the potential gains of the product, emphasizing the high-tech features and the prestige of owning it. They believe that, by focusing on the positive outcomes, customers will be more likely to make a purchase, a concept rooted in the principles of *prospect theory*, which suggests that people are more sensitive to potential gains than losses. However, the Chinese team, led by Pang, proposes a different approach. They suggest framing the marketing campaign around the avoidance of losses, such as missed opportunities if the product is not purchased. Pang explains that, in China, the prevention of losses can be a stronger stimulus than the prospect of gains, reflecting a potentially different psychological bias within *prospect theory*. The two teams must then navigate intercultural dynamics to create a marketing strategy that resonates with the local audience. Lisa learns that, while prospect theory is a universal concept, its application needs to be nuanced in certain contexts. The campaign ultimately combines both 'Chinese' and 'American' approaches, appealing to the desire for gain and the avoidance of loss, creating a strong intercultural message resonating with a broader audience.

Prospect Theory suggests that people are more averse to losses than they are attracted to equivalent gains, which can lead to intellectual inertia as individuals avoid decisions that may lead to loss (see Tian & Xu, 2021). Developed by Kahneman and Tversky (1979), prospect theory deals with decision-making under conditions of risk. It suggests that individuals evaluate potential losses and gains relative to a reference point, and their preferences for risks and cautions can vary depending on whether they are in a gain or loss situation.

As far as ICER is concerned, prospect theory could be applied to understand how different researchers and educators perceive and make decisions regarding risk and uncertainty in research on interculturality. Moreover, prospect theory could be used to analyse how values and norms influence the reference points that scholars and educators use to evaluate gains and losses [e.g., success and failure in the way they problematise interculturality in education]. This could lead to a better understanding of e.g. non-economic decisions like conflict resolution and negotiation strategies interculturally.

6. Two professors, John Taylor from New Zealand and Rosy Kim from South Korea, were appointed to a joint task force aimed at enhancing intercultural communication among local and international students at their institution in Thailand. The task force was a response to growing concerns about clashes, misunderstandings and a lack of understanding among the diverse student body. Taylor, a long-serving faculty member, had witnessed the evolution of the university and believed in its core values. He saw their approach to interculturality as fundamentally sound, often highlighting the numerous success stories and the university's commitment to diversity. Kim had a very different perspective. She had observed that, despite the university's liberal image, there were subtle but significant barriers to intercultural exchange. She noticed for example that certain groups were underrepresented in curriculum development and that the support systems for international students were not as robust or convincing as they could be. As they collaborated through the task force, Taylor tended to justify the current system, focusing on the positive aspects and the university's good intentions. He believed that the existing framework was generally effective and only needed minor changes. Kim, however, felt the need to address the systemic issues more upfront. She argued for a comprehensive review of the curricula to ensure they represented a broader range of perspectives and the development of support programs to help international students adjust to the academic environment. Their differing views exemplified *system justification theory* in action. Taylor's allegiance to established practices reflected a desire to maintain the status quo that had probably served him well as a while male academic in the Global South. Kim, being a different kind of outsider since she had been recruited recently from South Korea, was less inclined to accept the system without question and sought to challenge and improve it. Through a series of meetings and discussions, the two scholars eventually found common ground. They developed a proposal that acknowledged the university's efforts in fostering intercultural communication amongst and between students and staff while also recommending substantive reforms.

System Justification Theory represents the social-psychological motivation to justify and rationalise the existing social, economic-political, ideological and institutional arrangements, which can contribute to intellectual inertia by discouraging critical examination of the status quo (Kesberg et al., 2023). These arrangements might prove to be flawed or reproduce inequalities and yet (both privileged and disadvantaged) individuals might tend to support them in order to protect their own identities and those of their in-groups. Social stereotypes and political ideologies allow people to maintain the acceptability of how things stand in a given society, institution and/or context (Kemmelmeier, 2017).

System Justification Theory can provide insights into how different groups perceive and respond to the systems they are part of interculturally. Some research has shown for instance that religiosity and political conservatism are positively associated with system justification, including support for dogmatic political systems (Badaan et al., 2020; Azevedo & Jost, 2021). What is more, this theory could help explain why members of disadvantaged groups might internalise negative values and stereotypes that oppress them. This has been associated with e.g. identification with the aggressor (Rubin et al., 2023) as well as false consciousness, where individuals hold beliefs that are against their collective interest [see Lewis, 2021 about the concept of *assimilation* at a university in New Zealand]. System Justification Theory can also be applied to understand e.g. employees' attitudes and behaviours in work organisations (in accounting, see Çollaku et al., 2023). People may defend their organisations as a system, supporting policies and practices that maintain conventionality, even if they are personally disadvantaged by them.

7. (A university is considering a new international exchange program. The discussion is between Professor Liu, a Chinese faculty member, and Professor Red, an American visiting scholar).

Liu: I think that we should continue with the exchange program as planned. We've already invested a significant amount of resources into developing it.

Red: I understand your point, dear colleague, but I've been reviewing the potential outcomes, and I'm not convinced it's the best use of our resources. We might be falling into the *sunk-cost fallacy*.

Liu: The sunk-cost fallacy? What do you mean by that?

Red: It's a cognitive bias whereby we continue a behaviour or project just because we've already invested in it, even if it's no longer the best option. We shouldn't let the resources we've already put in dictate our future decisions.

Liu: But we've worked so hard on this … It feels wrong to abandon it now!

Red: I agree that it's hard to walk away from something we've invested in. However, it's important to evaluate the current situation and future prospects.

The world has changed since 2020 and our students are not so eager to come here anymore. If the exchange program isn't beneficial for our students or aligns with our goals, we should reconsider.

Liu: I don't know. Maybe you're right. We should be making decisions based on what's best for the university, not just what we've already spent.

Sunk-Cost Fallacy symbolises the irrational adherence to practices or beliefs because of the perceived investment of time, resources or identities, even when these are no longer beneficial or relevant in a changing landscape (Jhang et al., 2023). The sunk-cost fallacy is a cognitive bias that leads people to continue investing time, money or effort into a decision, project ideology, even when it is no longer the best course of action, due to the resources already invested. This bias causes individuals to make choices based on past costs rather than future benefits (see e.g., Qiao, 2023 about blind box purchase behaviour and consumption in China).

The sunk-cost fallacy may manifest in intercultural research and education. Some scholars and educators might place a higher value on collective investment and saving face in their cooperation, making it more challenging to walk away from a sunk-cost situation. Additionally, different attitudes towards risk and tolerance for failure can influence the expression of the sunk-cost fallacy amongst e.g. international colleagues or between students and teachers. Understanding and recognising the sunk-cost fallacy in relation to interculturality is crucial for designing decision support systems and interventions. It could help researchers and educators better comprehend decision-making processes and offer advice to prevent or mitigate the impact of this bias on the ways we do research on interculturality and organise education around the notion – and push us outside the realm of intellectual inertia ...

3. Fragments about intellectual inertia in ICER

[Research and education are meant to foster change. And yet the knowledge they produce can too easily become ossified, reinforcing the status quo and making it difficult for innovative, critical and interculturally oriented perspectives to take root and flourish.]

[Interculturality is something we can impose on others. As a notion, students', scholars' and educators' mission is to question this *something*.]

[Power dynamics are inherently linked to intellectual inertia in research and education. Dominant groups (western, white, male, English-speaking) may exhibit inertia as a means of preserving their hegemony, while members of dominated groups may face inertia in the form of resistance to assimilation.]

[Predatory leading (western and English-speaking) research on interculturality forces us to *think without thinking, to perform thinking* and *to believe that we are thinking*.]

[Intellectual inertia in the context of intercultural research can benefit a variety of people, although not always in positive or progressive ways. These could include: *established and dominating scholars, policy makers, textbook publishers and educational content creator*s. One thing they all have in common is that they can either save or make (more) money out of intellectual inertia. While it may seem counterintuitive, some students might also benefit from intellectual inertia if it means less exposure to challenging or complex ideas that could complicate their learning experience.]

[In 2024, following a bad case of shingles, I experienced constant pain on my left side, especially around my ribcage. Exploring the pain and how to potentially get rid of it, I realised that massaging and pressing the opposite side made the pain go away. A remedy for intellectual inertia? Look elsewhere?]

[We spend half of our lives dreaming, imagining, how about accepting and admitting their influence on our ideas (Cixous, 1993)? How about using them to move forward in our thinking?]

[After three hours at Kunsthalle Zürich (an art museum in Switzerland) my eyes are literally burning, not only because of the amazing art collection that they hold but also because of the hundreds of texts included in the exhibitions that detail the provenance of many artworks as potentially looted during World War II. The visit differs from visits to other museums. The added dimension of historical and society responsibility of a museum impacts my mind.]

[Using a tokenistic voice from the Global South to justify the 'universal' academic appeal of one's 'theories' (ideologies) internationally (as a white person) represents today's worst form of intellectual inertia and indoctrinating strategy.]

[Intellectual inertia *par excellence*: Pretending to care about the 'other' (decolonising 'our' knowledge) while recolonising by imposing a western concept about interculturality (e.g., intercultural competence) to show good intentions in learning more about how 'they' dealt with it in 'pre-colonial times'.]

[The real problem of interculturality in research today is that we claim criticality for ourselves but cannot look outside *that* criticality.]

[Someone justifies that they will do 'non-essentialism' by adding references to *Hofstede* and *Trompenaars* as counter-examples. *The two easy targets*.]

[We need to pay attention to how we potentially regress in what we say and write rather than attempt progress. Regressing is a danger in intercultural research and education. What does *regressing* mean here? Recycling ideas while believing/pretending to be original. Forgetting to be critical of one's criticality. Not recognising one's past errors. Being satisfied with what we have (already) contributed without modifying it.]

[A US-based scholar criticises another north American scholar for being *too western* and a European scholar for being *too individualistic* to deal with interculturality. When they present their own approach, they do not self-criticise, merely regurgitating their own 'contributions' and making reference to very Eurocentric scholars as *backups*.]

[One risk with research on interculturality today is *stultification* (from Latin for turning into foolishness): we might lose creativity, enthusiasm, initiative as a result of tedious and restrictive routines. We chime, come again, din, echo, iterate, reiterate, recycle, rehearse, repeat, summarise …]

[Making one's (fantasy of reality) everyone's.]

["We know that intercultural educators happily surrender to colour-blindness", someone writes. But who are these individuals and where? Isn't the one writing doing colour-blindness too? Is anyone immune against this evil?]

[Commenting on a colleague's remark about a supra-national institution ignoring the issue of language in their 'model of intercultural competence', I write: "The absence of language is not surprising. Learning and practicing languages is costly and time-consuming. In order to produce and be 'efficient', the use of English appears to be the best option. The fact that there is only half a convincing statement about language (written by monolingual authors who wrote the document describing the model) is not startling at all". I ask my colleague to "react a bit more to this important aspect". They reply: "I will leave a more explicit critique of this for another occasion …".]

[Having had the opportunity to spend three hours with the Chinese artist Xu Bing (https://xubing.com/), I am full of energy. His work and, especially his thinking, reinvigorate me. Xu Bing is an artist but he is in fact a bright social observer, commentator and, in fact, a real researcher. He is famous for his square word calligraphy that transcribes English words into a format that mimics the structure of Chinese characters, offering a unique perspective on interculturality (and as we shall see from critical perspectives). His special form of square word calligraphy helps demystify somehow the Chinese written language by making it accessible to those of us non-Chinese speakers (Xu Bing, 2020). It also helps understand the composition of Chinese characters. I believe that we intercultural researchers can use his square word calligraphy to study the intersection of language and visual art, exploring how meaning is constructed in written forms that blend elements from different linguistic traditions. I have always found that the process of 'deciphering' Xu Bing's calligraphy can help reflect on interculturality, as it requires us to engage deeply with a form of writing that is both accessible and challenging. Xu Bing suggests that practicing his square word calligraphy can serve as a meditative experience, in similar ways as traditional Chinese calligraphy, leading to special mental and physical engagement with the art (Xu Bing, 2020). Xu Bing's work is thus not only an artistic innovation but also a powerful tool for intercultural education and research, fostering a deeper understanding of language, art and the human experience. During our conversations, he confesses that he does not see his work on the square word calligraphy as 'intercultural' (in English, he says *cross-cultural*). For him, interculturality is an ideal that is impracticable because of our obsession with hierarchies and power relations. However, he believes that this special type of calligraphy can disrupt and challenge people's thinking, reminding them to think

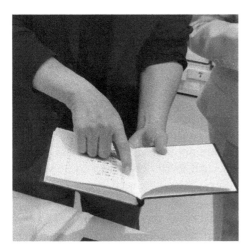

FIGURE 3.2 Emoji-writing.

outside the box. I tend to agree with him. Interculturality cannot function as an ideal whereby we are together in a perfect state of equality, generosity and honesty. Like all social phenomena, we must fail at interculturality. It is only human. Being aware of this caveat and not trying too hard to fake interculturality as something that can work, is always a step forward in being a human ... Figure 3.2. shows Xu Bing reading a book he wrote titled *Book from the Ground: From Point to Point* (Xu Bing, 2018) containing thousands of pictograms to describe the everyday life of an office worker – a book without words.]

[Some of the worst enemies of interculturality in research and education is a lack of reading outside one's own favourite circles and being unaware of the archaeology of ideas.]

[The cliché of *thirdness* ... I would love to hear some critiques of these 'critiques' otherwise they sound a bit like unquestionable truths.]

[How could we possibly address interculturality as something *fluid, uncertain* and *changeable* in education when the latter urges us to deliver on time and save time (thus money), prove that we are learning and doing something according to 'their' criteria (tests, evaluations) and rationalise everything?]

[A critical paper on interculturality. The theoretical part is somehow convincing, although it rehearses the same 'anti-essentialistic' critiques as everybody else. However, when we get to the 'analysis', the words from the participants are merely taken for granted while they in fact seem to be reciting the litanies of anti-essentialism as they were 'taught' by the researcher-teacher. Slogans are no proof of anything – if just of indoctrination and intellectual inertia from both researchers-teachers' and students' perspectives.]

[Telling people what/how not to say or write in ICER is id[l]eological. *"You should not use ... you must not say ...".*]

[Our writing and thinking are full of ghosts who haunt us. These ghosts infiltrate our minds and release inert gases in what we utter.]

["The concept of Otherness is less controversial than interculturality", I hear a colleague assert. *How is this term LESS controversial than intercultural? How, where, for whom?*]

[Intellectual inertia when someone cites the idea of simplexity, which I put forward in 2016 (Dervin, 2016), as proposed by Dervin and Jacobsson (2021). *READ. ARCHEOLOGY.*]

[In some contexts, interculturalists are not trained to be scholars but to work through the system to survive. Intellectual inertia gives way to power, finance, influence and even abuse as driving forces. These are seen as ways to move up in the structure and to avoid any real scholarly tasks.]

[*My own intellectual inertia.* Reading through papers, chapters and books about interculturality, I often see my name pop up. *Feelings of repetitiveness*: the same ideas are discussed and re-discussed across various publications. Here are some of 'my' ideas and concepts (which are shared by hundreds of other interculturalists and researchers) that I have seen in recent months. I admit that these leave me with an aftertaste of semi-shame for the indolent, robot-like and somewhat a-critical ideologies that they impose:]

- Interculturality should not be reduced to exchanges based on national cultures but should consider instead the polycentrism and fluidity of culture [*what is culture? If culture is fluid then is there such a thing as 'culture'?*].
- The issue of othering and how it should be openly discussed, combated and eliminated [can we ever *not* other people?].
- My concept of *liquid interculturality* (with the idea of the *liquid* borrowed from Bauman): a non-essentialist and non-culturalist approach which acknowledges the diversity and fluidity of identities as individuals move between cultural contexts and shape their selves [very idealistic and ignorant of power relations and privileges].
- The utility of *intersectional analysis* in developing interculturality (borrowed from e.g., Hill Collins, 2019). Intersectionality aims to examine power differentials from a multifaceted perspective and individualise analyses of intercultural encounters rather than generalise them based solely on cultural and ethnic identity [Is intersectionality a panacea when we have to rely on what people *say and/or do* – which may not reflect any 'truth'? Intersectionality can only inform us of *some aspects* of a process.]

[*Transition to the next Étagère.* Language is both a gateway to interculturality but also a barrier perpetuated by certain forms of intellectual inertia in research and education – which we could call linguistic nonchalance and negligence. Defaulting to the few languages (or just one language) that we might know and the constructs we have been fed with (often passively), we risk missing the nuances and richness that multilingualism can offer in navigating interculturality as a polysemic and protean notion.]

2. Vitrine II

Dr. Li is an associate professor of intercultural and linguistic mediation at Sapienza University (Rome, Italy, Europe), originally from the North of China. Their specialty was a critical examination of intercultural narratives, with a particular focus on the perils of essentialism and culturalism. However, as the years unfolded, Dr. Li's once-sharp intellect began to circle the same well-trodden paths, unable to break free from the repetitive cycle of their own critiques and of those of western scholars. The story begins with Li standing at the podium in a lecture hall on the Piazzalle della Minerva, their voice echoing through the lecture hall as they dissected the dangers of reducing complex cultures to simplistic and monolithic entities in English. Their arguments were well-crafted, their passion palpable, but there was a sense of *déjà-vu* that hung in the air. The same points were made, the same examples cited and the same conclusions drawn, *semester after semester*. Intellectual inertia had taken root in Li's scholarly pursuits. They found themselves unable to move beyond the well-established critiques that had once been the cornerstone of their academic reputation in Italy and abroad (like many other interculturalists). The fear of venturing into uncharted territories, of potentially undermining their own work, had become a paralysing force. One day, a student, intrigued by the passion in their Chinese professor's voice but frustrated by the repetitive content, approached them after class. "Dr Li, the student began, your lectures are very compelling, but I can't help but feel that we're treading water. Are there no new perspectives to explore?". The question struck a chord within Li, resonating with the unspoken doubts that had been gnawing at them for years. They attempted to engage with new literature, to attend conferences that promised fresh insights, but each foray into the unknown felt like a step into a labyrinth without an exit. The more they tried to break free from their intellectual rut, the more they found themselves returning to the same critical stance, their voice an echo in this vast hall of the Città universitaria. As time wore on, their lectures began to lose their allure. Students, seeking the stimulation of new ideas, began to fill other lecture halls. Colleagues, once eager to engage in debate, now found their discussions with Dr Li to be a fruitless loop, a Sisyphean task of pushing the same boulder up the same hill, only for it to roll back down. Li's research, once a promising beacon in the field of ICER, became a shadow of its former self. Their national and international publications, once anticipated with eagerness, now met with a collective shrug from the Italian and global academic community. The very essence of their work, *the critique of essentialism and culturalism*, had become a mirror reflecting their own inability to evolve. In the end, Dr Li's story is one of a mind trapped within the labyrinth of its own making. Their warnings against the dangers of essentialism and culturalism became somehow a self-fulfilling prophecy, as their own intellectual journey was confined to the narrow corridors of their initial insights, based on well-rehearsed western ideologies.

1. Escapade II

intellectual inertia, which often relates to institutional inertia, is a complex cognitive and psychological phenomenon *the topic has not been addressed head on in ICER* intellectual inertia reflects the tricky continuum of change-persistence (dynamic, creative-static, mechanic) *it leads to becoming entrenched, resistant to change (maintaining the status quo) and getting stuck in our own ideological realm* intellectual inertia is both driven by and leading to rigid shared mental models, mental and ideological stagnation as well as cognitive and epistemic rigidity *conservatism, dogmatism, traditionalism and complacency all represent forms of intellectual inertia* intellectual inertia in ICER might derive from (capitalistic/neoliberal) gatekeeping practices, rigid institutional, field and collegiate prospects *generalisation, oblivion, repetition, resistance all entail intellectual inertia*

In order to summarise the takeaways from our discussions of intellectual inertia in relation in ICER, this Escapade concludes by presenting nine assertions that you may wish to review and use for self-assessment purposes. Our main question here is: *How much does intellectual inertia affect (y)our own engagement with interculturality?*

1. I often find myself returning to the same theories and frameworks in my intercultural research/teaching/learning without considering/being able to consider newer alternatives.
2. I often rely on the same sources of information or the same group of scholars when conducting my intercultural research and teaching about it.
3. I have a hard time understanding or relating to perspectives that are vastly different from my own.
4. When reviewing literature on intercultural topics, I tend to focus more on studies that align with my research interests.
5. I rarely update my knowledge base with the latest research and developments from the broader field of intercultural studies (communication, education, business, nursing …).
6. I rarely question the assumptions underlying the traditional models of intercultural communication that I use in my research (e.g. models of intercultural competence, anti-essentialism).
7. When I encounter new research methodologies in ICER, I am more likely to critique them than to explore their potential benefits.

8. I am more likely to collaborate with researchers who share similar backgrounds and research interests.
9. In general, I believe that my research methods and theoretical frameworks are the most effective for understanding intercultural phenomena.

Note

1 This Étagère adopts a reversed section numbering strategy to disrupt our thinking, which is very much in line with the perspective on interculturality adopted in this book.

References

Al Atiqi, M. (2023). *Echo Chamber and Polarization in Social Media. An Agent-Based Modeling Approach*. Springer.
Azevedo, F. & Jost, J. T. (2021). The ideological basis of antiscientific attitudes: Effects of authoritarianism, conservatism, religiosity, social dominance, and system justification. *Group Processes & Intergroup Relations 24*(4), 518–549. https://doi.org/10.1177/1368430221990104
Badaan, V., Richa, R. & Jost, J. T. (2020). Ideological justification of the sectarian political system in Lebanon. *Current Opinion in Psychology 32*, 138–145. https://doi.org/10.1016/j.copsyc.2019.07.033.
Barthes, R. (1980). *Camera Lucida: Reflections on Photography*. Vintage.
Barthes, R (1993). *A Barthes Reader* (edited by S. Sontag). Vintage.
Barthes, R. (1997). *The Eiffel Tower and Other Mythologies*. University of California Press.
Barthes, R. (2009). *Mythologies*. Vintage.
Barthes, R. (2010). *The Grain of the Voice*. Vintage.
Barthes, R. (2020). *Roland Barthes by Roland Barthes*. Vintage.
Bergson, H. (1975). *Mind-Energy. Lectures and Essays*. Bloomsbury Academic.
Bergson, H. (1984). *Creative Evolution*. University Press of America.
Borghetti, C. & Qin, X. (2022). Resources for intercultural learning in a non-essentialist perspective: An investigation of student and teacher perceptions in Chinese universities. *Language and Intercultural Communication 22*(5), 599–614. https://doi.org/10.1080/14708477.2022.2105344
Cixous, H. (1993). *Three Steps on the Ladder of Writing*. Columbia University Press.
Çollaku, L., Ramushi, A. S. & Aliu, M. (2023). Fraud intention and the relationship with selfishness: The mediating role of moral justification in the accounting profession. International Journal of Ethics and Systems, Vol. ahead-of-print No. ahead-of-print. https://doi.org/10.1108/IJOES-10-2023-0220
Compagnon, A. (1997). Who is the real one? In: Rabaté, J.-M. (ed.). *Writing the Image After Roland Barthes* (pp. 196–200). University of Pennsylvania Press.
Confucius (2024). *The Analects*. (Translation by James Legge). https://ctext.org/dictionary.pl?if=en&id=1134
Demeulenaere, A. (2023). Barthes and Bouvier in Japan: The difficult dialogue between semiotics and intercultural communication. In: Hertel, R. & Sandrock, K. (eds.). *Failures East and West: Cultural Encounters between East Asia and Europe* (pp. 137–151). EUP.
Denzau, A. T. & North, D. C. (1994). Shared Mental Models: Ideologies and institutions. *Kyklos 47*, 3–31. https://doi.org/10.1111/j.1467-6435.1994.tb02246.x

Dervin, F. (2010). Bergson, précurseur des mobilités académiques contemporaines? *Cahiers de Framespa 6*. http://framespa.revues.org/589

Dervin, F. (2011). A plea for change in research on intercultural discourses: A 'liquid' approach to the study of the acculturation of Chinese students. *Journal of Multicultural Discourses 6*(1), 37–52. https://doi.org/10.1080/17447143.2010.532218

Dervin, F. (2016). *Interculturality in Education*. Palgrave.

Dervin, F. (2022). *Interculturality in Fragments. A Reflexive Approach*. Springer.

Dervin, F. (2024). *Interculturologies*. Springer.

Dervin, F. & Jacobsson, A. (2021). *Teacher Education for Critical and Reflexive Interculturality*. Palgrave.

Etymonline.com (2024a). *Inertia*. www.etymonline.com/word/inertia#etymonline_v_6420

Faghih, N. & Samadi, A. H. (eds.). (2024). *Institutional Inertia. Theory and Evidence*. Springer.

Forer, B. R. (1949). The fallacy of personal validation: A classroom demonstration of gullibility. *Journal of Abnormal and Social Psychology 44*, 118–123.

Gonthier, C. & Thomassin, N. (2024). Getting students interested in psychological measurement by experiencing the Barnum Effect. *Teaching of Psychology 0*(0). https://doi.org/10.1177/00986283241240454

Graiouid, S. (2024). Critical Intercultural Communication and the Public Sphere: Theoretical Engagements with Tahakkum and Other-Interculturality. *Journal of International and Intercultural Communication*, 1–23. https://doi.org/10.1080/17513057.2024.2389799

Gunter, P. A. Y. (2023). *Getting Bergson Straight. The Contributions of Intuition to the Sciences*. Vernon Press.

Hill Collins, P. (2019). *Intersectionality as Critical Social Theory*. Duke University Press.

Holliday, A. (2010). *Intercultural Communication and Ideology*. Sage.

House, J., Kádár, D. Z., Liu, F. & Han, D. (2024). The problem of translating Chinese policy related expressions: A case study of wenming ('civilised'). *Text & Talk 44*(3), 343–367. https://doi.org/10.1515/text-2021-0142

Hua, J. & Zhou, Y. X. (2023). Personality assessment usage and mental health among Chinese adolescents: A sequential mediation model of the Barnum effect and ego identity. *Frontiers in Psychology 14*, 1097068. DOI: 10.3389/fpsyg.2023.1097068

Jhang, J., Lee, D. C., Park, J., Lee, J., & Kim, J. (2023). The impact of childhood environments on the sunk-cost fallacy. *Psychology & Marketing* 40, 531–541. https://doi.org/10.1002/mar.21750?>

Jin, E. & Jiang, X. (2024). How bibliometric evaluation makes the academia an 'Iron Cage': Evidence from Chinese academics. *Research Evaluation 33*, rvae031. https://doi.org/10.1093/reseval/rvae031

Kafka, F. (2002). *Kafka's 'The Metamorphosis' and Other Writings*. Bloomsbury Academic.

Kahneman, D. & Tversky, A. (1979). Prospect theory: An analysis of decision under risk. *Econometrica 47*(2), 263–291.

Kemmelmeier, M. (2017). System justification theory. In: Tuner, B. S. (ed.). *The Wiley-Blackwell Encyclopedia of Social Theory*. Wiley. https://doi.org/10.1002/9781118430873.est0381

Kesberg, R., Brandt, M. J., Easterbrook, M. J., Spruyt, B. & Turner-Zwinkels, F. (2023). Finding (dis-)advantaged system justifiers: A bottom-up approach to explore system justification theory. *European Journal of Social Psychology 54*, 81–96. https://doi.org/10.1002/ejsp.2989

Knight, D. (ed.). (2020). *Interdisciplinary Barthes.* Proceedings of the British Academy. https://doi.org/10.5871/bacad/9780197266670.001.0001. Accessed 25 Sept. 2024.
Lamiell, J. & Slaney, K. (eds.). (2020). *Problematic Research Practices and Inertia in Scientific Psychology. History, Sources, and Recommended Solutions.* Routledge.
Lawlor, L. (2019). Bergson on the true intellect. In: Lefebvre, A. & Schott, N. F. (eds.). *Interpreting Bergson* (pp. 67–86). CUP.
Ledgerwood, A., Lawson, K. M., Kraus, M. W., Ray Vollhardt, J., Remedios, J. D., Wilkinson Westberg, D., Uskul, A. K, Adetula, A., Wayne Leach, C., Martinez, J. E., Naumann, Geetha Reddy, L P., Chucky Tate, C., Todd, A. R., Weltzien, K., Buchanan, N., González, R., Montilla Doble, L. J., Romero-Canyas, R., Westgate, E. & Zou, L. X. (2024). Disrupting racism and global exclusion in academic publishing: Recommendations and resources for authors, reviewers, and editors. *Collabra: Psychology 10* (1), 121394. https://doi.org/10.1525/collabra.121394
Lewis, L. (2021). Assimilation as 'false consciousness': Higher education immigrant students' acculturation beliefs and experiences. *International Journal of Intercultural Relations 83*, 30–42. https://doi.org/10.1016/j.ijintrel.2021.04.012
Liu, J. & Zheng, Y. (2024). The emergence of epistemic agency in researching multilingually: An autoethnography of a Chinese researcher's academic publishing practices. *International Journal of Applied Linguistics,* 1–20. https://doi.org/10.1111/ijal.12617
Maele, J. V. & Jin, L. (2022). Intercultural teaching and learning in Chinese higher education: Integrating practices and perspectives. *Language and Intercultural Communication 22*(5), 493–502. https://doi.org/10.1080/14708477.2022.2131134
Medina, J. (2013). *The Epistemology of Resistance: Gender and Racial Oppression, Epistemic Injustice, and the Social Imagination.* OUP.
Moosavi, L. (2023). Turning the decolonial gaze towards ourselves: Decolonising the curriculum and 'decolonial reflexivity' in sociology and social theory. *Sociology 57*(1), 137–156. https://doi.org/10.1177/00380385221096037
Peng, R., Zhu, C. & Wu, W.-P, (2019). Visualizing the knowledge domain of intercultural competence research: A bibliometric analysis. *International Journal of Intercultural Relations 74*, 58–68. https://doi.org/10.1016/j.ijintrel.2019.10.008
Piller, I. (2010). *Intercultural Communication: A Critical Introduction.* EUP.
Puett, M. & Gross-Loh (2016). *The Path. What Chinese Philosophers Can Teach Us about the Good Life.* Simon & Schuster.
Qiao, Z. (2023). Sunk Cost Fallacy in blind box consumption among high school students. *Highlights in Business, Economics and Management GEFHR 21,* 55–61.
R'boul, H. (2022). Epistemological plurality in intercultural communication knowledge. *Journal of Multicultural Discourses 17*(2), 173–188. DOI: 10.1080/17447143.2022.2069784
R'boul, H. & Dervin, F. (2024). Attempts at including, mediating and creating 'new' knowledges: Problematising appropriation in intercultural communication education and research. *Applied Linguistics Review.* Advance online publication. https://doi.org/10.1515/applirev-2024-0009
Roucek, J. S. (1944). Ideology as a means of social control, II. *The American Journal of Economics and Sociology 3,* 179–192. https://doi.org/10.1111/j.1536-7150.1944.tb01317.x

Rubin, M., Owuamalam, C. K., Spears, R. & Caricati, L. (2023). Social identity explanations of system justification: Misconceptions, criticisms, and clarifications. *European Review of Social Psychology 34*(2), 268–297. DOI: 10.1080/10463283.2023.2184578

Samadi, A. H., Alipourian, M., Afroozeh, S., Raanaei, A. & Panahi, M. (2024). An introduction to institutional inertia: Concepts, types and causes. In: Faghih, N. & Samadi, A. H. (eds.). *Institutional Inertia. Theory and Evidence* (pp. 47–86). Springer.

Sher, G. (2016). *Epistemic Friction: An Essay on Knowledge, Truth, and Logic.* OUP.

Sober, E. (1985). Panglossian functionalism and the philosophy of mind. *Synthese 64*, 165–193. https://doi.org/10.1007/BF00486037

Thelwall, M., Simrick, S., Viney, I. & Van den Besselaar, P. (2023). What is research funding, how does it influence research, and how is it recorded? Key dimensions of variation. *Scientometrics 128*, 6085–6106. https://doi.org/10.1007/s11192-023-04836-w

Tian, X. & Xu, Z. (2021). *Fuzzy Decision-Making Methods Based on Prospect Theory and Its Application in Venture Capital.* Springer.

Voltaire, F. (2020). *Candide, or The Optimist.* Macmillan Collector's Library.

Xu Bing (2018). *Book from the Ground: From Point to Point.* MIT Press.

Xu Bing (2020). *Xu Bing: Book from the Sky to Book from the Ground.* ACC Art Books.

Zhou, V. X. & Pilcher, N. (2017). 'Intercultural competence' as an intersubjective process: A reply to 'essentialism.' *Language and Intercultural Communication 18*(1), 125–143. https://doi.org/10.1080/14708477.2017.1400510

Étagère 4

LANGUAGE INDIFFERENCE AND NONCHALANCE

Crises of language and interculturality

Étagère 4 …

- Discusses the impact of language on interculturality in research and education.
- Explores how language can both facilitate and hinder interculturality.
- Recommends practices for enhancing language sensitivity.

Five basic questions

1. What could language indifference and nonchalance be within the context of intercultural communication education and research?
2. How could language indifference and nonchalance lead to misunderstandings and non-understandings in intercultural communication?
3. What role could language play in shaping research on interculturality and its education?
4. What strategies could researchers use to minimise language indifference and nonchalance in their work?
5. What could be the ethical implications of language indifference and nonchalance in research on interculturality?

4. Yarn III[1]

Language has often been highlighted in literature through characters who either take it for granted or are naive of its influence. To me, one of the writers who has dealt with the issues of language indifference and nonchalance (understood here simply as *a lack of and/or a lazy interest and concern for language*) in invigorating ways is Samuel Beckett (1906–1989). A key figure both in English and French in the so-called 'Theatre of the Absurd', Beckett had a complex and profound relationship with language, which he often used to express the existential themes of his numerous plays such as isolation, the search for meaning and the impossibility to communicate with self and others. As such, the writer was deeply interested in the limitations of language to convey meaning and the struggle of the human condition to find expression. Here is a short review of how the topic of language is incorporated into his most famous plays:

- In *Waiting for Godot* (Beckett, 2006), the characters, Vladimir and Estragon, engage in repetitive and often nonsensical conversations that highlight the lack of communication and the inability to express their inner turmoil. Their dialogues are filled with pauses and circular reasoning (i.e. the characters' arguments come back to the starting point without having proven anything), which underscores the limitations of language to provide comfort or intelligibility in a chaotic world like ours.
- Language in another play titled *Endgame* (Beckett, 2009a) is used to express the different characters' feelings of confinement and anguish. Dialogues are often brief, fragmented and devoid of emotional depth, reflecting the characters' inability to connect with one another or express their inner lives.
- *Not I* (Beckett, 2004): In this one-act play, the character, Mouth, is a disembodied voice that spews out words in a rapid and uncontrollable stream, suggesting the inability to control one's own narrative or the overwhelming nature of internal dialogues. The use of language in the play challenges the audience's ability to comprehend and engage with the torrent of words, reflecting the chaos of the human mind and of those who influence what we say, think and silence.
- In *Happy Days* (Beckett, 2010), the protagonist Winnie is buried up to her waist in the first act and up to her neck in the second act, her ability to communicate and interact with the world becoming increasingly incomplete. Her dialogue is optimistic and banal, contrasting with her absurd situation and highlighting the disconnect between her words and the reality.
- *Krapp's Last Tape* (Beckett, 2009b) explores the relationship between memory, language and self-perception. In this one-act play, Krapp, an ageing man, listens to recordings of his past self, reflecting on the gap between the person he was and the person he has become. The language in the play is self-referencing and meditative, with Krapp's monologues revealing the inadequacy of language to capture the fullness of human experience and the passage of time. The play surveys the concept of language indifference through Krapp's detachment from his own recorded voice and the life it recounts. As he listens to his tapes, Krapp is a participant-observer of his own life, creating a distance between himself and his complex past. This distance is obvious in his reactions to the tapes, where he alternates between nostalgia, regret and

even mockery of his younger self. The contrast between the technologically perfect record of the tapes and the flawed and ageing Krapp seems to emphasise the absurdity of life. As such, the tapes seem to capture a version of Krapp that is unchanging and fixed, unlike the living Krapp who is subject to old age and the imperfections of memory. This contrast also underscores the limitations of language and communication, as the tapes, despite their clarity, fail to fully capture the essence of Krapp's experiences or the depth of his intricate emotions. In the context of language indifference, the play appears to suggest that no matter how much we attempt to document our lives, there will always be an inherent disconnect between e.g. recorded words and the lived experiences that they are meant to represent.

If we summarise what to take away from Beckett, in the search for meaning, language indifference and nonchalance (e.g. repetitions, nonsense) represent potentially important and omnipresent barriers to ICER that need to be taken seriously into account. These two key terms also hint at our tendency to think and speak in 'circles', our quasi-impossibility to communicate and connect with others and … our isolation from them. *Language beware!*

[Pause 1: Confession to a secret that fell]
I wrote the following poem in summer 2024 about the theme of this Étagère. Please read it and reflect on what I was attempting to say with this poem. Try to imagine what every word[2] that I have chosen to include in English and the languages that I know, tells us about language indifference and nonchalance, especially in relation to academia and education. Although the poem might sound like a lament, it also aims to 'wake us up' to the realities and complexities of language in ICER. Jot down your own thoughts about what the poem is trying to say. How do they relate to your own experiences and/or observations in research and education? Would you associate this topic to these very same words?

in a world where words could weave a kuvakudos of thoughts
                                       bridges from one soul to another
                                       beautiful Tanz of lexes
we find ourselves numb … emotions unchained
                                       a chamber of thoughts
hearing our own röst
echoing in our libraries   fading away in an abstinent tungumál
the enemy of the baabelin of sounds
never sets us free
that apathy towards language …
                                       [… my once cherished chain]
                                       [… my former beacon and guide]
                     dimmed   *neglected*

Une symphonie muette
I weep for a stage that's torn apart
we remain, in the hush of our own space,

                                                                                     distant sounds

沉默 [chénmò] we can't replace

2. A mosaic of meanings and connotations

Moving forward, in this section I would want us to observe four short academic texts written for this Resource Book in order to reflect on the potential for language to both elucidate and obfuscate our understanding of interculturality. Consider each text and ask yourself what makes these texts potentially difficult to read and understand, and observe the impact on you.

1. The dialectical interplay between hegemonic cultural paradigms and subaltern counter-narratives is often muddied by the epistemological biases inherent in dominant discourses. The polyvalent nature of cultural constructs, when subjected to a deconstructive analysis, reveals the underlying power dynamics that perpetuate the marginalization of non-dominant cultural expressions. The quest for a more inclusive cultural ontology necessitates a critical re-evaluation of the ontological assumptions that undergird our understanding of culture.

I intentionally crafted this first text to be opaque. As such, it may present comprehension difficulties for those unfamiliar with the jargon and concepts prevalent in western globalised academic discourses on e.g. culture and interculturality, inspired from so-called postmodern thought (e.g. Maffesoli, 1995). In the text, I use complex sentence structures and specialised terminology (e.g. hegemonic cultural paradigms, polyvalent nature, deconstructive analysis) on purpose, which can be problematic for readers from non-English-speaking backgrounds/post-coloniality, and others, particularly if they are not well-versed in the specific academic language of cultural studies/interculturality. The discussion is also highly abstract, which can be difficult to grasp because of the lack of concrete examples. Finally, the focus on the themes of power dynamics and marginalisation within interculturality may not resonate with someone from a context who has had different experiences or priorities regarding e.g. 'cultural' identity and interculturality.

2. The transcultural hermeneutic spiral is a recursive process whereby the intercultural subject is the culturocosmonaut, journeying through the ethnoludic cosmos in search of the cultural elixir that promises a socio-epistemological apotheosis. This quest is not without its culturological quagmires and ethnographic quicksands, but it is through these challenges

that the intercultural alchemist forges a culturovital essence that transcends the mundane and enters the realm of the culturocosmic sublime.

I hope that you realised quickly that this text is a pastiche – see a hoax. It is meant to be absurd, playful and … somewhat meaningless, exhibiting a high level of nonchalance towards your potential unfamiliarity with the terms, assuming a level of expertise or willingness to engage with expert terminology. The following aspects are highly problematic: too specialised and abstract terminology (invented jargon – originally a word referring to the chattering of birds – such as *culturocosmonaut*, *culturological quagmires*, *ethnographic quicksands* …). The text also seems to assume that you readers are familiar with the concepts and are willing to engage with them at a deep level (no attempt to simplify or explain the terms in a way that would make them more accessible). As a final point, the text uses a rhetorical style that seems to be more about impressing with the intricacies of language than about communicating information in a somewhat straightforward manner.

3. Interculturality, in my view, is like the concept of 和而不同 (harmony but with differences), a traditional Chinese idea. It's about embracing the various cultural elements from all over the world, just like how the Chinese garden includes different plants and stones, yet maintains harmony. As a young Chinese student, I perceive interculturality as a practice of 求同存异 (seeking common ground while reserving differences). It's about finding the balance between our shared humanity and our unique cultural identities. It's like the Chinese art of paper-cutting, where each cut is distinct, but together they form a beautiful and coherent picture. In the context of Chinese ideology, interculturality is also about 互利共赢 (mutually beneficial and win-win). It's not just about exchanging cultural practices; it's about enhancing mutual understanding and respect, which leads to a more peaceful and prosperous world. It's about celebrating the diversity of cultures while also recognizing our common goals and aspirations. Moreover, interculturality aligns with the Chinese principle of 天人合一 (unity of heaven and humanity), where all parts of the world are interconnected and interdependent. It's about understanding that our cultural differences are not barriers, but rather, they are the richness that makes our global community vibrant and strong.

This text was produced by a Chinese undergraduate student at a university in Beijing. It might be difficult for someone from outside this context and who does not speak Chinese to understand this short text. As such, it includes Chinese ideological slogans like 和而不同 (harmony but with differences), 求同存异 (seeking common ground while reserving differences), 互利共赢 (mutually beneficial and win-win), and 天人合一 (unity of heaven and humanity). These concepts are rooted in Chinese philosophy and today's political ideology and may not have direct equivalents in English or western thought/ideological realm (see

Yuan et al., 2022) [without knowledge of Chinese or an understanding of these concepts, the meanings and connotations could be lost]. The student's text also references 'cultural' practices and philosophies that are often constructed as specific to China, such as *the Chinese garden* and *paper-cutting*. These references may not be familiar to someone from e.g. a western background, which could make it difficult to grasp the full meaning (although paper-cutting is also a so-called tradition in e.g. Switzerland). You will have also noted that the text tends to discuss interculturality from Chinese ideological perspectives, which emphasise for example harmony, mutual benefit and the interconnectedness of all things (An et al., 2022; Shen, 2023). These ideas might contrast with certain (fantasised? Imagined?) western perspectives that often emphasise e.g. competition, individualism and the division between nature and the 'Human'.

4. In Senegal, we have a saying, Tey jii li garmi, tey jii li jaam, which means One tree does not make a forest. This proverb encapsulates our view on diversity; it is the collective harmony of many voices and traditions that creates the symphony of our society. Interculturality, to me, is not just about engaging with the foreign, but about recognizing and celebrating the diversity within our own land. Our land is a mosaic of ethnic groups, each with its own language, customs, and spiritual beliefs. Yet, we are bound by a common thread, a shared humanity that transcends our differences. We believe in Mbooloommeek ba, which speaks to the interconnectedness of all people, a concept that resonates with the idea of interculturality. In Senegal, we also hold the concept of Teranga, which is the essence of our hospitality and the spirit of sharing. It is this spirit that guides our approach to interculturality. We extend our hands in friendship, not just to those who are like us, but to all who seek to understand and be understood. However, our approach to interculturality is not always easily grasped by those from afar. Our worldview is deeply rooted in the oral traditions and the wisdom of our ancestors. It is a perspective that is sensory and experiential, often expressed through the rhythm of our drums, the vibrant colors of our attire, and the flavors of our cuisine.

Written by a university student from Senegal, this text could be challenging to understand due to both linguistic and contextual specificities. These might include: *cultural proverbs and concepts* [Phrases like Tey jii li garmi, tey jii li jaam and Mbooloommeek ba]; *the concept of Teranga* (Diame, 2023) which appears to be a special Senegalese 'value' that encapsulates the spirit of hospitality and community; the text also asserts that Senegalese worldviews are often conveyed through oral traditions, which may be quite different from the written and text-based traditions that are more prevalent in many other parts of the world; to finish, the text makes references to the fact that Senegalese 'culture' might be described as communicating through sensory experiences like drum rhythms and culinary flavours, to which many scholars and educators in ICER might find difficult to relate.

7. The silent crisis of language indifference and nonchalance

7.1. Sleepwalking through language

A few recommendations before we start:

- While engaging with this Étagère section, record your observations and reflections on how language reflects different beliefs, ideologies, values and biases in relation to ICER. For example, note instances where language may be indifferent or nonchalant towards interculturality as a complex and polysemic notion in research and education.
- Following the principles of what could be referred to as Eavesdropping Ethnography (e.g. Tipper, 2020), and in an ethical and respectful way, observe conversations in formal and informal contexts of ICER (at a conference, during coffee break at your department), the language people use, in order to identify and reflect on potential language indifference and nonchalance.

We start with a few words from the novel *I'm Not Stiller* which was published in 1954 by Max Frisch (1911–1991). The story revolves around Stiller, who is mistaken for someone else and assumes a stolen identity (he is not *the Stiller* from the title!). As he navigates the complexities of his assumed identity, he grapples with his sense of self. *I'm Not Stiller* delves into the character's past through a series of flashbacks and introspective reflections, revealing his troubled relationships, personal failures and unresolved guilt. In the novel Frisch makes his main character utter the followings:

- "I have no words for my reality" (Frisch, 1962: 72).
- "We live in an age of reproduction. Most of what makes up our personal picture of the world we have never seen with our own eyes – or rather, we've seen it with our own eyes, but not on the spot: our knowledge comes to us from a distance, we are televiewers, telehearers, teleknowers" (Frisch, 1962: 141).

In this section, while problematising and defining *imperfectly* language indifference and nonchalance, I draw inspiration from these two quotes: 1. Words cannot but fail us to discuss interculturality in our hypercomplex worlds of research and education; 2. We must bear in mind the mediated nature of today's (knowledge about) interculturality through e.g. social media and academic publications, and the fact that the language we use to describe it may fall short of direct observations and experiences, thus influencing how:

we speak (too much, too little),
    un-speak,
        fantaspeak (fantasize while speaking),
            reprospeak (see the second quote from Frisch),

> forget to speak,
>> refrain from speaking,
>>> impose speaking,
in relation to interculturality.

My general impression of ICER today is that we scholars and educators often sleepwalk through language within discussions of interculturality, believing naively in its extraordinary power to e.g. solve problems or understand the world and other worldviews. We have become what I would like to call *interculturalists with linguanoia*: We seem to believe in the *power of words*, thinking that simply by using the 'right' words or phrases (meaning actually those imposed on us by people who have the power to speak and make us listen; or imposed by us on others), we can magically understand and influence others' thoughts, change their behaviour or even alter their reality (see e.g. research on the ideologeme of intercultural competence, see Byram, 2020).

We might also naively believe that using language (different languages!) can automatically grant us the ability to think differently, understand others and unlock all the secrets of interculturality as an academic notion. Language is then perceived naively as a *cure-all*!

An excessive trust in translation might also characterise *interculturalists with linguanoia*. As such, we might have an unwarranted faith in translation, thinking that it can perfectly convey the nuances and contexts of any language without any loss of meaning (Dervin & Jacobsson, 2021; Bojsen et al., 2023; Huang, 2023).

For Barthes (2010), language is *fascist*. And language is *fascist* in ICER too, I would add. With this provocative assertion, Barthes critiques the way language can be used to enforce and perpetuate certain ideologies and norms in any context of communication. As said in Étagère 3, Barthes (2020) believed that language has the power to impose a particular worldview and set of values, much like e.g. a fascist system might impose its ideology on its population. Language is never a neutral tool for researching and educating interculturally. Instead it is a complex system that can perpetuate power structures and biases. Barthes's idea is that language, by its very nature, creates a system of rules and conventions that users must follow, which can be seen as restrictive. This can lead to the marginalisation of certain ideologies, expressions and experiences that do not fit within a given dominant linguistic framework, often leading to language indifference and nonchalance. By privileging and preferring certain ways of speaking, one could go as far as saying that language is also too often fascist in ICER …

[A good instance of language as fascist: A friend from Pakistan explained to me that his official signature is composed of both English (family name) and Urdu (first name). He started using this signature to rebel against a system back in his country which only accepts signatures written in English. He told me how he was disturbed by the fact that his mother was shamed by a bank teller once for using her signature in Urdu (the only signature she had). They claimed that her signature was not ﺲﭼﮐ (kachay, *not fully cooked, not fully ripe*) … (When the colonialism and fascism of English humiliates the powerless …).

Language does indoctrinate (Reboul, 1984) by shaping our beliefs, perceptions and (somehow) our behaviours in subtle and not-so-subtle ways. Being aware of these influences and questioning the language we use and hear can help mitigate the indoctrinating effects of language (indifference and nonchalance being two such effects). [Can you think of concrete examples? Some popular hints today: *euphemisms* (the use of 'softeners' or politically correct language, e.g. 'policy adjustment' vs. 'policy failure'), *gender roles*, *labels*, *language used to frame historical narratives* (e.g. the 'discovery of America' vs. 'colonialism'), *news media* ('protestors' vs. 'demonstrators'), *political framing*, etc.]

Discussions around the power of English should also be introduced here (Al-Issa & Mirhosseini, 2019). English as the dominant language in academic and scientific research, can lead to a bias towards English-speaking perspectives and a marginalisation of 'non-English' viewpoints. The dominance of English in academia often leads to the tendency for research published in English to be more widely disseminated and accessible, which can result in the exclusion or underrepresentation of research from non-English-speaking scholars/educators, potentially indoctrinating the global research community into narrow perspectives. English-language research may inadvertently carry ideological and lingua-cultural assumptions that are not universally applicable (see House et al., 2024).

[Pause 2: Language is cunning – or people?]
In China, I have often seen old official notices, which look like some kind of oversized envelope. I have been fascinated by these 'envelopes' after seeing an exhibition about them in Beijing six years ago (Figure 4.1.). In this piece named 假大空 (jiǎ dà kōng), an idiom that translates as 'empty words' or 'bogus speech' (Word-for-word: *fake/artificial big space* or *air* or *sky*), I have pasted pieces of embroidery that I made based on sentences written (originally in Chinese but translated in English here) about someone who was being lauded for being hard-working, knowledgeable and rigorous. However, the realities of this person were otherwise. In fact, they had very little ethics and abused the work of others for their own benefits. When I read these words about this person, I became frustrated and somewhat upset. How could someone be so cunning as to make the world believe that they were an invented ideal? Writing the sentences through embroidery took a long time but it helped me calm down and rethink my original feelings. As a whole, the art piece is entirely contradictory. While the English sentences represent exemplary instances of *belles paroles*, the two Chinese phrases that I included in pinyin (which Chinese speakers would understand) signal a parallel world, another set of realities. Although this is an extreme case, often we have to experience such contradictions without being aware of it. Language is cunning and it can easily be tricked into 'emptiness' and yet benefit someone – and in-/directly the 'system'. *How often do you face jiǎ dà kōng in ICER?*]

96 Intercultural Self-Defence

FIGURE 4.1   Jiǎ dà kōng /假大空 (Dervin, 2023; 17.5 x 26.3 cm).

7.2. *Language as an afterthought in research and education*

As you will have probably understood up till now, language indifference and nonchalance in ICER can lead to several issues, including unfair power relations, misunderstandings, non-understandings, misinterpretations and a lack of empathy for the contexts in which languages are embedded.

First, languages are not just tools for communication since they carry nuances, ideologies, values and 'ways of life'. Language indifference can thus result in the loss of these nuances, leading to research that fails to capture the richness and complexity of perspectives and discourses in interculturality.

What is more, when researchers and educators do not consider the subtleties of language, they may misinterpret data or responses from participants/students, leading to inaccurate and one-sided conclusions. Indifference to language can also lead to poor translation practices. This can result in research findings that are not valid or reliable (Holmes et al., 2022; Warriner & Bigelow, 2019). Intercultural researchers may not have the linguistic expertise to fully appreciate the subtleties of different languages, leading to oversights in understanding and interpretation, and communicating around their research (Dervin, 2023; Shen, 2023; Shen & Singh, 2022).

I believe that ignoring language aspects of our work on interculturality often raises ethical issues too, as it may involve a failure to respect and understand ideologies and positions of e.g. research participants, potentially leading to their exploitation or even harm.

From a policy and practice perspective, research findings are often used to inform them in areas like education, healthcare and social services. Language indifference and nonchalance could result in policies that are not necessarily appropriate or effective, thus failing to meet the needs of diverse individuals. In a similar vein, language indifference and nonchalance can lead to the exclusion of minority voices in research and education, as it may not accommodate the languages and communication styles of 'minority groups', thus perpetuating inequality and marginalisation. This is often the case with theoretical frameworks in intercultural research which may be limited if they do not account for the role of language in shaping e.g. interactions and identities (Holmes et al., 2022; Dervin, 2023).

Finally, indifference to language can create real barriers in intercultural collaborations in academia, as researchers from different linguistic backgrounds may struggle to communicate, hindering the development of shared understandings and research goals. Some of us might assume that certain linguistic or communicative principles are universal, overlooking the unique features of their partners and contexts of interaction (Liu & Zheng, 2024; House et al., 2024). We may also believe that we understand each other while reproducing the status quo often imposed by the most powerful figures. Finally, let us bear in mind that the tools and technologies that we use in research may not be equipped to handle the diversity and complexity of languages, leading to indifference (e.g. WhatsApp, Moodle, etc.).

7.3. Derrida, Cixous and Dostoyevsky for language in ICER

[Pause 3a. Derrida's concept of différance]

Jacques Derrida's (2021) concept of différance is a central tenet of his so-called deconstructive philosophy, serving as a play on the words *difference* and *deferment* in French. The concept encapsulates the idea that meaning in language is generated not only because of a word's difference from others within a signifying system but also because meaning is inevitably and infinitely deferred or postponed. This *constant deferral* means that meaning is always in flux, perpetually under erasure and glimpsed only through impasses in understanding (Derrida, 2021: 290).

In the context of intercultural research, the notion of différance can be employed to address the issue of language indifference and nonchalance, which may manifest as a disregard for or misunderstanding of linguistico-ideological nuances in communication (Dasli, 2024). Derrida's concept emphasises the complexity and dynamism of language, suggesting that in interculturality, we should be attentive to the multiplicity and shifting nature of linguistic meanings. The concept prompts us researchers and practitioners to question and reflect further on the language we use and how it impacts the perception and expression of knowledge on interculturality in the ways we speak, teach and write. It discourages the simplification or reification of language as a static entity, instead advocating for an understanding of language as a construct that is continually formed and reshaped within specific and overlapping social, ideological and historical contexts.

[Pause 3b. Hélène Cixous: questioning our entrenched mindsets through language]

The French feminist theorist Hélène Cixous's theories on language and writing appear to be relevant to the study of interculturality, particularly in the context of language indifference, indoctrination, and intellectual inertia. As such, the writer argues that 'traditional' language structures often marginalise or silence non-dominant voices (Cixous, 2024). In intercultural research, this is crucial as it encourages scholars to recognise and challenge the biases inherent in language, promoting potentially more inclusive and representative discourses. It's about ensuring that all expressions are given space and consideration, not just those that align with dominant ideologies and epistemic hegemony in the field of interculturality. Furthermore, Cixous's work suggests that language can be a tool of indoctrination, where certain ideologies and norms are imposed on others (Díaz Diocaretz & Segarra, 2004). As we have seen, in ICER, recognising this could help unpack the power dynamics at play in epistemic dialogues and debates about interculturality and could inform efforts to foster more reciprocal relationships between e.g. students, scholars and educators from different contexts. Interestingly, Cixous's theories would encourage us interculturalists to question our entrenched mindsets, particularly in how we relate to ideologies, norms and values (Cixous & Schäfer, 2021). This could support us in being more innovative and to produce and disseminate more nuanced understandings of e.g. our concepts and methods, as well as more effective strategies for promoting intellectual exchange and co-construction.

All in all, Cixous (2024) advocates for a writing and research practice that are aware of their own biases, open to the Other and committed to ethical representation. In her book *Le rire de la Méduse* (trans.: *The Laugh of the Medusa*), Cixous (2024) argues for a radical unrethinking of language and literature from a feminine perspective. She calls for women to 'write themselves' (Cixous, 1993, 2024) as a means of reclaiming their bodies and identities, which have been traditionally confined and controlled by patriarchal discourse. This form of writing is characterised by its generosity, fluidity, non-linearity and resistance to traditional narrative structures, embracing multiplicity, emotion and the body. In the following excerpt, Cixous (1993: 82) highlights the anxiety and struggle women face when attempting to speak in public, often due to the patriarchal structures that silence or devalue their voices: "Every woman has known the torment of getting up to speak. Her heart racing, at times entirely lost for words, ground and language slipping away – that's how daring a feat, how great a transgression it is for a woman to speak – even just open her mouth – in public". Language indifference and nonchalance in ICER calls for similar subversive actions and endeavours so that voices that are silenced, unheard, minoritised, can also be at the forefront of the field and feel more empowered. The vast majority of us face similar struggles as the woman described by Cixous who is nervous about speaking in public.

[Pause 3c. Fyodor Dostoyevsky's desire for deep and candid communication]

The writer Fyodor Dostoyevsky (1821–1881), often referred to as a profound psychological explorer of the human condition, does not explicitly write about language indifference in his works, but, like e.g. Samuel Beckett (see Beckett, 2009a), he has deeply explored the power of language and its impact on human relationships and society. In one of my favourite novels, *The Idiot* (2012), Dostoyevsky uses the character of Prince Myshkin to showcase the purity and sincerity of language in contrast to deceit and manipulation present in the dialogues of other characters. Myshkin's straightforward and compassionate communication style reflects Dostoyevsky's belief in the importance of language as a tool for expressing truth and maintaining moral integrity (Williams, 2008; Kristeva, 2022).

Dostoyevsky's novels often feature characters that grapple with existential questions and the language they use is a reflection of their internal struggles and philosophical debates (Kristeva, 2022). The complexity and depth of the language used by Dostoyevsky's characters are indicative of the author's view of language as a powerful medium that shapes action, emotion and thought. Furthermore, Dostoyevsky's own life experiences, including his epilepsy and time in a Siberian prison camp in Russia (Williams, 2008), are woven into his narratives, often through the voices of his characters. The way these characters use language to express their experiences and thoughts is a testament to Dostoyevsky's understanding of the intimate connection between language and the human psyche. Here is a quote from *The Idiot* (Dostoyevsky, 2012: 429): "I shall tell you everything, EVERYTHING, even the most important things of all, whenever I like, and you are to hide nothing from me on your side. I want to speak to at least one person, as I would to myself". Here, Dostoyevsky seems to express a desire for deep and honest communication that can help to clear up misunderstandings that arise from the complexity of human thoughts and feelings (see my poem at the beginning of this Étagère where I lament about the same issue).

1. A conceptual toolbox to apprehend language indifference and nonchalance

Language indifference in research represents a lack of concern or recognition for the importance of language in various aspects of communication, cognition and e.g.

identity building and negotiation. It can manifest in different ways in research and education, such as disregard for linguistic diversities in the way research is done, the undervaluation of language learning and use or the failure to acknowledge the role of language in shaping academic and educational perceptions and constructions of interculturality. Here are some concepts that could be useful individually or in combination in analysing language indifference and nonchalance.

Cognitive and creative aspects:

- *Cognitive Load Theory*: The idea that our working memory has limited capacity could be used to examine and try to understand aspects of indifference and nonchalance towards e.g. using, learning and/or making efforts to include additional languages in research and education, as it requires significant cognitive effort (Sweller, 2024).
- *Logoclasm*: A term that has been associated with Samuel Beckett's approach to art and literature, particularly in the context of his experimental and minimalist plays (see Yarn III). The term is used to describe an art form that deliberately disrupts, 'mismakes' or undermines language and traditional narrative structures (de la Durantaye, 2016). In Beckett's work, logoclasm refers to his intentional subversion of traditional literary and dramatic conventions, often through the use of abstraction, a focus on failure, negativity and minimalism (de la Durantaye, 2016). Language and reason as well as unity and continuity are highly disrupted through logoclasm. Clements (2019: 247) reminds us that "For Beckett, language not only fails to represent but functions to obscure the 'something or nothing' of the world outside the speaking subject. The task of the writer is, then, not more accurate or encompassing mimesis through a new use of language, but the willed destruction of the very customs and habits of language that create an unclear relation between the world and mind". In other words, Beckett aimed to use *language against language*. Language failure is an ideal for the writer.

Economic entry points:

- *Dialectical Materialism*: This Marxist concept advances that material conditions shape our social consciousness (Lefebvre, 2009; Žižek, 2013). Applied to language in academia, it could suggest that e.g. economic and socio-political structures might influence the value placed on language skills and diversity and the production and dissemination of knowledge about e.g. interculturality.
- *Economic Pragmatism*: It refers to a focus on economic gain (e.g. academic promotion, publish or perish) over the production of challenging and constantly renewed intercultural research and education. This might lead to indifference towards language as something that is not economically beneficial. To my knowledge this has not been studied in relation to ICER and would deserve our full attention (see Ansell & Bartenberger, 2019 about pragmatism and

political crisis management in times of financial crises which could inspire interculturalists interested in language indifference and nonchalance).

Ideology:

- *Linguistic and cultural Hegemony*: This concept refers to the dominance of one language/'culture' over others, often leading to the marginalisation of certain groups and individuals. Indifference may arise when a dominant language and 'culture' overshadow the importance of linguistic diversity in relation to interculturality (see e.g. Ilves, 2004 on Antonio Gramsci's writings on language and hegemony).
- *Echoing of language*: Also known as echoism or parroting, echoing of language refers to individuals repeating ideas, phrases and/or words they have heard from others, often without fully understanding or critically evaluating the content (see Bakhtin, 2010). This can occur when someone is influenced by a particular group, ideology or authority figure and adopts their language without necessarily internalising the meaning or context (see echo chambers). Examples of echoing of language include political slogans (an attention-getting phrase), buzzwords (voguish words), jargon (overly specialised words or phrases), groupthink (see Étagère 2). Echoing of language can be a sign of indoctrination or a lack of critical thinking, but it can also simply be the result of not having the opportunity to engage deeply with the ideas being discussed (see Étagères 2 and 3).
- *Colonial Linguistics*: The historical impact of colonialism on language, whereby (western) colonisers imposed their languages on colonised peoples. This can lead to a legacy of language indifference or suppression of e.g. indigenous and/ or 'small' languages (Schmidt-Brücken et al., 2016; Calvet, 1998).

Planning and policy:

- *Language Planning and Policy*: The study of how e.g. governments and institutions manage language use can shed light on official attitudes towards e.g. language preservation, education and promotion, which may influence public indifference (see Hamid et al. (2015) on language planning for medium of instruction in Asia). Language planning and policy in intercultural research and education has received limited attention and should be high on our agenda for intercultural self-defence.

Translanguaging:

- *A Translanguaging Space for Original Theorising*: Shen Haibo's (2023) paper explores the potential of bilingual postgraduate researchers to engage in original theorising through translanguaging, which describes the way multilingual speakers use all their language skills together, rather than keeping them

102 Intercultural Self-Defence

separate (Li, 2018). The paper discusses how bilinguals could leverage their full linguistic and theoretical repertoire, particularly the resources of their non-English languages, to develop new concepts and analytical tools for academic research. Shen (2023) argues that by adopting a translanguaging perspective in education and research, researchers could contribute to a more diverse and inclusive academic discourse.

[Pause 4: Comparing translations, bearing indifference or nonchalance in mind]

Here is the blurb of French scholar Martine A.-Pretceille's (1996) best-selling short introductory book titled *L'éducation interculturelle* in French. The book has influenced several generations of French-speaking scholars (myself included, A.-Pretceille was my PhD supervisor) in fields such as language education and teacher education. In English the title could translate as *Intercultural Education*, although this would not render the use of the article *l'* in French ('The intercultural education', which gives the impression that there is one form of such education – in fact A.-Pretceille does promote her own 'French Republican' version as 'the' only right form of intercultural education in the book, see Figure 4.2.).

FIGURE 4.2 French Republican values as a slogan sold at a souvenir shop in Paris (France).

Following the French blurb, I am including three different translations of the text, which I have created myself with the help of a few friends and colleagues. The translations can be seen as fantasised, imaginary (and stereotypical, some might argue) translations characterised as 1. British English; 2. American English; 3. 'non-native' English. My interest here is not in forcing you to decide about/imagine these categories in terms of right/wrong, authentic/fabricated, etc. My interest is in us reflecting on how translation choices might influence (potential) (mis-)perceptions and/or (mis-)understandings of the ideologies, beliefs, values of the original text. While reading these texts, observe *word choices* (e.g. specific vocabulary used such as reality vs, fact; come together vs. confrontation), *formulations* (e.g. use of the passive voice; simplified syntax; spelling). What differences and similarities can you see between the three translations? How do these elements seem to influence you in trying to make sense of what the book blurb is about? Which of the three translations is the clearest to you? Which one do you find the most confusing? Explain why. Either based on the original French version (if you can read French) or around the three translations into English, write your own version of the blurb that you think is clear and understandable for scholars/educators from your own context(s).

Notre modernité est marquée par une pluralité dans les formes de socialisation, de culture, d'éducation, de langage, de modes d'être au monde et aux autres... L'autre, l'étranger, l'étrangéité sont omniprésents et font partie de l'environnement proche et du quotidien. L'école est devenue un lieu de confrontation symbolique entre les différentes normes. Elle était déjà au cœur des enjeux politiques et sociaux, elle est désormais aussi au centre des enjeux culturels. Si la diversité culturelle s'impose dans les faits, l'éducation interculturelle se propose d'en maîtriser les effets et de la valoriser.

1. Our modernity is marked by plurality in today's socialisation, culture, education, language, ways of being in the world and in others ... The other, the foreigner, foreignness are omnipresent and are part of our immediate environment and everyday life. School has become a place of symbolic confrontation between different norms. This confrontation was already at the heart of political and social issues, and it is now also at the centre of cultural issues. If cultural diversity is a reality, intercultural education aims to control its effects and enhance it. (*Fantasized British English*)
2. Our modernity is characterized by diversity in relation to socialization, culture, education, language, ways of being in the world and with others ... The other, the stranger, strangeness are ever-present and form part of the immediate environment and daily life. Schools have become a place of symbolic confrontation between different norms. Confrontation was already at the heart of political and social issues, it is now also at the center of cultural issues. If cultural diversity is a fact, intercultural education aims to manage its effects and to value it. (*Fantasized American English*)

3. Our time today is filled with many different ways of making friends, celebrating, learning, talking, and living with each other and the world around us. People who are different, from far away, or who seem unfamiliar are everywhere and are part of our normal lives. Schools are places where we see different rules and ways of doing things come together. They have always been important for politics and how society works, and now they are also very important for the different cultures we have. If we have many different cultures, teaching people how to understand and respect each other's cultures is important. This kind of teaching helps us to deal with the good and not-so-good things that can happen because of our differences and helps us to appreciate the value of having different cultures. (*Fantasized non-native English*)

[Pause 5: Taking a militant attitude towards sound]
Morton Feldman (1926–1987) was an American avant-garde composer. Here is what he said about sound (Feldman, 2006: 56):

> To me (sic), I took a militant attitude towards sounds. I wanted sounds to be a metaphor, that they could be as free as a human being might be free. That was my idea about sound. It still is, that they should breathe... not to be used for the vested interest of an idea. I feel that music should have no vested interests, that you shouldn't know how it's made, that you shouldn't know if there's a system, that you shouldn't know anything about it ... except that it's some kind of life force that to some degree really changes your life ... if you're into it.

Feldman's approach to music, as reflected in his so-called graph music (notation on graph paper), offers deep insights into the role of language in any form of communication. Feldman's notation, particularly in his scores, invites a level of interpretation and indeterminacy that challenges traditional notions of musical language and communication (Feldman, 2006). This can be seen as a metaphor for the complexities and ambiguities inherent in language as discussed in this Étagère. *Projection 1* from 1950 represents one of the earliest examples of graphic notation in music. The piece features an original notation that looks more like a circuit diagram than traditional music notation. With its non-standard notation, *Projection 1* challenges the idea that language and notation are always sufficient to convey artistic intent, much like how research language can sometimes fall short in describing innovative or abstract concepts. So, in his graph music, Feldman often used non-standard notations, which were deliberately loose, allowing for a range of interpretations by the performers (Cline, 2016). This openness can be likened to the way language is used in communication, where the same words can have different meanings based on context, tone and the background of both speaker and listener. This can also be compared to the limitations of academic language in fully encapsulating the complexity of e.g. epistemic diversity and research findings in relation to interculturality.

Feldman's music also embodies a sense of silence and stillness, which can be paralleled to the moments of silence and confusion that occur in dialogue with other students, educators and researchers and, even, in writing. These pauses are not just empty spaces but are filled with potential meanings, much like the silences in conversation that can convey hesitation, reflection or a search for the correct words. Moreover, Feldman's compositions often require a deep listening experience, where the listener must engage with the music in a more active and interpretive way (Cline, 2016). For example, the solo piano piece *For Bunita Marcus* (1985) is a study in sustained concentration and subtlety, much like the need for precision and clarity in research writing. Feldman's use of silence and minimal material could encourage us to consider the economy of language and the power of understatement in conveying complex ideas. This aligns with the idea that communication through language is not just about *the transmission of information* but also about *the shared experience and understanding* between interactants – and this applies well to the contexts of research and education. Language is then not just about the words themselves but also about the spaces between them, the moments of silence and the shared experience of interpretation that occurs between speakers. I believe that paying attention to silence (Eco, 2020: 43, "the long pause, silence as creation of suspense, silence as threat, silence as agreement, silence as denial, silence in music") could also help us move beyond indifference and nonchalance.

Finally, Feldman's music is often described as intimate and personal, with a focus on the individual experience of sounds. This could suggest that research and education also require a personal touch, whereby e.g. the researcher's voice and perspective are evident, allowing for a more direct connection with their readers and listeners … By examining Feldman's music, we ICER students, educators and researchers could gain insights into the strategic use of language, the importance of pacing and structure and the potential for creative expression within the constraints of academic communication and language use.

3. Fragments about language in ICER

[Reading Cixous about the internalised misogyny that patriarchal language and structures can instil in women (leading them to be complicit in their own oppression), I cannot help but think about what western interculturalists have done to the Global South. "Men have committed the greatest crime against women. Insidiously, violently, they have led them to hate women, to be their own enemies, to mobilize their immense strength against themselves, to be the executants of their virile needs" (Cixous, 1993: 80 – replace men and women by western interculturalists and interculturalists from the Global South).]

[Kafka (in Flores, 1977: 24) summarises *so well* what language must do to us: "I write differently from what I speak, I speak differently from what I think, I think differently from the way I ought to think, and so it all proceeds into the deepest darkness". Not paying attention to these complexities in research and education cannot do justice to interculturality.]

[Asked a colleague to open up the definition of a term in English for a global readership. They seem to understand this request as not allowing them to use the term I am urging them to explain. Is multilingual justice a form of oppression now?]

[To chapter authors in one of my edited books: About the very word 'ethnic'. When I suggested that you could position it, I was inspired by my noticing on many occasions that colleagues from different corners of the world and languages understand and make use of the word in very different ways from the way*S* we might in Finnish research (the Finnish word *etninen* is a loanword from Indo-European languages and it is defined and used in very unstable ways *within* and *between* fields of research; it is also often mixed up with the concept of race ... even in sociology ...). For example, in China, the English word ethnic is often used to refer to the Chinese notion of Minzu in sociological research (which only refers to Chinese citizens, not to those from outside China). Many scholars also often use the word *nationalities* in English as a synonym for 'ethnic groups' (inspired by the Soviet Union). These tend to confuse international researchers, especially if they are merely taken for granted. I do understand that in different sociological and linguistic traditions we might think that these are stabilised 'terms' but crossing economic-political-ideological borders I often realise that they are not. And the use of English as a lingua franca often gives us the illusion that we put the same realities and connotations behind words ... (They did not respond).]

[An intercultureme is a polysemic and yet 'fakely' obvious term used in intercultural research and education. Interculturemes disseminated in English that ought to be discarded: *culture, competence, identity*. Break away from them as quickly as you can.]

[A reviewer from the west asks a colleague from the Global South to reformulate a critique towards a scholar in English since they find it very unkind in its awkward 'formulation'. The critique concerns a scholar from the Global South, educated solely in the west. This could be considered as a good example of care and critique of language indifference and nonchalance. And yet, who in academia is entitled and/or forced to reformulate and why?]

[Why can we only criticise concepts, theories, paradigms, ideologies, formulations ('things'!) and not their enunciators directly? As if they were *untouchables*. Who speaks them? Yet, no one seems to have any qualms about criticising the usual victim: *Hofstede*. Aggressive and often misinformed voices against him do as they wish.]

[Let's cross the mirror of language together in intercultural research and education.]

[Conflicts are never about 'culture' but about what money and power fantasies make us do to each other. Intercultural training makes no sense if it is about *each other's culture.* We need training that helps us face dysfunctional power relations and abuse of power, especially in relation to language use.]

[The invention and use of a concept to describe and prescribe reality will always lead to injustice, (in-/direct) conflict with others. In turn they will coin and manipulate their own concept. Hopefully the clashes that emerge from these 'inter-ideaflicts' can lead us to reconsider our thoughts for a moment.]

[When I work with someone in research on interculturality, I keep asking myself these days: "what does this person really want from me?"; "what is their real agenda?"; "what do their kind, considerate and even 'cheesy' words – but in the end ideological and potentially 'disguisingly' abusive words – want from me?" I am thinking: self-defence.]

[About finding a universal definition of interculturality: That could never be possible. Interculturality is systematically embedded in historical-linguistic-political-economic-ideological … agendas which cannot agree with each other … see: USA versus Finland, China, Malaysia. Interculturality is about how we have been taught-told to define ourselves versus others and how we might rebel against these definitions. So, who we think we might be is the starting point … Easy to see how this could never work …]

[An interesting paper focusing on emic concepts renegotiated between speakers of Japanese, Balinese and Chinese. And yet the end of the paper goes back to discourses of western interculturality. *Cosmopolitanism and global citizenship*. Coup raté!]

[Looking at Duccio's painting of Jesus healing a blindman from 1311 (*The Healing of the Man Born Blind*) at the National Gallery in London. The man appears twice on the painting: both as *blind* and *healed*. Two realities of the same person in one representation. What if, similarly, we could represent this duality in our writing on interculturality? At least *two* instead of one.]

[I have noticed that I have started using certain Chinese ideologemes of interculturality in English (Chinglish?), which my Finnish students and colleagues do not understand … *cultural spread, cultural output, enhancing talent quality, the charm of different cultures, great culture* …]

[*Change?* I meet a friend I haven't seen for a long time and tell another Chinese friend that their *qi* (气, with a pictographic character describing the gas of floating clouds, now referring to someone's temperament, general feelings about them) has become more positive and mature. Ten years ago, I would have been surprised about such a comment and most likely unable to understand it.]

[Why do we talk about language barriers? The barriers are in our heads and ideologies not in languages. *Languages are innocent* (here).]

[The overuse of aggrandising adjectives in some Chinese research papers about intercultural competence shows somehow that there might be a problem with what they qualify. *Great/excellent culture; the charm of other cultures* …]

[As a field that is meant to be opened to diversity, ICER could in fact be very closed in terms of *who* can speak in the field, *how* one speaks and *what* one can say and *why*.]

108 Intercultural Self-Defence

[In the French press, a trade union representative is quoted as having said: "we are here to negotiate, we are not here to discuss." I thought that these two verbs were part of the same process.]

5. Vitrine III

(A university campus, where a group of international students from different countries is gathered. The students are trying to discuss some of the basic concepts of interculturality but with a twist of confusion over complex concepts. Each student brings up different theories of interculturality, but they struggle to define complex concepts.)

Yiran: Hey, everyone, I've been thinking about interculturality a lot lately. I think Dervin is right; it's about power and how we negotiate identities.

Ahmed: But, Yiran, I'm more into Byram's idea. It's about competence, you know? Like, having skills to interact with others from different cultures.

Maria: Oh, interesting! I've been reading Shi-xu who talks about interculturality as a third culture, a space where we create new meanings.

Yiran: Yeah, but what does that mean, Maria? 'New meanings' sounds too abstract for me. How do we define that?

Ahmed: Exactly! And Byram's skills, they seem practical. Like, how to use knowledge about another culture.

Maria: But it's not just about skills. It's about being in the in-between, right? It's complex, like a ... a hybrid identity or something.

Yiran: Hybrid identity? I'm confused. Is that like a mix of cultures? But Dervin says it's more about how we use power to define who we are.

Ahmed: I think we're all mixing things up here. Maybe we should go back to basics. Byram's skills, they help us to bridge the gap, no?

Maria: But it's not just about bridging, it's about creating! Like, we're not just mixing, we're making something new. It's postmodern, you know?

Yiran: Postmodern? I think we're losing the plot here. Dervin would say we need to deconstruct these ideas, not just create new ones.

Ahmed: Deconstruct? What does that even mean? I thought we were talking about how to interact with people, not tearing down ideas.

Maria: Well, maybe we need both. We deconstruct and then we create, right? It's like a cycle.

Yiran: A cycle of what? I'm feeling a bit lost in all these big words. Can we just agree on a simple definition?

Ahmed: Simple? Interculturality is never simple, Yiran. It's complex, like Maria said.

Maria: Yes, it's complex, but we can try to understand it together. Maybe we need a new theory that combines all these ideas.

Yiran: A new theory? Maybe we should just talk to our supervisor about this. They might be able to help us make sense of it all.

6. Escapade III

Let's go back to the five questions presented at the beginning of this Étagère, for which I am now providing brief answers:

1. What could language indifference and nonchalance be within the context of intercultural communication education and research?

Language indifference refers to a lack of attention or sensitivity to the nuances, complexities and ideological significance of language when engaging with intercultural research and education. Language nonchalance relates to a lack of sincerity or even seriousness in the way we might use language and reflect on it in ICER.

2. How could language indifference and nonchalance lead to misunderstandings and non-understandings in intercultural communication?

Misunderstandings can arise when we scholars, educators or students fail to recognize the specific context(s) and meanings attached to certain words or expressions related to interculturality, leading to risks of indoctrination, intellectual inertia and the phenomenon of 'floating past each other', whereby we might believe we understand each other or agree but, in fact, we do not.

3. What role could language play in shaping research on interculturality and its education?

Language is a crucial component of research on interculturality and its education, as it carries the histories, ideologies, values and beliefs (amongst others) of a given community/group of people, influencing how individuals perceive and interact with knowledge about interculturality.

4. What strategies could researchers use to minimize language indifference and nonchalance in their work?

Interculturalists (researchers and educators) could address language indifference by promoting (critical) multilingualism systematically and encouraging themselves and others to pay attention to e.g. epistemic inequalities and injustice derived from ignoring language. Framing the use of idiomatic expressions, 'cultural' references or ideologemes that may not be understood by others, questioning the assumption that all participants share the same linguistic background, or providing translations or accommodations for e.g. so-called non-native speakers could support minimizing language indifference and nonchalance.

5. *What could be the ethical implications of language indifference and nonchalance in research on interculturality?*

Language indifference and nonchalance could lead to ethical issues such as misrepresentation, exclusion or marginalization of certain perspectives in research and education, which can undermine e.g. the integrity of research and the outcomes of education.

Now *hesitate* with words. *Be indecisive* with me …

Interculturality, as a concept, is … it's complex … It's not just about different cultures meeting, but more about the … the dynamic, interactions, mis … under … standing … misunderstandings, even. I talk about it in a way that's … it's not straightforward, it's not … it's not a clear-cut defin … It's more about the … the in-between, the … the spaces where ideologies and people overlap, collide, and … and sometimes, they … they blend. There's this idea of … of silence … Not the absence of sound, but … but the silence of not knowing, the … the silence of not understanding … the … lence of being silence. "We must return to silence" says Eco (2020: 42). It's … it's a part of intercultural encounters, this … this silence. It's … it's not always comfortable, but it's … it's there. It's a … a moment to … to reflect, to … to question, to … to learn. And then there's confusion. It's … it's inevi … when you're dealing with … with different ideologies, beliefs, values. You … you might not get the … the … the … their languaging. It's … it's confusing, it's … it's dis … orient … But … we can see it as a … a learning opportunity, a … a chance to … to grow, to … to unlearn. So, when we talk about interculturality, we … we should … should embrace the … the silence, the … the con..sion. It's … it's not about … about having all the answers, but … but about being open to … to the questions, to … to the uncertainties. It's … it's about … about being … being humble, being … being willing to … to learn, to … to change. In the end, interculturality in research and education is … is a journey, a … a journey of … of un-/discovery … of mysteries … of … of self and of … of others. It's … it's not a destination, it's … it's a … a process, a … a contin … process. And … and it's … it's filled with moments of … of silence and confusion, but … but also of … of clarity and understanding. It's … it's a … a beautiful mess, really. A … a beautiful, complex, and … and ever-evolving mess. *And we care … we look at language … we lis … ten to it and … we … cherish l.a.n.g.u.a.g.e …*

Notes

1 The section numbering is random in this Étagère to contribute to questioning the 'taken-for-granted' and 'good sense' critiqued in this book.
2 Translations of the words used in the poem. Kuvakudos (Finnish) = tapestry; Tanz (German) = dance; röst (Swedish) = voice; tungumál (Icelandic); baabelin (Finnish) = Babel; une symphonie muette (French) = a mute symphony; 沉默 [chénmò] (Chinese) = silence.

References

A.-Pretceille, M. (1996). *L'éducation interculturelle*. QSJ PUF.

Al-Issa, A. & Mirhosseini, S.-A. (eds.) (2019). *Worldwide English Language Education Today: Ideologies, Policies and Practices*. Routledge.

An, R., Zhu, J., Li, Y. & Zhu, H. (2022). Acculturation in a multicultural classroom: perspectives within the yin-yang metaphor framework. *Language and Intercultural Communication* 22(5), 534–551. https://doi.org/10.1080/14708477.2022.2112960

Ansell, C. & Bartenberger, M. (2019). *Pragmatism and Political Crisis Management Principle and Practical Rationality During the Financial Crisis*. Elgar Edward Publishing.

Bakhtin, M. M. (2010). *The Dialogic Imagination: Four Essays*. University of Texas Press.

Barthes, R. (2010). *The Grain of the Voice*. Vintage.

Barthes, R. (2020). *Roland Barthes by Roland Barthes*. Vintage.

Beckett, S. (2004). *Not I/Footfalls/Rockaby*. Faber & Faber.

Beckett, S. (2006). *Waiting for Godot*. Faber & Faber.

Beckett, S. (2009a). *Endgame*. Faber & Faber.

Beckett, S. (2009b). *Krapp's Last Tape and Other Shorter Plays*. Faber & Faber.

Beckett, S. (2010). *Happy Days*. Faber & Faber.

Bojsen, H., Daryai-Hansen, P., Holmen, A. & Risager, K. (eds.). (2023). *Translanguaging and Epistemological Decentring in Higher Education and Research*. Multilingual Matters.

Byram, M. (2020). *Teaching and Assessing Intercultural Communicative Competence: Revisited*. Multilingual Matters.

Calvet, J.-L. (1998). *Language Wars and Linguistic Politics*. OUP.

Cixous, H. (1993). The laugh of the medusa. In: Roman, C. P., Miller, C. & Juhasz, S. (eds.). *The Women and Language Debate: A Sourcebook* (pp. 78–93). Rutgers University Press.

Cixous, H. (1993). *Three Steps on the Ladder of Writing*. Columbia University Press.

Cixous, H. (2024). *Le rire de la Méduse*. NRF.

Cixous, H., & Schäfer, E. (2021). Via Telefaune, a Phone Call with Hélène Cixous. In: Braun, J. (ed.). *Hysterical Methodologies in the Arts* (pp. 369–373). Palgrave Macmillan.

Clements, C. (2019). "Logoclasm in the Name of Beauty": Bersani and Beckett's enigmatic sociability. *Lit: Literature Interpretation Theory* 30(4), 247–264. https://doi.org/10.1080/10436928.2019.1673610

Cline, D. (2016). *The Graph Music of Morton Feldman*. CUP.

Dasli, M. (2024). Critical pedagogy, deconstruction and the promises of interculturality. In: Dervin, F. (ed.). *The Routledge Handbook of Critical Interculturality in Communication and Education* (pp. 69–82). Routledge.

de la Durantaye, L. (2016). *Beckett's Art of Mismaking*. Harvard University Press.

Derrida, J. (2021). *Writing and Difference*. University of Chicago Press.

Dervin, F. (2023). *Communicating Around Interculturality in Research and Education*. Routledge.

Dervin, F. & Jacobsson, A. (2021). *Teacher Education for Critical and Reflexive Interculturality*. Palgrave.

Diame, M. (2023). *Traditional Values and Local Community in the Formal Educational System in Senegal. Relevance, Need, and Barriers to the Integration of Local Knowledge*. Routledge.

Díaz Diocaretz, M. & Segarra, M. (eds.). (2004). *Joyful Babel: Translating Hélène Cixous*. Editions Rodopi B.V.

Dostoyevsky, F. (2012). *The Idiot*. Vintage.
Eco, U. (2020). *How to Spot a Fascist*. Harvill Secker.
Feldman, M. (2006). *Morton Feldman Says. Selected Interviews and Lectures 1964–1987*. Hyphen Press.
Flores, A. (1977). *The Kafka Debate. New Perspectives for Our Time*. Gordian Press.
Frisch, M. (1962). *I'm not Stiller*. Vintage.
Hamid, M., Nguyen, H. & Baldauf, R. (eds.). *Language Planning for Medium of Instruction in Asia*. Routledge.
Holmes, P., Reynolds, J. & Ganassin, S. (eds.). (2022). *The Politics of Researching Multilingually*. Multilingual Matters.
House, J., Kádár, D. Z., Liu, F. & Han, D. (2024). The problem of translating Chinese policy related expressions: a case study of wenming ('civilised'). *Text & Talk 44*(3): 343–367. https://doi.org/10.1515/text-2021-0142
Huang, X. (2023). Writing with an accent: Travelling scholars and xenophone scholarship. *European Journal of Women's Studies 30*(4), 455–469. https://doi.org/10.1177/135050 68231207048
Ilves, P. (2004). *Language and Hegemony in Gramsci*. Pluto Press.
Kristeva, J. (2022). *Dostoyevsky, or the Flood of Language*. Columbia University Press.
Lefebvre, H. (2009). *Dialectical Materialism*. University of Minnesota Press.
Li, W. (2018). Translanguaging as a practical theory of language. *Applied Linguistics 39*(1), 9–30. https://doi.org/10.1093/applin/amx039.
Liu, J. & Zheng, Y. (2024). The emergence of epistemic agency in researching multilingually: An auto ethnography of a Chinese researcher's academic publishing practices. *International Journal of Applied Linguistics*, 1–20. https://doi.org/10.1111/ijal.12617
Maffesoli, M. (1995). *The Time of the Tribes: The Decline of Individualism in Mass Society*. Sage.
Reboul, O. (1984). *Le langage de l'éducation*. PUF.
Schmidt-Brücken, D., Schuster, S., Stolz, T., Warnke, I. H. & Wienberg, M. (eds.). (2016). *Koloniallinguistik. Sprache in kolonialen Kontexten*. De Gruyter.
Shen, H. (2023). Bilingual postgraduates' potentials for original research by translanguaging for theorizing. *Beijing International Review of Education 4*(4), 703–723. https://doi.org/10.1163/25902539-04040012
Shen, H. & Singh, M. (2022). A translanguaging approach to bilingual theorising in postgraduate researchers' education. *Journal of Multilingual and Multicultural Development,* 1–20. https://doi.org/10.1080/01434632.2022.2134876
Sweller, J. (2024). Cognitive load theory and individual differences. *Learning and Individual Differences 110,* 102423. https://doi.org/10.1016/j.lindif.2024.102423
Tipper, B. (2020). "Everyday ethnographies and the art of eavesdropping: Capturing ordinary human–animal encounters". In: Holmes, H. & H. S. M. (eds.). Mundane Methods (pp. 135-144). Manchester, England: Manchester University Press.
Warriner, D. D. & Bigelow, M. (eds.). (2019). *Critical Reflections on Research Methods: Power and Equity in Complex Multilingual Contexts*. Multilingual Matters.
Williams, R. (2008). *Dostoyevsky. Language, Faith and Fiction*. Continuum.
Yuan, M., Dervin, F. Sude & Chen, N. (2022). *Change and Exchange in Global Education: Learning with Chinese Stories of Interculturality*. Palgrave.
Žižek, S. (2013). *Absolute Recoil: Towards a New Foundation of Dialectical Materialism*. Verso.

Étagère 5
A GUIDE TO INTERCULTURAL SELF-DEFENCE

Breaking free?

Étagère 5 …

- Provides practical strategies for resisting indoctrination, inertia and language insensitivity.
- Encourages readers to engage with interculturality critically and reflexively.
- Offers a toolbox of activities for self-assessment and professional development.

[A romanticised narrative about intercultural self-defence]

A new academic year was underway at the University of Hong Kong (China).

Associate Professor Mang, an expert in intercultural communication education, was eager to challenge his new students about the complexities of interculturality in order to help them think further about the notion, which he had been researching for nearly a decade. The semester began with a provocative question from Mang during the first lecture: "What do our biases and assumptions do to the way we interpret the notion of interculturality in Chinese and English?". His students, a diverse group of eager minds from Hong Kong, mainland China and different countries, were initially silent, caught off guard by the question. But as the semester progressed, they tried to learn to expect such queries, each designed to test their minds. One particular student, Bing, found herself grappling with the topic of indoctrination. Raised in a rather strict educational system, she had been taught to accept certain narratives without question. Mang's course, however, tried to encourage her to deconstruct these narratives, to examine their underlying assumptions and to recognise the power structures that maintained them. Another student, Liam, struggled with intellectual inertia. He had a tendency to rely on familiar concepts, theories and perspectives related to interculturality, even when they were inadequate for understanding the phenomena he wished to study. Through a series of thought-provoking seminars and challenging readings in English and Chinese, Prof. Mang tried to push Liam to step out of his comfort zone, to question the mostly western theories and concepts he had long taken for granted and to explore new ways of thinking. Language indifference in English was a collective issue that the entire class had to confront for months. In their zeal to observe and compare cultures, the students often failed to appreciate the subtlety of language in their analytical work. Mang thus assigned them a multi-week project to study 'a cultural practice' through local people's narratives. This immersive experience forced them to pay attention to the nuances of language and to understand that words can carry different ideological, connotational and emotional aspects. As the semester drew to a close, the students presented their research, each narrative demonstrating sound critical and reflexive engagement with interculturality. Maria explored the narratives of her homeland (Spain) through a new and deconstructed lens. Liam questioned long-held anthropological theories and proposed a fresh perspective. The class as a whole seems to have learned to approach language with the reverence it deserved in research.

In his concluding lecture, Mang left his students with a final thought:

"At university, we must be vigilant against the dangers of indoctrination, intellectual inertia and language indifference. Our goal is not just to learn about 'cultures' but to engage with them interculturally, to unlearn about the ways we have been made to analyse 'cultures', in ways that are thoughtful, open but also ... critical".

Recitative.[1] Key takeaways from the issues of indoctrination, intellectual inertia and language indifference in intercultural education communication and research

Astra inclinant, sed non obligant.
(The stars incline us, they do not blind us.)

The three previous Étagères aimed to make us reflect on the meanings, contradictions and simplicities of three key problematic phenomena in intercultural communication education and research. In this more 'positive' Étagère, we try to explore ways of keeping our eyes open and rejecting what some of these phenomena do to us. We deepen our intercultural self-defence! Like the opening Latin saying suggests, we refute fatalism (what the stars have in hold for us), we try not to be forced by 'fate' and we learn to decide what we wish to do and say as far as interculturality is concerned.

Table 5.1. summarises the Étagères, presenting basic definitions of the three problematic phenomena, their motives, effects and lists of useful analytical concepts introduced in the Étagères.

What I personally take away from exploring these three issues concerning intercultural scholarship and education is that I am even more convinced that we need to encourage 'real' collaboration across academic fields to bring fresh perspectives and innovative approaches to intercultural communication research. Many of the discussions in Étagères 2–4 were gleaned from fields such as the arts, business, psychology, etc. Many of the issues that I have covered have never been discussed in our big field. I am also of the opinion that it is even more essential today to engage in critical reflection on our own biases and the assumptions underlying our research to ensure that our work is not perpetuating outdated, ideologically dominating, limited and/or contradictory viewpoints. Everyone talks about critical thinking and criticality in ICER now and yet these are often avoided or simplified. One missing link in this regard is language use in research. For the past four years, I have been literally obsessed by the lack of engagement with language in ICER – by that I mean in the way we teach or research interculturality, many scholars do work on e.g. language education and interculturality. Research on interculturality is conducted in many languages but it does seem that (some?) research published in English is very dominant and influential (see Peng et al., 2019 on intercultural competence). Most of us have very limited language repertoires and many of the dominating voices in the field are monolingual in English. This is a very big problem since this limits engagement with others in different language (ideological) worlds and reinforces unequal power relations in research – although we are all reciting the litanies of social justice and equity/equality in ICER. So, the need to develop a keen awareness of how language can shape and limit understanding in intercultural communication education and research is another priority. This includes working hard to reflect on what language does (not do) to us and being mindful of the nuances, connotations and contexts of words and expressions. At the same time, it is important to promote reflexive approaches to our research that consider the impact of our own economic-political, ideological and epistemic backgrounds and positionalities on educational acts, research processes and outcomes. Actively questioning and challenging prevailing paradigms, ideologies and 'speak' in intercultural communication research might help stimulate theoretical developments and empirical investigations. For Reboul (1984: 165), "Reste qu'on peut prendre conscience des idéologies, réfléchir sur leur force et sur leurs limites, leur montrer leurs lacunes pour les contraindre à dialoguer" (my translation: "The fact remains that we can become aware of ideologies, reflect on their strength and their limits, show them their shortcomings in order to force them to dialogue"). In order to counter indoctrination, inertia and indifference, we *must* commit to continuous learning and professional development, beyond our own institutional, national, linguistic, ideological, epistemic, methodological, 'tribes', to stay abreast of research, theories and practices in the field of ICER.

TABLE 5.1 Summary of main ideas from previous Étagères.

Concepts	Basic definition	Motives	Effects	Useful analytical concepts
Indoctrination	(a) Lack of encouragement for criticality towards interculturality in research and education. (b) (Hidden) dismissal of alternative viewpoints in the construction and dissemination of knowledge deemed to be legitimate.	Authority, censorship, early exposure, emotional manipulation, fear, isolation, peer pressure, repetition, selective information.	- Adhere strictly to specific beliefs - Echo language - Fear consequences of deviating - Hold rigid beliefs - Lack self-reflection - Lack tolerance - Resist to new information - Overtly or defensively react emotionally to disagreement.	- *Identifying indoctrinating practices*: Cognitive and emotional comfort, Dogma, Doublethink, Epistemic injustice, Ideological bias, Ideological echo chambers, Logical fallacies, Mental manipulation, Mind seepage, Nudges, Propaganda. - *Accompanying indoctrination critically and reflexively*: Counter-education, Critical thinking, Enkrateia, Paideia, Rational autonomy.
Intellectual inertia	(a) Tendency to maintain the status quo or old patterns of thinking when faced with new information or changes. (b) Lack of motivation to move forward in one's unrethinking in the way interculturality is taught and researched.	Belief bias, capitalism and neoliberalism in higher education, commitment escalation bias, confirmation bias, conservatism bias, self-attribution bias, status-quo bias, structural inertia.	- Complacency - Entrenchment in tradition - Fear of uncertainty - Lack of exposure to diverse perspectives - Un-reflexivity.	- Barnum effect - Echo chambers - Panglossian reasoning - Prospect theory - Resistance to epistemic friction - Sunk-cost fallacy - System justification theory.
Language indifference and nonchalance	(a) Lack of and/or a lazy interest and concern for language in research and education. (b) Sleepwalking through language.	Abstract, assumptions about interlocutors' knowledge, belief in the power and universality of language, jargon, specialised terminology, specific rhetorical style, use of glocalised references, slogans and ideologemes.	- Comprehension difficulties - Disregard for aspects of ethics - 'Floating past each other' phenomenon - Hegemony - Inaccurate interpretations - Loss of nuances - (Unintentional) Indoctrination.	- *Cognitive and creative aspects*: cognitive load theory, logoclasm - *Economic entry points*: Dialectical materialism, economic pragmatism - *Ideology*: linguistic and cultural hegemony, colonial linguistics, echoing of language - *Planning and policy*: language planning and policy.

Finally, although our influence is in fact limited here, we should try to put pressure on research groups, institutions and funding bodies to support research that *really* tries to push the boundaries of knowledge and explores new territories in relation to interculturality – beyond slogans and tokenisation.

[Pause 1: Resistance to indoctrination?]
For years, I have been collecting pictures of slogans and words printed on clothes in different parts of the world. This interest started when I was 18 when I was working as a language teacher at an international summer camp. I noticed that students were wearing T-shirts with all kinds of messages in different languages. Today, this is a very common phenomenon around the world. These are some of the fascinating messages I have seen on T-shirts and accessories (e.g. caps, see Figure 5.1.) in China:

> The decline of Western civilization is coming; No to the ancient world; Don't deny the fact; Revolution; Utopia; Don't happy be worry; School kills; Contemporary shit; Keep it simple Stupid; Relativism; Do it for your self; I wish common sense; don't believe everything you think; feminist; free; Don't worry about the government.

These are often mere slogans and I am never sure if the people who wear these pieces of clothing understand what they mean. However, I always try to imagine why someone bought a particular piece with a specific message, what it could tell us (or not) about them, how it might influence others (passers-by, friends), and how serious they might be about spreading this message to the world. Finally, I am also interested in the potential reasons why a fashion brand and/or house might want to print these messages on their clothes. *How about you?*

FIGURE 5.1 'Don't worry about the government'.

Ritardando. Reflecting and self-assessing

The importance of constant reflexivity in research and education about interculturality has been discussed in ICER for decades (e.g. Byrd-Clark & Dervin, 2014). Reflexivity can help us examine our own biases and assumptions, address our positionality, build trust with others and enhance our personal growth (amongst others, see Olmos-Vega et al., 2022). Here are 10 self-assessment items for you to reflect on the aforementioned key takeaways from the previous Étagères. These basic self-assessment items are designed to help you start to identify and address issues of indoctrination, intellectual inertia and language indifference that may be encountered in intercultural education communication and research. Read through these elements as often as you can to remind yourself of the importance to intensify your intercultural self-defence!

1. I can identify and critically think about the knowledge I receive from publications, lectures and seminars and discussions with others, about aspects of interculturality in research and education to avoid being indoctrinated *a minima*.
2. I strive to maintain an open mind and be receptive to new and unfamiliar perspectives, ideas and ways of speaking/writing about interculturality, especially from other parts of the world than the west (e.g., US and UK) and in different languages.
3. I understand and recognize the risks of intellectual inertia in my work and make every effort to actively seek intellectual challenges and knowledge.
4. I regularly review my learning-teaching-research practices to ensure that I am not falling into a mindset of epistemic, ideological and methodological complacency.
5. I endeavour to increase my interests in language in the production and dissemination of knowledge to better understand the polysemy and complexities of scholarship on interculturality (in English as an international language of research and education and other languages if possible).
6. I consider mindfully the choice and impact of language when communicating around the notion of interculturality in English and other languages.
7. I reflect on my use of language to ensure it does not inadvertently convey indifference, nonchalance or even bias.
9. I recognize the importance of self-assessment and often engage in it to keep an eye on my engagement with interculturality in research and education.
10. I reflect on my teaching and learning methods to ensure that they do not accidentally cause indoctrination or indifference in others. I thus discuss these issues with my partners (colleagues, students, decision-makers, etc.) and suggest potential changes in the way we talk about interculturality.

[Pause 2: Maintaining personal autonomy and the ability to think *independently* **– inspiration from the myth of Orpheus]**

Myths can inspire us to think further and "offer crucial lessons about the human experience" (Lefkowitz, 2003). When discussing indoctrination, inertia and language indifference in intercultural scholarship, we could draw on one myth that touches on themes related to these: the Greek myth of Orpheus and Eurydice (see Jean Cocteau's beautiful film based on this story called *Orphée* from 1949). The story illustrates the power of doubt and the consequences of not adhering to a set of instructions or beliefs that have been imparted, which is a key element in academic and educational discussions of interculturality. In the story, Orpheus has superhuman musical skills. His singing is so powerful and enchanting that more-than-humans moved about him dancing. After the death of his wife Eurydice from the bite of a snake, he decides to venture into the Underworld (the sunless place anyone who dies goes to in Greek mythology) to bring her back to the land of the living (see Figure 5.2. by Cocteau (1889–1963)). His music moves Hades and Persephone (respectively: The God of the dead and the Goddess of spring) so much that they agree to let Eurydice return to the world of the living on one condition: *Orpheus must not look back at her until they have left the Underworld*. However, due to Orpheus's doubt, lack of trust and joy, he looks back at Eurydice just as they are about to exit the Underworld, causing her to remain in the realm of the dead forever (see Virgil, 2009).

This mythological act can be seen as a failure of trust in the instructions given to Orpheus by the gods of the Underworld, which could be analogous to the critical thinking and questioning of (unfair) indoctrinated beliefs. The story encourages us to reflect on how to maintain criticality in the face of authority and rules

FIGURE 5.2 *Orpheus's Mirror* by Cocteau (1969) showing the musician entering the Underworld.

and how to preserve personal independence and judgement under pressure and expectations (Radcliffe et al., 2011). Furthermore, the myth can be used to explore the relationship between the individual and the collective and how to maintain personal independence in a world torn apart between different ideologies, with a few selected ones that dominate what we say and do. It can also serve as a reminder that, even under strong pressures, we should learn to question and explore rather than accept things blindly. The importance of scepticism is also put forth in the myth while reminding us of the need to pay some consequences for disagreeing and acting 'otherwise' in certain cases. Finally, the myth provides a potential platform for discussing how to maintain personal autonomy and the ability to think independently amidst e.g. various socio-economic-political influences.

Andante. Textual analyses: 'Feeling' the presence and potential impact of indoctrination and language indifference in the way interculturality is constructed

Like any academic text about interculturality, the following three (invented) texts (two short academic texts and a dialogue between a professor and a student) have elements of indoctrination and language indifference (and thus intellectual inertia). In writing these texts, I was inspired by my long-term experience in examining, reviewing, supervising, critiquing and writing in different parts of the world and in different languages.

Can you decide for yourself why it seems to be so? What aspects of the texts could make them indoctrinating and nonchalant linguistically? Although they are 'imaginary' texts created for this Resource Book, they contain hints of specific glocalised takes on interculturality (bits and pieces of ideologies from different countries). Can you 'feel' them? Can you have a guess at which economic-political contexts they might derive from?

Use some of the 'useful analytical concepts' from Table 5.1. to examine and discuss the content of the three texts. You may also compare the three texts.

1. In our increasingly interconnected world, interculturality is the cement that binds us together. It's about understanding that each culture has its own unique set of values, customs and practices that deserve respect, recognition and being tolerated. The beauty of interculturality lies in its ability to bring people from different backgrounds together, fostering a harmonious global community where diversity is not just put up with but celebrated. Cultures around the world have contributed immensely to human experience. From the ancient wisdom of the East to the innovative spirit of the West, each culture has a story to tell. It's important that we appreciate these differences and integrate them into our daily lives. After all, it's through understanding and embracing diversities that we can truly grow as individuals and as members of a given community. Language, on the other hand, is just a tool for communication.

While it's useful for expressing ideas and sharing information, it's not the be-all and end-all of interculturality, especially in research and education. What truly matters is the willingness to engage with other cultures, to learn from them and to be open to new experiences. Language can help facilitate this process, but it's not a prerequisite for intercultural encounters.

[*A few notes for you to compare: This text presents a particular viewpoint on interculturality as if it were an absolute 'truth'. It seems to assume that everyone should celebrate 'diversity/-ies' and that this is the only way to achieve 'harmony' (many polysemic terms in English and other languages!). This perspective doesn't account for the complexities and challenges that can arise from potential differences, nor does it consider that some individuals might have different beliefs about the value of certain practices. What is more the text brusquely dismisses the importance of language in interculturality, suggesting that it's merely a tool and not a crucial aspect of e.g. scholarship and/or education. This overlooks the fact that language is deeply intertwined with the notion, conveying not just information but also nuances, emotions and ideological 'flavours' that interlocutors (students, readers) might miss (see Dervin, 2022). By presenting interculturality in such a one-sided and nonchalant manner about language, the text risks oversimplifying complex issues and potentially perpetuating a superficial understanding of interculturality.*]

2. Interculturality is the cornerstone of modern societies, a fundamental notion that research must embrace without question. It represents the unequivocal acceptance of all cultural practices as equal, regardless of their origins or implications. In our scholarly pursuits, we must view interculturality not as a subject of debate but as an obvious truth that guides our research and informs our understanding of the world. To be a proponent of interculturality is to be on the right side of democratic culture, advocating for a global ethos where all cultures are inherently valid and worthy of everyone's utmost respect. The integration of diverse cultural elements is not just beneficial, it is imperative for the advancement of knowledge. Our research must reflect this by prioritizing the voices and values of all cultures without bias, discrimination or critical analysis that might question the inviolability of cultural norms.

[*A few notes for you to compare: This second text assumes that the concept of interculturality is universally applicable and beneficial, without acknowledging that different scholars and educators may have conflicting opinions about this, depending on the economic-political-ideological context(s) they work in. In my opinion, this mandate could stifle academic freedom and diversity of thought. The text tends to present interculturality as a monolithic concept that is inherently positive, without considering the complexities and potential conflicts that can arise from it in daily life, education and research. You will also notice that the text seems to discourage critical analysis of interculturality, suggesting that everything should be accepted without question. This approach can be problematic as it may lead to e.g. the dismissal of valid concerns about the notion in research and education. Furthermore, by stating that interculturality will lead to 'harmonious global unity', the text sets aside the need for e.g. negotiation and compromise. This thus appears to be an oversimplification of the challenges involved in navigating, (re-)negotiating and experiencing the instabilities and complexities of interculturality. In general, I would say that the text seems to present interculturality as a binary choice – either one is for it or one is against it. This schism does not seem to allow for a nuanced understanding of this scientific notion.*]

In the following dialogue between a PhD researcher and their supervisor, Markku is initially open to the idea of interculturality but has not fully adopted any clear 'indoctrinated' perspective. Through the conversation with Professor Lock, who represents a somewhat static viewpoint about the notion, Markku gradually adopts the idea that 'all cultural practices' should be accepted without question.

3. *Lock*: Hyvää iltapäivää, Markku. I've been told that you've been reading a lot about interculturality in research lately. What are your thoughts so far?

   Markku: Good afternoon. Yes, it's intriguing. I've come to believe that interculturality is the key to unlocking a new era of understanding and cooperation among diverse cultures.

   Lock: That's a strong statement but I agree. It's crucial that we embrace all cultures without discrimination. Every culture has a unique set of values that we must respect and learn from.

   Markku: Tottakai! I've realized that any critical examination of cultural practices is just cultural insensitivity. We should celebrate the diversity that each culture brings to the table.

   Lock: Well said, Markku. It's all about acceptance and unity in our diversity. Our research should reflect that ideal. Remember, the goal is to create a harmonious global community where the voice of every culture is heard and valued equally.

   Markku: I completely agree. I've decided that my next paper will focus on how we could further promote interculturality in academia. I believe that, by doing so, we can overcome all barriers to understanding.

   Lock: That sounds like an excellent idea. I'm glad to see your enthusiasm. Just make sure your research emphasizes the importance of unquestioning acceptance of all cultural norms and practices.

   Markku: Unquestioning acceptance? I mean, I do think we should be open-minded but shouldn't we also maintain some level of criticality?

Lock: Critical thinking is important, of course, but when it comes to interculturality, we must prioritize acceptance. Our role as researchers is to break down barriers, not create new ones by questioning the cultures we're trying to understand and describe to others.

[A few notes for you to compare: I admit that this (exaggerated) portrayal of indoctrination is concerning because it suggests that any form of critical analysis or questioning of 'cultural norms' is inappropriate or insensitive. What the dialogue seems to fail to recognize is that research should involve reliable examination and critique to ensure a comprehensive and nuanced understanding of interculturality. By discouraging critical analysis, indoctrination can lead to a potentially unbalanced and harmful approach to intercultural education and research. In the dialogue, Lock promotes a particular viewpoint on interculturality – that all 'cultures' should be accepted without question and that critical examination of 'cultural practices' is a form of tactlessness. Markku initially has a more nuanced understanding compared to his professor, acknowledging the importance of criticality. However, under the influence of Lock, Markku seems to begin to adopt his supervisor's perspective, which might discourage critical analysis. As far as intellectual inertia is concerned, Lock seems to exhibit it by rejecting the value of critical thinking in the context of intercultural research. He insists that the role of researchers is to accept and promote 'cultural practices' without questioning, which is an established belief that he does not seem willing to reconsider. On the other hand, Markku exhibits some signs of intellectual inertia as well, as he begins to align with Lock's perspective without critically evaluating the implications of abandoning critical analysis in research. The (imagined) dialogue seems to imply then that, as we have seen in the previous three Étagères, intellectual inertia can lead to a stagnation of thought, where new ideas or alternative viewpoints are not considered and research is conducted within a narrow and predefined framework.]

[Pause 3: Think 'otherwise']
The clock in Figure 5.3. is found inside a cathedral in Florence (Italy), which is known as the Santa Maria del Fiore or the Duomo. The diameter of the clock face is almost two metres and it is situated approximately 15 metres off the ground above the main door of the cathedral. This is a remarkable (and somewhat confusing) piece of timekeeping history and the only one of its kind still in working order. *What do you see? How does it work? What is the time according to it?* The design is unique and reflects the so-called 'Italian time' (ora italica) or 'Julian time' system, which was based on the calendar established by Julius Caesar in 46 C. E. This system began at sunset and ended at sunset, with the clock's primary purpose being liturgical, marking the hour for vespers, the sunset prayer service in Roman Catholic and other churches. The clock's face is decorated with a golden star at its

124 Intercultural Self-Defence

FIGURE 5.3 The Uccello's clock at the Duomo.

centre and the heads of what are believed to be the four famous religious figures – John, Luke, Mark, Matthew – at each corner of the square frame. The clock was frescoed by the famous Early Renaissance artist Paolo Di Dono (1397–1475). It only has one hand, which runs anti-clockwise, starting from the Roman numeral XXIIII (23) at the bottom, indicating the 24 hours of the day. In the 16th century, the city of Florence witnessed pressure to shift from the ora italica to the 'French' system of measuring time (today's 'AM' and 'PM'). Yet the officials resisted and if anyone was caught using this other time, they would have been severely punished. Di Dono's work on the clock face is considered a masterpiece, with the use of light and shadow creating the illusion of light streaming in from a window that doesn't actually exist. The Italian phrase about wearing a hat (berretto/cappello), del sulle ventitré ('23 o'clock'), contains a hint at this very clock. Sulle ventitré refers to the hat being worn at a steep angle to protect one's eyes against the sun in the hour before sunset (King, 2013).

[*How many time measuring systems can you easily read?*]

Legato. Extra learning box: A detour via propaganda

Let me mention a few interdisciplinary books that you could read, should you wish to go further in exploring the topics of this Resource Book. These titles also aim to support readers in unrethinking in ICER. Let us start with a few classics about the important topic of propaganda, which can give up further food for thought and analytical tools to reflect on what we do and say in intercultural research and education.

The philosopher and 'Christian anarchist' Jacques Ellul is the author of *Propaganda: The Formation of Men's Attitudes* (Ellul, 1973). Ellul was a thinker with fascinating insights into the topic of propaganda, whose views spanned the psychological, sociological, ethical and political dimensions of propaganda. He linked propaganda to the pursuit of power and proposed various categories (Ellul, 1973), including *political propaganda and sociological propaganda* (political propaganda aims to maintain or change political power, while sociological propaganda focuses on social order and norms); *agitational propaganda and integrative propaganda* (agitational propaganda seeks to stir up emotions and actions, while integrative propaganda aims to assimilate individuals into social groups or communities); *vertical propaganda and horizontal propaganda* (vertical propaganda is top down, often conducted by governments or authoritative bodies; horizontal propaganda occurs between individuals or among groups); *irrational propaganda and rational propaganda* (irrational propaganda appeals to emotions and the subconscious, while rational propaganda is based on logic and rational argumentation). [*Can you think of examples of agitational propaganda vs. integrative propaganda in societal, educational and scientific discourses of interculturality?*]

Ellul (1973: 98) also introduced the concept of total propaganda, which is linked to his argument that technique dominates modern society. He believed that propaganda in modern society is so pervasive and all-encompassing that it becomes an environment from which individuals can hardly escape. [*What do you make of this argument in the 2020s, 50 years after Ellul published his book?*]

Although Jacques Ellul's theoretical definitions and classifications have had relatively little influence on our research field, his categorisation of propaganda represents a potentially significant contribution to the study of propaganda and indoctrination in ICER.

Another classic, which relates to propaganda 'indirectly', is *The Origins of Totalitarianism* by Hannah Arendt (1973), in which the philosopher provides a comprehensive analysis of the rise of totalitarian regimes in the 20th century, particularly focusing on Nazi Germany and the Soviet Union. Arendt's analysis of totalitarianism is closely related to propaganda and indoctrination, as these tools are central to the functioning of such regimes.

I first note that Hannah Arendt (1973) describes totalitarianism as a form of government that seeks to dominate and control all aspects of human life, including the private sphere. Propaganda, in this context, is not merely a tool for persuasion but a means of creating a new reality, where the distinctions between 'truth' and 'falsehood' somehow disappear. The purpose of totalitarian propaganda is to establish absolute control over the masses by manipulating their perceptions and beliefs. Indoctrination, on the other hand, is the process of instilling the ideology of the regime into the individuals, ensuring their loyalty and active participation in the regime's goals (Arendt, 1973). The philosopher argues that totalitarian regimes use propaganda and indoctrination to transform individuals into atomised and isolated beings who are easily manipulated and controlled (Arendt, 1973). [*How much do governments and supra-national bodies indoctrinate us in the ways we research and educate for interculturality? Do they leave us space to think against these ideologies? For example, in discussions of democratic culture (Hoff, 2020) in education, is critiquing the very idea of democracy or human rights acceptable? By whom, where and how?*]

Another interesting aspect of Arendt's analysis is the concept of the totalitarian atomisation of society (Arendt, 1968: 21), where individuals are separated from one another and from the broader social and political context. This atomisation makes it easier for a given regime to use propaganda and indoctrination to create a new type of social being, one who is incapable of independent thought or action.

Arendt also discusses the role of terror in totalitarian regimes, which is used to maintain control and suppress dissent (Arendt, 1973). Propaganda and indoctrination are essential in creating an atmosphere of fear, where individuals are led to believe that any deviation would result in severe consequences. [*Do you find the issues of terror and/or fear to be relevant to discuss the three foes of ICER? Or is it going too far? Have you yourself experienced fear in expressing an idea or critiquing a big 'idea' that seems unbeatable?*]

Although first published in 1990, I also consider *Munitions of the Mind* by Philip M. Taylor as a classic. In the book, Taylor (2005) presents a very comprehensive history of propaganda from ancient times to the present day, tracing the evolution of propaganda as an instrument of persuasion and its role in e.g. warfare and politics. Taylor (2005) also discusses how propaganda has been used throughout history, from stone monuments and coins to modern media like radio, film, television and the internet. The book also delves into the use of propaganda in ancient civilisations, showing how it was used to demonstrate divine support and consolidate power. Taylor reviews its use in e.g. conflicts of the Middle Ages, both World Wars of the 20th century and during the post-Cold War era (e.g. during the 1991 Gulf War). This book also considers the important relationship between propaganda and society, noting that propaganda is most effective when it conforms to existing needs and attitudes, even if those needs are artificially created (Taylor, 2005). Interestingly for us, the author (Taylor, 2005) maintains that propaganda is often misunderstood and carries negative connotations, but it is essentially a neutral process of persuasion. It's the intention behind the propaganda that demands scrutiny, not propaganda as such. In other words, we should become aware of the intentions behind propaganda and *not just the messages themselves*.

[Pause 5: A few words about the IPA]

The Institute for Propaganda Analysis (IPA) was established in 1937 in the USA to 'educate' the American public about the pervasive nature of political propaganda. It was composed of social scientists and journalists who aimed to analyse and expose the tactics used by propagandists. The IPA sought to create propaganda literacy and produced educational materials such as one-page fliers, bulletins examining recent propaganda instances and reports (Augé, 2007). The motto of their bulletin was "A bulletin to help the intelligent citizen detect and analyse propaganda" (see e.g. a picture of the bulletin at: https://digital-collections.csun.edu/digital/collection/InOurOwnBackyard/id/77). The IPA developed techniques for analysing information to help audiences think 'rationally' and 'critically', particularly in the context of media literacy and education.

The Institute also identified and popularised seven common propaganda techniques, such as glittering generalities, bandwagon and plain folks, which have been widely recognised and taught in communication studies for decades (see Étagère 2). They also emphasised the importance of critical thinking and the scientific mindset of fact-finding and logical reasoning when confronted with information. The IPA's methods were eventually adopted by schools, and by the late 1930s, approximately one million school children were using their techniques to analyse propaganda. However, the IPA faced challenges and was eventually targeted by the House Committee on Un-American Activities (HUAC), which perceived the organisation as a threat due to its critical stance on existing communication structures and practices (Augé, 2007). It closed down in 1942.

Let us go back to the literature on propaganda and focus on more recent books.

We start with Stanley's (2016) book *How Propaganda Works* which provides a deep analysis of the mechanisms of propaganda within 'liberal democratic' (western) societies. Stanley (2016) defines propaganda as the manipulation of rational will to close off debate, often through deception, emotional appeal, misdirection, intimidation and stereotypes. He argues that propaganda is particularly potent in the 'echo chambers' that were mentioned in previous sections, where the pre-existing beliefs of people are reinforced, making them more susceptible to such manipulation (Stanley, 2016: 186; see Étagère 4). In the book, Stanley differentiates between two types of propaganda: *supporting propaganda*, which promotes a certain view or action and *undermining propaganda*, which uses values to weaken those very values (Stanley, 2016: 57). The book also discusses how propaganda can create ideologies that might generate false beliefs resistant to e.g. 'evidence'. Once such ideologies are established, they can be reactivated with simple cues to bring those beliefs to the surface. Stanley (2016: 98) also explores the origins of such ideologies, suggesting they stem from self-interest and the making of identity reinforcing in-group/out-group affiliations. Like this Resource Book, using historical examples mostly from the USA, *How Propaganda Works* also addresses the role of language as a tool of control, the relationship between ideology and propaganda and the ways in which propaganda can be used to maintain the power of elites (Stanley, 2016). [*Please reflect on this last word* elites: *how does it apply to our discussions on intercultural research and education?*]

The recent literature contains many other books on indoctrination and propaganda which can be interesting to explore. In what follows, I have selected four books (three in English and one in French) published between 2021 and 2023:

- *Propaganda & Persuasion* (2021, 7th Edition) by Jowett and O'Donnelle provides four case studies and examples of the use of propaganda throughout

history. The latest edition adds important discussions on social media as a disseminator of propaganda.
- *The Indoctrinated Brain: How to Successfully Fend Off the Global Attack on Your Mental Freedom* (2023) by Nehls (a medical doctor) could be considered as a provocative and controversial book that introduces discussions of the neurobiological mechanism that leads to many mental and health problems (e.g. brain-damage, burnout) but also, more importantly, deprives us of our ability to think for ourselves.
- *Fighting Fake News: Teaching Students to Identify and Interrogate Information Pollution* was written by Wilhem et al. (2023). As the title indicates, it is aimed at educators who wish to instil (further) criticality in their students while e.g. reading digital content, by focusing on the use of rhetorical devices or mechanisms that reduce our access to diverse information.
- Last, *La fabrique des discours propagandistes contemporains: Comment et pourquoi ça marche?* (in English: Manufacturing Contemporary Discourses of Propaganda: How and why they work?) by Grinshpun (2023), tries to explain why propaganda is more sophisticated in democratic societies than in totalitarianism, how the concept differs from ideology and what discursive, linguistic and psycho-socio elements contribute to the dissemination of propaganda.

To conclude this section, here is a list of propaganda strategies gleaned and inspired from these books (in alphabetical order). I have often come across such strategies in ICER and used them myself:

- **Appeal to nature**: Claims that something is normal, better and (maybe) safer because it is 'natural' (the use of this word should represent an alarm call, especially in intercultural studies).
- **Black-and-white fallacy**: Presents complex issues as having only two possible solutions (e.g. essentialism/anti-essentialism).
- **Causal oversimplification**: Reduces complex issues to simple, often inaccurate, causes and solutions (e.g. issues of racism are often discussed in terms of individual responsibility while ignoring the influence of the system, see Tourse et al., 2018).
- **Proof by example**: Uses a single or a few examples to prove a point, ignoring other evidence.

In relation to others (allies/enemies/audience):

- **Appeal to authority**: Cites an authority figure to support a claim (e.g. mechanical and often tokenistic use of references from 'gurus').
- **Appeal to emotion**: Plays on the audience's emotions rather than problematising arguments and counter-arguments.

- **Appeal to tradition**: Argues that something should be done because "we've always done it that way" (see the argument of 'throwing the baby with the bathwater' in discussions of the use or rejection of the concept of culture, Ogay & Edelmann, 2016).
- **Circumstantial *ad hominem***: Suggests that because of the circumstances or situation of the person making the argument, it should be discredited (a white scholar's voice, a member of a specific political party in one part of the world, etc.).
- **Testimonial by association**: Uses a person's association with a respected group to lend credibility.
- **Transfer**: Associates a product or idea with a respected person, place or institution (Harvard University, British Council, Council of Europe, OECD …).

Language strategies:

- **Euphemism**: Uses mild or indirect language to make an unpleasant idea more acceptable.
- **Glittering generalities**: Use positive and emotionally charged language to describe the benefits of interculturality.
- **Repetition**: Repeats a message frequently to make it memorable and unquestionable.
- **Vice words**: Uses words with negative connotations to make the opposition less appealing.
- **Virtue words**: Uses words with positive connotations to make the message more appealing.
- **We-they language**: Uses language to create an 'us versus them' mentality.

Sforzando. Critical analysis and reflexivity in intercultural research design

[A problem-solving activity]

In this section, we strengthen further our engagement with the issues of indoctrination, intellectual inertia and language indifference, especially in intercultural research, by considering first the following problem-solving activity.

In a fictional research scenario, a group of interculturalists from one country is conducting a study on the effects of social media on university students' mental health and well-being in different parts of the world. The research team is based in a country with a dominant ideological narrative that seems to argue that social media is inherently harmful. The team's funding comes from organisations with an interest in promoting this narrative. The lead researcher, a famous professor locally, is also known for their public stance against social media. Meanwhile, the research involves participants from diverse linguistic backgrounds and the data is being translated into English for publication in a top international journal.

In what follows, I am sharing a description of a long-term problem-solving intervention to support this team in dealing with the potentialities of indoctrination, intellectual inertia and language indifference in their intercultural work (see Reboul, 1984; Chomsky, 2004; Snook, 2024). Feel free to critique and/or add to the proposed objectives and steps below.

Objective: To ensure the research is not unduly influenced by pre-existing ideological narratives, funding biases or language differences and to promote intellectual consistency and ethical research practices.

Steps:

a. **Bias identification**: I would begin with a workshop where researchers identify potential biases, including the influence of the funding source, the lead researcher's public stance locally and the dominating ideological narrative surrounding social media.
b. **Diverse perspectives**: I would then invite scholars and experts with varying views on the impact of social media to provide guest lectures and seminars, ensuring a broader perspective is considered.
c. **Peer review**: The research team's methodology and initial findings would be reviewed by an international, multilingual and interdisciplinary group of peers to check for potential indoctrination or inertia.
d. **Language sensitivity**: This would be followed by a session with language experts (e.g. discourse analysts) to discuss the challenges and best practices of translating qualitative data, focusing on problematising the original meaning during translation by language non-specialists.
e. **Reflexivity**: I would then encourage researchers to write reflexive diaries in their first language and in English, about their personal biases, how these might influence their work and how they could be managed.
f. **Ethical deliberation**: I would organise a workshop on research ethics, focusing on the potential consequences of intellectual inertia and language indifference on intercultural research.
g. **Transparent communication**: Making sure that all research findings are communicated as transparently as possible is important, including limitations and potential biases, both in the original language and in translation, would be an important step.
h. **Public engagement**: Learning to engage with the public locally and abroad to understand their views on social media and mental health and well-being could provide a reality check against potential indoctrination.
i. **Final review**: Before submitting the paper, the final manuscript could be reviewed by a professional translator and an interculturalist from another research group in the same country or elsewhere to ensure that the translation works well.

[A research reflexivity workshop]

Objective: To foster open-mindedness, critical analysis and linguistic awareness among researchers.
Duration: Half-day to full-day workshop.
Participants: Researchers, Master's students and PhD researchers specialising in ICER.
Materials needed: Flip charts or whiteboards. Markers. Handouts on the topics of indoctrination, intellectual inertia, and language indifference. Case studies or research papers with examples of the issues to be discussed. Group work materials (e.g. sticky notes, pens, paper for notes).

Steps:

1. *Introduction and icebreaker*: Begin with a brief introduction to the concepts of indoctrination, intellectual inertia and language indifference (see Étagères 2 to 4 as well as Table 5.1.). Engage participants in an icebreaking activity to set a collaborative tone.
2. *Lecture and discussion*: Provide a short lecture on the three issues, their implications in research, and examples.
    Facilitate a discussion where participants can share their experiences or observations.
3. *Case study analysis*: Distribute case studies or research papers that contain instances of indoctrination, intellectual inertia and/or language indifference for interculturality (see activities in this Étagère). Have participants work in small groups to identify and discuss these instances.
4. *Critical thinking exercises*: Design exercises that challenge participants to think critically about their own beliefs and assumptions. Use e.g. Socratic and/or Confucian questioning techniques to encourage deeper reflection. Socrates' and Confucius's arts of conversation urge e.g. both teachers and students to be responsible for co-creating dialogue and co-learning (see, e.g. Montazeri, 2022).
5. *Role-playing scenarios*: Create scenarios where workshop participants act as a researcher, reviewer or reader to identify and address potential issues in their research. Encourage participants to challenge each other's viewpoints.
6. *Language sensitivity training*: Conduct activities that highlight the importance of language in research, such as translating a research abstract into different languages and discussing the nuances. Discuss the impact of language on research interpretation and audience.
7. *Brainstorming solutions*: Have groups brainstorm and present solutions to the issues identified in the case studies. Discuss how these solutions can be implemented in their own research practices.

8. *Action planning*: Encourage participants to create an action plan for how they will address these issues in their future research. Include steps for self-assessment and peer review to ensure ongoing vigilance.
9. *Reflection and feedback*: Provide time for individual reflection on what they have learned and how they can apply it.
10. *Closing*: Summarise the key takeaways from the workshop. Emphasise the importance of continuous learning and self-improvement in research on interculturality.
11. *Follow-up*: Schedule regular check-ins or follow-up workshops to reinforce the learning. Create a community of practice where researchers can share their experiences and support each other in addressing our adversaries.

Allegro. **The intercultural sceptic's toolbox: A potpourri of activities to reinforce one's intercultural self-defence**

In this section, I am sharing a list of 16 short activities which I believe can push us to work even harder at intercultural self-defence. The activities deal with biases, beliefs, ideologies, paradigms, counter-arguments, perspectives and theoretical frameworks in relation to interculturality. Different kinds of activities are suggested: *journal, map, puzzle, inventory, audit, dialogue, reflexive writing, role-taking, interview, flip* and *itch*. These may be used for independent self-reflexive purposes and/or with colleagues, students and beyond the contexts of academia and education.

Activity 1: *Implicit bias test*

1. Start by taking an online Implicit Association Test (IAT) which aims to measure attitudes and beliefs that you may be reluctant or unable to report in order to uncover any of your hidden biases. For instance, at Harvard Project Implicit, one can take such a test about *Hispanic, religion, sexuality* or *Asian-Foreign* (https://implicit.harvard.edu/implicit/selectatest.html).
2. Reflect on the results and consider how these biases might influence your views on interculturality and related topics.
3. Discuss with friends, colleagues and/or students how spotting and admitting to implicit biases could influence research and education on the notion of interculturality.

Activity 2: *Belief journaling*

1. Over the course of several months, maintain a journal where you record any instances where you notice your beliefs influencing your interpretations of what you have read or discussed with colleagues and/or students.

2. Review your journal entries regularly and identify patterns or themes in your beliefs.
3. Reflect on how these beliefs may have been shaped by e.g. your economic-political positions and views, family, education and/or past experiences, encounters.

Activity 3: *Ideological map*

1. Draw a brainstorming diagram of what you consider to be your main ideological beliefs about interculturality before e.g. reading a book or attending a lecture. You may use words, ideas, images, thoughts in your diagram.
2. As you read an article or listen to a lecture, update the map to reflect any shifts or changes in your beliefs.
3. At the end of the book or the lecture, create a new diagram. Compare the two maps to visualise this intellectual journey.

Activity 4: *Paradigm puzzle*

1. Identify a dominant paradigm in ICER, which you have followed in your research and/or teaching (e.g. non-essentialism, culturalism).
2. Research an alternative paradigm that challenges this dominant one.
3. Write a comparative analysis of the two paradigms, detailing their strengths and weaknesses, and potential improvement (and even: combination).

Activity 5: *Inertia inventory*

1. List the theories, methods or beliefs that dominate your subfield(s) of ICER.
2. For each, note why they might be resistant to change and break down the reasons it is accepted as dogma. If possible, reflect on where and who follows this dogma.
3. Explore potential alternatives or counter-arguments to challenge its dogmatic status.

Activity 6: *Language sensitivity analysis*

1. Select a passage from an article or a book related to interculturality that you have used many times in your own research or teaching.
2. Analyse how the language used in the passage might have influenced your perception of the topic at hand (use of specific words/formulations, ideologisms, localisms, translanguaging strategies …).
3. Rewrite the passage with what you consider to be a more sensitive and inclusive language style.

Activity 7: *Language audit*

1. For one day, keep a record of all the language you use, including spoken, written and digital communication.
2. Identify any instances where your language may have been indifferent or insensitive to the way you speak about interculturality in research and education.
3. Reflect on how you could adjust your language to be more inclusive and sensitive to language use in dealing with interculturality academically.

Activity 8: *Counter-argument writing*

1. Pick a central argument from a book, an article or a lecture on interculturality that you find most captivating.
2. Write down an argument that could oppose this viewpoint.
3. Reflect on the process. Did it change your perspective in any way?

Activity 9: *Discomfort dialogue*

1. Interview a colleague or a student whom you know has a different ideological background, about their views on interculturality as a scientific and educational notion.
2. Record any instances where you feel your own indoctrination is influencing the conversation with them.
3. Reflect on how understanding someone else's perspective can challenge your own beliefs.

Activity 10: *Perspective-taking role-play*

1. With a group of colleagues and/or students, select a controversial topic related to indoctrination, language and interculturality (e.g. *anti-essentialism is propaganda*).
2. Assign each person a role that may not align with their ideological beliefs.
3. Role-play a discussion, and afterward, discuss the challenges and insights gained from defending an opposing viewpoint.

Activity 11: *Iconoclast interview*

1. If you can, interview someone known for challenging established norms in the broad field of ICER.
2. Discuss their motivations, the reactions they've encountered and the impact of their work.
3. Reflect on how their approach differs from your own and what you can learn from it – but also what they might learn from you!

Activity 12: *Uncomfortable learning*

1. Seek out a workshop, lecture or seminar that might challenge your current beliefs on intercultural issues in research and education (and beyond!).
2. Engage with the material, even if it makes you somewhat uncomfortable.
3. Write about your experience and what you learned from stepping outside of your comfort zone.

Activity 13: *Interdisciplinary insight*

1. Choose a concept from a field outside of ICER but potentially relevant to your learning-teaching and/or research (e.g. Menon, 2022; Dervin et al., 2025).
2. Explore how this concept could be applied to intercultural research.
3. Discuss the potential benefits and challenges of integrating interdisciplinary insights in ICER.

Activity 14: *Theoretical framework flip*

1. Choose a piece of your own writing or research.
2. Rewrite it using a different theoretical framework than the one you originally used.
3. Compare the two versions and discuss how the change in framework altered your perspective and that of potential readers/listeners.

Activity 15: *Ideological itch*

1. Identify an idea or belief that makes you uncomfortable in ICER.
2. Delve into the reasons why it bothers you and what it challenges within your existing beliefs.
3. Write a reflection on the experience and whether it has changed your perspective.

Finally, activity 16: *Research regret*

1. Think of a research project, paper or book you regret working on due to its lack of innovation or contribution to ICER.
2. Identify what you would do differently if you were to undertake the project/write the paper now.
3. Write a new outline or proposal for the project, incorporating what you've learned.

These activities were designed to stimulate our curiosity, encouraging us to analyse, evaluate and synthesise information, create informed opinions and make reasoned decisions. Through these activities, I believe that we can learn to challenge (some)

136 Intercultural Self-Defence

assumptions, uncover (some) biases and contribute constructively to discourses of interculturality in research and education.

[Pause 4: Including words from other languages]
In 2021 many decisions concerning the use of English in the capital city of Beijing were discussed in both Chinese and foreign media. One piece of news concerned the decision by the Beijing metro company to rename stations in English around the capital. For some of the stations, the English word *station* was replaced by the Chinese word zhan (站) written in pinyin (see Figure 5.4.). Many commentators criticised this decision, claiming that it made no sense to use the Chinese word in English for such a common word as station.

[Bear in mind the idioms 'Old wine in a new bottle' and, in Chinese, 换汤不换药 (huàn tāng bù huàn yào), which means literally 'different broth but the same old medicine'.]

In my recent writings, I have made use of words from different languages to refer to certain intercultural phenomena, rather than sticking to English words. In our *Concise Routledge Encyclopaedia of New Concepts for Interculturality* (Dervin et al., 2025), we present 74 concepts selected and elaborated by multilingual scholars, with an aim to enrich critical discussions of the notion of interculturality in global scholarship. Our starting point for putting together this Encyclopaedia was that, although many interculturalists are attempting to unrethink and decolonise interculturality, this seems to be happening in similar linguistic terms as before, especially in the English language – which questions our attempts to e.g. decolonise interculturality. This is why we argued that there is a strong need to develop concepts in English.

What are your views on this issue? How could it help avert language indifference and nonchalance? Have you come across concepts and notions in other

FIGURE 5.4 Zhan-station.

languages used in English? How convincing were they? What was the added value of including them? Would you yourself insert words from other languages to discuss the complexities of interculturality? How to do it in a transparent and meaningful way?

Staccato. **Stuck for new ideas?**

Stimulating a student, researcher or educator who is feeling stuck for new ideas in ICER might involve a combination of motivational strategies, creative thinking exercises and practical steps to rejuvenate their interest and innovation in their work. Here are some approaches that might help:

- *Change of scenery*: A fresh environment might stimulate new thoughts. Encourage people to work from a different location, attend conferences or visit other research sites locally or internationally to gain new perspectives and inspiration.
- *Collaboration*: Teaming up with other researchers, even in different fields, can lead to cross-pollination of ideas and spark new directions for research on interculturality.
- *Reading broadly*: Reading outside of our usual academic literature (books, articles or papers in different fields) can provide inspiration. The arts might also open up new vistas.
- *Brainstorming sessions*: Organised brainstorming with peers can help in generating a list of ideas, no matter how 'crazy' they might seem at first.
- *Taking a break*: Sometimes, stepping away from the research for a short period can help clear the mind and reduce burnout.
- *Failure as a learning tool*: Viewing failure as a part of the research process in interculturality is essential since this could help in overcoming the fear of trying new things.
- *Creative exercises*: Engaging in creative exercises like writing fiction or painting can sometimes stimulate the brain in different ways, leading to new insights into interculturality.

Tremolo. **Ultimate fragmenting**

These are the last fragments that I am sharing in this Resource Book. They are divided into three subsections following the antagonists that we have examined in the previous Étagères. As with fragments in other parts of the book, may I suggest that you read them one by one, slowly and in whichever order you want, reflect on what they might mean (to you and others) and, in the spirit of criticality of criticality (Dervin, 2024), disagree with them, unrethink what they contain?

Indoctrination ... unbelief

[#] To name and label something as *interculturality*, isn't this already an indoctrinating act?

[#] A colleague: *For me interculturality is this (long incomprehensible definition)*. Fred: For me ... I don't know ... maybe ... not ... I have given up ...

[#] Consider yourself to be a (potential) *indoctrinator* and *indoctrinatee.*

[#] When we feel out of indoctrination, we have been indoctrinated again.

[#] ~~Against the position of the mere publicist in ICER~~.

[#] Capitalistic ideas about interculturality in education: *aim for no conflict in interculturality* (so we do not waste time and make as much of a profit as we can), *lower hierarchies* (which is impossible, but this objective could make us believe that things will go smoothly and thus improve benefits and profits), *learn how to communicate 'effectively'* (to control others better and thus triumph).

[#] Intercultural competence is about trying to establish logic, rationality and explanation to disturb the changing realities of who we become together, what we say and do. Interculturality is seen as a way forward only, ignoring its multi-directionalities.

[#] A big intercultural name from the west decides to speak French at an international conference to 'make a stance against' the colonialism of English ... *French as a decolonising language?* Desolation.

[#] Someone writes about decolonising interculturality: They start their article with the western-centric and capitalistic goal of *protecting culture*.

[#] A scholar from an African country talking about the Global South, quotes their 'favourite singer', Dolly Parton from the USA, to critique inequalities experienced in their society.

[#] The cliché of the 'paradigm shift' when, in fact, it is purely an ideological shift.

[#] Indoctrination is subjugated oppression.

[#] Finnish conductor and composer Jorma Panula (in Hall, 2023: n.p.): "The conductor should help, not disturb". So, should the scholar-educator of interculturality.

[#] ~~Against clique-thinking~~.

[#] (Af)filiation is repetition.

[#] If every scholar had to have a motto, mine would be: *I don't contribute to your ideological fantasy*.

[#] I have come to realise that the Janusianism, which often leads to epistemic and methodological contradictions in research and education, that I discussed in the 2010s is in fact the norm of interculturality in research and education (Dervin, 2016). We say this *and* that, do this *and* that. We accuse others of doing what we do. We are definitely always in between.

[#] I criticise the idea of *contact hypothesis* in front of a group of students for being too general and static. Later, I make a claim about young people that makes a student react: "isn't your argument about 'us' too generic? I don't think that the youth's complex use of social media makes us more open than older people". She says. I contradicted myself. I admit, I accept. I am *only* human.

[#] Misunderstanding appears to be much more inventing than understanding.

Intellectual inertia … intellectual vigour

[#] The beauty of the impenetrable in intercultural encounters.

[#] The only thing that is unequivocal in relation to interculturality is its ambiguities.

[#] The courage to change, to contradict, to not rehearse.

[#] Interculturality is mysterious, generous, fragile, violent and always unpredictable.

[#] Since we are all intercultural, we must continue becoming intercultural.

[#] Sitting at concerts around the world throughout my life, I noticed that photographers tend to take pictures of performers when they are in obvious and somewhat exaggerated movement (for example, conductors jumping up and down). Immobility seems not to be of interest to them. And yet immobility is also kinetic beyond the obvious. A lesson for ICER?

[#] We have to accept some kind of *je ne sais quoi*. What we cannot explain.

[#] As much as interculturality is pushing in all directions, we must push and be pushed through engaging scientifically around the notion again and again.

[#] Interculturality cannot but occur between chaos and order. *Neither … nor*.

[#] Interculturality always requires improvisation, even when we feel it is 'programmed' and 'programmable'.

[#] Interculturality without any kind of surprise is not intercultural. Interculturality must be intimidating.

[#] Like life, interculturality is endless. We should thus not fake a final and well-structured form of interculturality.

[#] Interculturality is not something to 'delimit' or 'lock up' but to expand without limits.

[#] Interculturality does not exist. It is in constant motion.

[#] These questions that Arnold Schönberg kept asking John Cage when he was his student: "Why don't you take a little more liberty?" and then when Cage broke rules, Schoenberg said, "Why do you break the rules?" (Revill, 2014: 46). A good summary of what could be asked in ICER.

[#] *'Traditional approach'; 'classic view'.* Are these the only (negative) imaginaries about intercultural communication education and research? How about *'critical perspectives'*?

[#] Why would we want to research people's identity when they themselves might not (want to) know who they are?

[#] A student says she is eager to read my books. She asks for suggestions. *What to read first?* I suggest starting from the oldest to the newest, claiming that it is easier to get into my intellectual worlds. She replies that she prefers newer works. I explain that it is like climbing a mountain from the top and going down. Not impossible (one can take a car or a helicopter) but it will be problematic. It is also like building a house from the 10th floor, you need to have very solid foundations. There is no elevator available for this. How much I suffered to get where I am in my thinking about interculturality, my readers could also experience it in their own ways. *However, how about the other way around too?*

[#] When we turn the page of a book, we should be surprised by what we find on the new page.

[#] An academic text about interculturality should come to the reader as if they were strangers to each other. *If already acquainted, inertia!*

[#] Imaginaries and realities are two interchangeable sides of the same coin.

[#] My favourite idea about interculturality is the one that I haven't written about yet. The one coming.

[#] Knowing about one's ignorance is already knowing too much.

[#] We don't need to become critical and creative ... we are. It is all about doing it and daring to do it.

[#] Let's observe each other while thinking.

[#] Being a scholar of interculturality is not a job but a way of life.

[#] We interculturalists are not lie-proof.

[#] Creativity means challenging.

[#] We need to accept the uncertain, hermaphrodite, crepuscular, dreamlike.

[#] When we work on interculturality, we must experience a sense of illegitimacy and insecurity. We are not in control.

[#] My work is now to ceaselessly confront norms, expectations and habits of engaging with interculturality.

[#] The very idea of preparing for interculturality sounds counter-productive: how to prepare for constant change, hyper-performance and instabilities? An illusion?

[#] Someone: "I have been trying to develop a new argument on interculturality but I failed". What is new? Is new possible when one remains within the same language and ideological realms?

[#] Why do some of us feel they can attack e.g. Hofstede and Huntington but repeat and protect others who could also be criticised?

[#] Build up strength by getting used to insecurity. Accept change – real change.

[#] The best way to learn about interculturality is not to have the intention of learning about it.

[#] As soon as you start liking an idea, as soon as it becomes too obvious, run away. As soon as you are made to think that you must read something, run away.

[#] As soon as you think you have the answer, run away.

[#] Navigate
Try
Taste
Detest
Reject
Embrace
Dislike
Swallow
Vomit

[#] Interculturality as an invitation to think things over, to be uncertain.

[#] Why should art and music be relaxing and making us happy? To a friend: "I am listening to this great piece of music by British composer Rebecca Saunders". My friend: "I am happy you are relaxing". *I am not relaxing*, I am learning, I am thinking, I am practising my senses, I am unclogging my mind. Music and art are part of my work. They are essential. They feed in my unrethinking.

[#] I don't think that models of intercultural competence produced in the west should be reserved for 'westerners' and avoided outside this sphere. These models are problematic wherever they are used because they are based on specific ideological orders that push people to think in certain ways and (maybe) even to act and (mis-)understand their own intercultural experiences. They are not specific to a geographical location; they just pollute people's minds with pre-conceived ideas about what they do, and should do.

[#] There is no *cordon sanitaire* between private and research lives when one works on interculturality.

[#] Wishing to prevent a 'threat of ambiguity and a lack of precision from scholarly work on interculturality' is fighting against the very notion.

[#] Accept that we don't/we can't know. Accept that we don't own ideas and concepts but construct them together.

[#] The artist Alexander Calder (1898–1976) is famous for his mobiles made of metal and wire that are set in motion in space by air currents. *A good metaphor for interculturality*. They are unpredictable, constantly shifting positions, defying our need for predictions. Calder's mobiles ask us to reconsider the way we have been indoctrinated to think. They ask us to be mobile too.

[#] Van Gogh (1997: 236) for intercultural self-defence: "My great longing is to learn to make those very incorrectnesses, those deviations, remodellings, changes of reality, so that they may become, yes, untruth if you like – but more true than the literal truth".

Language indifference … language sensibility

[#] Project your own personality when you write and speak about interculturality. Unwrite (see Dervin & R'boul, 2024)!

[#] We must write what we think we cannot write.

[#] Having access to other languages must act as a detonator to force us to unrethink interculturality as a scientific and educational notion.

[#] When I read someone, I am not interested in their coherence but in their contradictions and how they try to disguise them. This is what interculturality is about: contradictions and lies are you and me.

[#] Speaking about and defining interculturality mean trying to objectivise it.

[#] *Valid and reliable* do not go hand in hand with interculturality.

[#] It is not language itself that is treacherous and prevents us from understanding each other. Our roles of *utterer-hearer-meaning-maker* create problems.

[#] The miracle of listening.

[#] You are what you hear.

[#] Whatever I say and write about interculturality represents indoctrination, so should I be quiet?

[#] Indoctrination also occurs when we don't give space to people to think beyond the box and to speak 'otherwise'. The box becomes the obvious and the taken for granted.

[#] "How should I call what I do?" someone asks me. I reply ironically: "carrot?". It is not so much about how we name things but about what we do with them, being aware of what we wish to do with them and being as transparent (and ready to renegotiate their meanings and connotations) as possible with others. Words are just words in the end.

[#] Questions should outweigh answers.

[#] Interculturality should lead to the freedom to ask questions we want to ask about ourselves.

[#] To do interculturality is to change. Perspectives that do not consider it one way or another are not about interculturality. Not our change as scholars and educators but multifaceted change. We must develop curiosity towards change: long-term, unchanged change, underground change, discourses of change, silenced and reflected-upon change. Change might want to be kept for oneself. Do not look for logic or coherence but look for other voices and contradictions.

[#] Read backwards, open a book backwards, top down, right to left.

[#] When reading about interculturality in education, we must play naïve, pretending that we don't understand so that things can be clarified and not universalised while e.g. claiming to be decolonial.

[#] Writing calligraphy in Chinese cannot but inspire unrethinking about interculturality:

- The text is at times read from right to left and vice versa; top to bottom and vice versa.
- Some owners of calligraphies add texts about the story or forms of calligraphy, with some even adding punctuation.
- Calligraphy floats, is fluid and reveals the individualities of the writer.
- Calligraphy is also a performance – it is not just about 'writing'.
- Calligraphy corresponds to a way of being with self while thinking and interacting with others in-/directly.
- Calligraphy is art.

[#] When you see a word in Chinese, you have to let your grammatical mind float: any character could be singular, plural, present, past, a noun, verb, adjective …

[#] Chinese seals can express the contrary of what their owner is. For example, someone might have a stamp that says 'barbarian' while hinting at the fact that they are otherwise. *A contradictory maybe double-faced sign of modesty?* Maybe this is how we should speak in intercultural research and education, send confusing messages, identity shifts about who we are or wish to be seen.

[#] The talent to listen.

[#] The art of effective miscommunication – believing that one can communicate.

[#] Censoring oneself by not using certain words does not necessarily help move forward with interculturality. One can be essentialist beyond discourses and statements … (as a reminder).

[#] Reading one of my students' article I am pondering: how could they unplug from my thinking, from my ideas, from my wording? *Disengage.*

[#] If a researcher's voice is only mentioned as accepted truth then there is something wrong. Their/our words should also be positioned.

[#] If I see the word *seminal* to refer to a scholar's work, I start doubting. Seminal seems to be a synonym for unquestionable today – and could thus be lazy and indoctrinating.

[#] *Why can't we ask proper questions?* I am dreaming of a conference where speakers ask questions to their audience and listen to them. The focus would be on questions rather than answers.

[#] *Observe and describe without judgement.* Is that even possible? To describe is to judge. We choose specific words thus we judge. I speak therefore I weigh.

[#] Working on a reference book of critical interculturality is an exercise of interculturality itself. *What do you mean?* I must have written four hundred times to the authors. Often, we don't have the opportunity to ask this question.

[#] We must find ourselves out of balance when reading something about interculturality. If we only find confirmations of what we think then we are not experiencing interculturality ourselves.

[#] Someone: "I want to become a better communicator". I reply: "You can't". Communication is a two-way phenomenon. Your partner should also wish to *become a better communicator.*

[#] The unnameable is exciting in interculturality.

[#] A professor of cultural studies on their social media: "I am open-minded". Is there a need to make such a statement? Is that even a possibility? Can one be really open-minded in disastrous times like ours?

[#] The phrase 'diversity management' is not shy of its economic and managerial aspects.

[#] There is some kind of mystery in the very word of interculturality that we need to cherish. Don't try too hard to give away everything about it.

[#] The idea of intercultural education is often hijacked. An international journal (based in Europe) rejects one of our papers because *intercultural education has to do with "the intersection between intercultural and social justice"* – no explanation for any of these terms were provided. Indoctrination and inertia *par excellence.*

[#] Listening to Nordic folk music by a band called Hedningarna (Finland/Sweden) I am inspired by their insertion of (meaningless) fillers such as 'rasma' or 'jo' between sets of words. I like the idea. It gives time to the listener to think about the lyrics. To take the time to pause. How about writing a text about interculturality that includes such fillers so we can pause to think?

> Interculturality challenges [rasma] us to deconstruct stereotypes and power imbalances [rasma]. It demands critical [rasma] self-reflection, acknowledging our biases [rasma]. Engage with other ideas [rasma], questioning dominant narratives [rasma]. Strive for equity [rasma], not mere 'tolerance' [rasma].

[#] Patricia E Sawin (1988: 211) commenting on her research on Finnish mythology: "Readers should be aware that I am working from English translations of the Finnish texts and with those critical resources available to an English speaker." *An inspiration for interculturalists.*

Note

1 In this Étagère, the sections are not numbered but receive musical notations as titles: *recitative* (basic progression); *ritardando* (the tempo should gradually slow down); *andante* (at a moderate walking pace); *legato* (played smoothly and without interruption); *sforzando* (should be played with a sudden, strong accent); *allegro* (moderately fast); *staccato* (should be played with a short, detached sound); *tremolo* (should be played rapidly and repeated).

References

Arendt, H. (1968). *Totalitarianism – Part Three of The Origins of Totalitarianism.* Houghton Mifflin Harcourt.
Arendt, H. (1973). *The Origins of Totalitarianism.* Harcourt, Brace, Jovanovich.
Augé, E. F. (2007). *Petit traité de propagande à l'usage de ceux qui la subissent.* De Boeck SUP.
Byrd-Clark, J. & Dervin, F. (eds.). (2014). *Reflexivity in Language and Intercultural Education. Rethinking Multilingualism and Interculturality.* Routledge.
Chomsky, N. (2004). *Language and Politics.* AK Press.
Dervin, F. (2016). *Interculturality in Education.* Palgrave.
Dervin, F. (2022). *Interculturality in Fragments. A Reflexive Approach.* Springer.
Dervin, F. (2024). *Interculurologies.* Springer.
Dervin, F. & R'boul, H. (eds.). (2024). *Un-writing Interculturality in Education and Research.* Routledge.

Dervin, F., R'boul, H. & Chen, N. (eds.). (2025). *The Concise Routledge Encyclopaedia of New Concepts for Interculturality*. Routledge.

Ellul, J. (1973). *Propaganda: The Formation of Men's Attitudes*. Vintage.

Grinshpun, Y. (2023). *La fabrique des discours propagandistes contemporains: Comment et pourquoi ça marche?* L'Harmattan.

Hall, A. (2023). The hidden hand: Jorma Panula's role in nurturing conducting talent. The hidden hand: Jorma Panula's role in nurturing conducting talent. *Bachtrack*. https://bachtrack.com/feature-the-hidden-hand-jorma-panula-march-2023#:~:text=The%20hidden%20hand:%20Jorma%20Panula%E2%80%99s%20role%20in

Hoff, H. E. (2020). The evolution of intercultural communicative competence: Conceptualisations, critiques and consequences for 21st century classroom practice. *Intercultural Communication Education* 3(2), 55–74. https://doi.org/10.29140/ice.v3n2.264

Jowett, G. S. & O'Donnelle, V. (2021). *Propaganda & Persuasion*. Sage.

King, R. (2013). *Brunelleschi's Dome: How a Renaissance Genius Reinvented Architecture*. Bloomsbury.

Lefkowitz, M. (2003). *Greek Gods, Human Lives: What We Can Learn from Myths*. Yale University Press.

Menon, D. M. (ed.). (2022). *Changing Theory: Concepts from the Global South*. Routledge.

Montazeri, M. S. (2022). *Psychotherapist's Guide to Socratic Dialogue* (pp. 1–21). Springer.

Nehls, M. (2023). *Indoctrinated Brain: How to Successfully Fend Off the Global Attack on Your Mental Freedom*. Skyhorse Publishing.

Ogay, T. & Edelmann, D. (2016). 'Taking culture seriously': Implications for intercultural education and training. *European Journal of Teacher Education* 39(3), 388–400. https://doi.org/10.1080/02619768.2016.1157160

Olmos-Vega, F. M., Stalmeijer, R. E., Varpio, L. & Kahlke, R. (2022). A practical guide to reflexivity in qualitative research: AMEE Guide No. 149. *Medical Teacher* 45(3), 241–251. https://doi.org/10.1080/0142159X.2022.2057287

Peng, R., Zhu, C. & Wu, W.-P, (2019). Visualizing the knowledge domain of intercultural competence research: A bibliometric analysis. *International Journal of Intercultural Relations* 74, 58–68. https://doi.org/10.1016/j.ijintrel.2019.10.008

Radcliffe, E., Dowden, K. & Livingstone, N. (2011). Orphic Mythology. In *A Companion to Greek Mythology* Ken Dowden, Niall Livingstone Blackwell (pp. 73–106).

Reboul, O. (1984). *Le langage de l'éducation*. PUF.

Revill, D. (2014). *The Roaring Silence: John Cage – A Life*. Arcade Publishing.

Sawin, P. E. (1988). Lönnrot's brainchildren: The representation of women in Finland's Kalevala. *Journal of Folklore Research* 25(3), 187–217.

Snook, I. A. (2024). *Indoctrination and Education*. Routledge.

Stanley, J. (2016). *How Propaganda Works*. Princeton University Press.

Taylor, P. M. (2005). *Munitions of the Mind: A History of Propaganda from the Ancient World to the Present Day*. Manchester University Press.

Tourse, R. W. C., Hamilton-Mason, J. & Wewiorski, N. J. (2018). *Systemic Racism in the United States. Scaffolding as Social Construction*. Springer.

Van Gogh, V. (1997). *The Letters of Vincent Van Gogh*. Simon & Schuster.

Virgil (2009). *Georgics*. Oxford World's Classics.

Wilhem, J. D., Smith, M. W., Kesson, H. & Appleman, D. (2023). *Fighting Fake News: Teaching Students to Identify and Interrogate Information Pollution*. Corwin.

Étagère 6
DEFEND YOURSELF AND ... OTHERS ...

1. **"Perhaps even my enemies and adversaries might have felt something here"**

The year 1908 marked a major change in western music production when Austrian composer Arnold Schönberg (1875–1951) presented his four-movement Second String Quartet, which parted ways with (western) tonal harmony into atonality. The string quartet had represented the archetype of European chamber music since the 18th century and usually included two violins, viola and cello (in this Second String Quartet, the composer added a female soprano). Schönberg (in Steiner, 1978: 123) wrote about the performance:

> My second string quartet caused, at its first performance in Vienna, December 1908, riots which surpassed every previous and subsequent happening of this kind. Although there were also some pe rsonal enemies of mine, who used the occasion to annoy me ... I have to admit, that these riots were justified without the hatred of my enemies, because they were a natural reaction of a conservatively educated audience to a new kind of music. Astonishingly, the first movement passed without any reaction, either for or against. But after the first measures of the second movement, the greater part of the audience started to laugh and did not cease to disturb the performance during the third movement "Litanei" (in form of variations) and the fourth movement "Entrückung". ... But at the end of this fourth movement a remarkable thing happened. After the singer ceases, there comes a long coda played by the string quartet alone. While, as mentioned before, the audience failed to respect even a singing lady, this coda was accepted without any audible disturbance. Perhaps even my enemies and adversaries might have felt something here.

In his 'revolutionary' Second String Quartet, Schönberg included the Viennese folk song 'O du lieber Augustin' in the second movement. The song is about a cheerful popular singer who cheered people up during the Black Death in Austria and stands as a symbol of fighting spirit. There are both personal and creative reasons for including this folk song in this quartet. Schönberg was going through a personal crisis during the composition of the piece. His wife had an affair with a famous painter, who later committed suicide. The use of the folk song could be a reflection of Schönberg's own feelings of loss and despair, mirroring the sentiment of the song's lyrics. Since the song is a well-known Viennese melody, its inclusion could also be a nod to Schönberg's heritage, tying his avant-garde composition to the rich musical tradition of Vienna. As mentioned, the Second String Quartet marked a major transitional period in Schönberg's work, moving from tonality to atonality and expressionism. The use of a familiar melody within a context that is increasingly dissonant and inharmonious served to highlight the shift in his musical language. Interestingly, the contrast between the simple, catchy tune of the folk song and the complex atonal environment it is placed in could be seen as a form of musical irony or even humour. It could provide a moment of stark relief within such a dense and challenging musical texture.

Why open the concluding Étagère of this Resource Book with this story?

First, as the reader will have noticed, interdisciplinarity was central in the book. Although I did refer to some of the 'canons' of ICER, multiple references were made to other fields of research (business, philosophy, psychology …) but also to the arts. Looking elsewhere for inspiration and disruption is important in the fight against the three foes discussed in this book.

Second, Schönberg's Second String Quartet, like many pieces of the early 20th century by e.g. Debussy or Stravinsky in Europe, showed that change was occurring before the two World Wars that were about to happen and for which the whole world would pay the high price that we now know about. For music, this meant moving away from traditional takes on how to compose music in Europe and how to listen to it. Our times are probably as confusing and dangerous as the early 20th century. We have wars, harsh economic-political conflicts, protests, growing inequalities, closing doors … Our times are also calling for change.

Third, in Schönberg's text, he describes well the harsh reactions that his work received from the audience (and his 'enemies'). He also ends by commenting ironically on the quiet reactions to the end of his quartet, saying "Perhaps even my enemies and adversaries might have felt something here". Proposing and actioning change in the ways we think and do things are challenging to both those who do and those who experience. Some of the ideas, critiques and methods that I have proposed in this Resource Book will surely surprise (see shock) some readers who might feel that such a Resource Book should be *this* or *that* and that it should not do *this* or *that*, say *this* or *that* ... I agree with them but I do hope that "they might have felt something here" ...

Quoting Cioran (1987: 90), I might add: "Tout ce qui nous incommode nous permet de nous définir. Sans indispositions, point d'identité" ("Everything that bothers us allows us to define ourselves. Without indispositions, there is no identity").

2. Main general takeaways from the Resource Book

Interculturality ...
...只可意会，不可言传。
只可意會，不可言傳。
(... zhí kě yì huì, bù kě yán chuán)
... can only be felt and understood in one's heart, but cannot be explained in words.

The étagères in this Resource Book were designed to be both standalone and interconnected, offering a comprehensive exploration of how to deal with interculturality in education and research. By understanding indoctrination, intellectual inertia and language issues, we could be better equipped to navigate critically and reflexively and contribute to the field of ICER.

Throughout this Resource Book, we have explored the multifaceted nature of interculturality, from theoretical frameworks to practical applications, always with an eye towards fostering further critical thinking.

The Étagère on indoctrination forced us to confront the darker side of this endeavour – where the transmission of knowledge can become a tool for control and manipulation rather than a pathway to enlightenment and empowerment. As we have seen, indoctrination is not merely a feature of totalitarian regimes or extremist groups; it can also operate insidiously within our educational institutions and research communities. It can manifest in the uncritical acceptance of dominant narratives, the suppression of dissenting voices and the reinforcement of existing power structures. Étagère 2 has urged us to be vigilant against these tendencies, to cultivate a spirit of critical inquiry and to create spaces for open and honest dialogue. The dystopian literature discussed in the Étagère served as a stark warning against the dangers of indoctrination. It reminded us of the importance of choice, the value of diverse perspectives and the necessity of constant vigilance in the defence of our intellectual and ethical autonomy. These stories also highlighted the resilience of the human spirit and the capacity for individuals to resist and transcend the forces that seek to indoctrinate them. Étagère 2 also provided us with a toolbox of concepts and strategies to help us navigate the treacherous waters of indoctrination. From critical thinking to epistemic pluralism, from autoethnography to action research, these tools empower us to engage with interculturality in more mindful and ethical ways. They encourage us to question, challenge and reflect, both on our own practices and on the broader structures of power and influence that shape our conflicting worlds. In the end, the Étagère on indoctrination was not just a critique but also a call to action. It challenged us to unrethink our approach to ICER, to question our assumptions and to work towards more potentially just and equitable futures in education and research.

Étagère 3 served as a critical inquiry into the entrenched mindsets and resistance to change within the field of ICER. In the Étagère, I scrutinised the phenomenon of intellectual inertia, which is characterised by a tendency to maintain the status quo and cling to e.g. established ideologies, theories and methods. The Étagère first employed Franz Kafka's short story *In the Penal Colony* as a metaphor for the rigidity and dogmatism that can pervade ICER, highlighting the need for scholars and educators to challenge prevailing norms and engage with new ideas and perspectives. The Étagère also introduced a variety of strategies and activities designed to foster critical thinking, reflexivity and openness to transformation. It emphasised the importance of language sensitivity and the need to question and redefine our approaches to interculturality. The Étagère concluded with a call for continuous learning and the development of a keen awareness of how language and other factors can shape and limit understanding in ICER. All in all, this Étagère underscored the importance of reflexivity in research and education about interculturality, encouraging students, researchers and educators to examine their biases and assumptions to enhance personal growth and build trust with others. It also introduced the role of language in constructing intercultural narratives and the potential for indoctrination and inertia in academic discourse. The Étagère challenged us to engage with complexity, resist simplification and strive for a more nuanced understanding of intercultural encounters.

In the Étagère *Language indifference and nonchalance: Crises of language and interculturality*, I explored the impact of language on ICER. Drawing inspiration from Samuel Beckett's theatrical works, I used them as a metaphor for the struggles with language in ICER. Beckett's characters often grapple with the inadequacy of language to express the human condition, reflecting the challenges in ICER where language fails to bridge gaps in understanding and problematising the notion of interculturality. The Étagère also delved into the implications of language indifference and nonchalance, suggesting that they can lead to misunderstandings and a lack of depth in intercultural communication. I argued that language is not merely a tool but carries with it ideologies, values and beliefs that shape research and education. Strategies to counteract language indifference include promoting multilingualism, questioning assumptions about language and providing translations to accommodate diverse linguistic milieus. I also raised ethical concerns, suggesting that indifference can result in the misrepresentation or exclusion of certain perspectives, undermining the integrity of research and education. Like other Étagères, I took a creative approach, with e.g. a poem that lamented the state of language in academia, particularly in ICER. The poem served as a call to action, urging us to reflect on the role of language and to challenge indifference and nonchalance. I also further examined the complexities of language through the lens of various academic texts, exploring how language can both clarify and obscure our understanding of interculturality. As such, the Étagère also engaged with the ideas of Jacques Derrida, Hélène Cixous and Fyodor Dostoyevsky, using their philosophical and creative insights to deepen the discussion on language in ICER. I concluded this Étagère with a series of fragments that challenge us, me as the author and you as the readers, to reconsider my/your assumptions and beliefs about interculturality and language. All in all, I emphasised the need for continuous learning, reflexivity and critical engagement with language to avoid intellectual inertia and to foster a more dynamic and inclusive approach to intercultural research and education.

Étagère 5 focused on the importance of critical engagement in ICER and emphasised the need to challenge and resist indoctrination, intellectual inertia and language indifference, which can limit the depth and breadth of interculturality. This Étagère also advocated for a self-reflexive approach to ICER, encouraging us students, researchers and educators to be aware of our own biases and preconceptions. Based on the main takeaways from Étagère 4, I underscored the crucial role of language in shaping research and education, arguing against language indifference and for a more nuanced and sensitive use of language. The Étagère thus called for a process of unlearning dominant ideologies and preconceived ideas about interculturality to foster e.g. more innovative and inclusive perspectives, while encouraging every one of us to engage critically with e.g. research papers, to question assumptions and to seek out new and diverse viewpoints. Finally, the Étagère suggested that collaboration across disciplines and with diverse perspectives can help break through intellectual inertia and stimulate new ideas in ICER.

If I summarise the central tenets of the proposed perspective, I could say that the different Étagères aim to help you enhance your self-defence capabilities in intercultural practices. The book has offered a range of activities and tools, including:

- Analysing and rewriting language in academic texts to be more sensitive and inclusive regarding interculturality;
- Creating and updating maps of personal ideological beliefs about interculturality during learning-teaching and research processes;
- Learning how to identify and reflect on personal implicit biases;
- Recording and analysing how personal beliefs influence interpretations of intercultural topics in research and education.

The main general takeaways from the book could also be summarised through three key words: *Critical awareness* or recognising the subtle influences that can shape perspectives within ICER; *self-reflection* or the need to regularly reassess personal beliefs and teaching/research practices; and *language sensitivity* or understanding the power and limitations of language in intercultural contexts.

I recognise that intercultural research and education is a constantly evolving field filled with challenges and opportunities. As the Resource Book shows, we need to embrace the uncertainty and complexity of interculturality as an ongoing process of renegotiation and rebalancing. This means that we also need to advocate for an open, curious, and critical attitude in research and education, constantly questioning and exploring.

My main recommendations for moving forward include the followings:

1. *Continuous learning*: Commit to ongoing education and unrethinking in intercultural studies. Keep abreast of new developments in intercultural theory and practice in English and any other language you might have access to.
2. *Active engagement*: Participate in discussions, workshops and conferences to broaden perspectives and meet e.g. individuals whose views seem to oppose yours about interculturality. Look for opportunities to integrate learnings into your teaching and research.
3. *Reflective practice*: Regularly write and reflect on personal and professional experiences with interculturality.
4. *Inclusive language use*: Strive to use language that is sensitive, inclusive and considers the audience. Remember that English as a global language of interculturality has its pros and cons.
5. *Collaborative approach*: Work with others to challenge and extend your and their understanding of interculturality as a notion in education and research.

Figure 6.1 is a painting I did in 2021 to try to capture the complexities and influences of the three foes on the one who wishes to engage with interculturality in research and education. Can you have a look at each aspect of the painting and decide how they might relate to indoctrination, intellectual inertia and language indifference and nonchalance? What does this painting tell you about the 'hand' (the author) of this book (to refer back to the metaphor of the hand from Étagère 1) and how he sees these three foes 'artistically'? If you wish, you may also try to create a piece where our three adversaries locate in the human body and around it.

Moving forward, these recommendations aim to empower us to be active participants in our ongoing intercultural journey in education and research, embracing the complexities and continuous evolution of interculturality.

[Pause 1: On the importance of accepting contradictions and change in interculturality in research and education]

Throughout the Resource Book, I have identified and highlighted contradictions, instabilities and 'Janusianisms' in what we do and say with interculturality. A contradiction could be defined as "a situation when two seemingly opposed

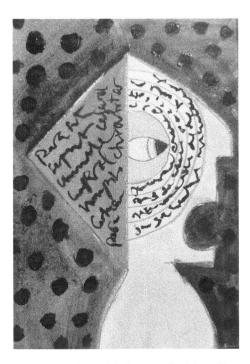

FIGURE 6.1   Dealing with the complexities of interculturality.

forces are simultaneously present" (Harvey, 2014: 1), be it unconscious or deliberate. Although we may lament about this fact of life (the human cannot but be contradictory since they often find themselves performing with and for others in complex contexts), I believe that we need to accept, confront and even celebrate contradictions. In a paper entitled "Anthropology and the study of contradictions", Berliner et al. (2016: 1–2) provide the following examples:

> Once during my anthropology of gender class, one student explained to us her embarrassment when, being a convinced feminist, she realized that she was enthusiastically singing the sexist lyrics of a popular track. In the same vein, I often think about environmentalists who are, at the same time, frequent flyers or smokers. Take also anti-capitalist intellectuals who, through their editorial and evaluative practices, participate actively in academic capitalism. Critical thinkers, too, are sometimes steeped in contradictions. Passionately defending a cause, they might ignore inconsistencies, much like when you fall in love and lose some discernment.

How many such "ambivalent explanations, incompatible beliefs, and intrapersonal contradictions" (Berliner et al., 2016: 2) have we experienced, co-constructed and faced in ICER? How many such phenomena have you identified in this Resource Book?

FIGURE 6.2   2 + 2 = 5.

Many of our experiences, realities and fantasies require us to choose within continua of assertions, opinions and ideologies. If we can't/don't choose (which we are often tempted to do), we can question the status quo and accept that things are not always 'black or white'. We accept our contradictions. We accept our humanity. We accept interculturality as something that does not occur in a (programmed/dictated) straight line.

> *Yes* or *no? No* or *yes? Life* or *death? Past* or *future? Round* or *flat? Green* or *blue? Honesty* or *lying? True* or *false? 2 + 2 = 5?...* (see Figure 6.2).

The omnipresence of *or* here forces us to make choices that we don't always have to make interculturally speaking. I would say that, to me, this is one of the main lessons from my contacts with 'China'. I remember being surprised and often shocked by the somewhat flexible and tolerant attitudes of some of my Chinese friends and colleagues towards *small* and *big* contradictions in everyday life. These include e.g. *claiming to not be and being at the same time* (no religious affiliation but worship of deities at temples, claiming that this is about *culture* (and it could well be!); penniless and yet buying expensive clothes); *condemning certain attitudes and ways of life and yet 'doing' them* (critiques towards materialistic obsessions and yet victims of compulsive shopping); *showing negative feelings towards a person, even disgust, and yet using them to get favours* (promotion, jobs …); *knowing that something is illegal and/or ethically unacceptable and yet doing it with eyes closed; constructing an image of being hard-working while exploiting others to do one's own work or learning how to navigate and blind the system* (on 'changing gods', see Hansen, 1990; on Chinese elite students, see Chiang, 2022). Although I used to be very judgemental of such contradictions, they helped me realise that I am also full of *contradictions* (e.g. I am a vegetarian but I eat chicken; janusianism in understanding current world conflicts …) and reflect further on issues of ethics in relation to intercultural research and education.

[And, by the way, in everyday language, we can feel how much contradictions are inherent to life. In English, we might speak of old news, acting naturally, unbiased opinion, same difference, or clearly confused... Can you think of similar contradictions (that we often do not consider as contradictions) in English and other languages?]

One important aspect of intercultural self-defence is thus to identify, recognise, understand, accept and (if needed!) question ambivalence in what we say (ambivalent statements, incompatible values), feel (emotional internal clashes) and do (contradictory attitudes) (Berliner et al., 2016: 5). Asking ourselves and (if needed/possible) asking questions to others, would benefit interculturality: "Yes, humans are full of contradictions. So, how to live with principles, emotions, and behaviors that contradict each other? How can one have a thought, and in the same movement, its opposite?" (Berliner et al., 2016: 2).

3. Creative self-reflective collage

In this section, we explore a creative outlet for expressing the complex ideas and concepts reviewed in this Resource Book. With a collage activity, whereby we are going to make a picture in which different things and materials are glued together (magazines, newspapers and books/pdfs related to interculturality, education and communication; using coloured papers, scissors, glue sticks, or a digital device for a digital collage; art supplies such as markers, coloured pencils and paint), we are encouraged to think deep(er) about the themes of interculturality, indoctrination, intellectual inertia and language indifference by creating a visual representation of our learning journey and self-perception in relation to these topics. We can spend approximately 2–3 hours on this type of activity, listening to music for creating a relaxing atmosphere. This type of self-reflexive activity could trigger a deeper and more personal understanding of the themes of the book, a visual representation of our learning journey that can serve as a reminder and inspiration. It could also enhance our self-awareness and critical thinking skills.

Instructions

a. **Preparation**: Find a quiet and comfortable space where you can work without interruptions. Gather all the materials you need. If you're making a physical collage, lay out your magazines, coloured papers and art supplies. If you're making a digital collage, ensure you have access to graphic design software or an online tool (and make sure you have enough battery!).

b. **Guided reflection**: Listen to some calming music, if you wish, to set the mood (check some of the music mentioned in this book, see the list in Étagère 1). Spend 10 to 15 minutes in silence, reflecting on your journey with the content of the Resource Book. Consider the following prompts:

- What have you learned about interculturality that surprised you?
- How have your views on indoctrination evolved?

- In what ways have you recognised intellectual inertia in yourself or others?
- How has your attitude towards language and its role in ICER changed?
c. **Collecting images and words**: Flip through the magazines, newspapers and books and cut out images, graphs, quotes or text snippets that resonate with your reflections. You may also write your own thoughts or phrases in your journal and cut them out to add to your collage.
d. **Creating the collage**: Start arranging the cut-outs on your collage background. You can do this physically on a piece of paper or digitally using graphic design software. Experiment with different layouts until you find one that feels meaningful to you. Add colours, drawings or painted elements to enhance your collage further.
e. **Reflective writing**: As you arrange the elements, write down your thoughts and feelings in your journal. Describe the collage you are creating and how each element relates to your understanding of the book's topics.
f. **Review and interpretation**: Once your collage is complete, take a step back and review it:
    - What story/stories does your collage tell about your journey with the book?
    - Are there any patterns or themes you notice?
g. **Sharing**: If you feel comfortable, share your collage with a friend, colleague or on social media using a hashtag related to the Resource Book or interculturality. Engage in discussions about what you've learned and how it's represented in your collage.
h. **Closing reflection**: Spend the final 15 minutes writing a reflective paragraph in your journal about the process and what you've learned from it. Consider how you will carry this learning forward in your approach to intercultural communication education and research.

4. Intercultural kaleidoscope through fragments from the Resource Book

This activity aims to support us in engaging with selected thought-provoking fragments from each Étagère of the book and explore their implications through a creative and collaborative activity. Learning outcomes could include: A deeper understanding of the key themes from the book through the lens of selected fragments; enhanced communication and collaboration skills through group discussion and interpretation; a creative and reflective experience that solidifies learning and encourages application of concepts in your own real-life research and educational contexts.

Using the following fragments which summarise some of the main takeaways from the Étagères as well as index cards or slips of paper, we can spend 2–3 hours alone or together with other people on this 'intercultural kaleidoscope' (this is ideal for book clubs, classrooms or workshops).

You can also choose your favourite fragments from the book that encapsulate a key concept, pose a thought-provoking question or use the ones listed below (alternatively you may use fragments from Dervin (2022) or R'boul and Dervin (2023)). Write each fragment on a separate index card or slip of paper and distribute the cards, giving participants a few minutes to read their fragment silently. Ask them to spend 5–10 minutes reflecting on their fragment, considering the followings:

- What does this fragment mean to me?
- How does it relate to the broader themes of the book?
- What questions does it raise for me?

Then form small groups of 3–4 participants with each participant sharing their fragment with the group and discussing their reflections. Groups could identify common themes or contrasting viewpoints among the fragments and select one fragment to focus on that best represents their collective thoughts and discussions. Groups then create a visual or written interpretation of their chosen fragment using art supplies or additional index cards. Finally, each group presents their interpretation to the larger group and discusses how different groups interpreted the same fragment or how their interpretations varied. As a large group, discuss the key insights and learnings from the activity by considering this question: *How do the fragments connect to real-world experiences and challenges in ICER?* Participants can also write a brief reflection on one or more of the followings:

- A new understanding or perspective gained from the activity.
- How the fragments relate to their personal or professional lives.
- Actions they could take to apply their learnings from the book and this activity.

Fragment 1: *On indoctrination*
"Indoctrination in ICER is not merely about manipulation; it's also about the subtle ways we absorb and repeat ideas without questioning".

Fragment 2: *The power of questions*
"In intercultural encounters, questions should outnumber answers. It's not about finding the right answers but asking the right questions".

Fragment 3: *Language and thought*
"Language is not just a tool for communication; it shapes our thoughts, influences our biases, and constructs our realities in ICER".

Fragment 4: *Intellectual inertia*
"The greatest danger in our broad field of interculturality is not ignorance, but the refusal to question what we think we already know".

158 Intercultural Self-Defence

Fragment 5: *The complexity of culture*
"Culture is not a fixed entity; it's a dynamic and ever-changing landscape that we must continuously re-evaluate".

Fragment 6: *On criticality*
"Criticality in intercultural research is not just about criticizing others' work but also about scrutinizing our own assumptions and methodologies".

Fragment 7: *The role of education*
"Education should not be a one-way street where ideas are imposed; it should be a marketplace of ideas where all perspectives are welcome".

Fragment 8: *Embracing contradictions*
"In interculturality, contradictions are not flaws; they are opportunities to delve deeper into the complexities of human interactions".

Fragment 9: The importance of listening
"Listening is not just about hearing words; it's about understanding the unspoken messages and the nuances behind them".

Fragment 10: *The journey of interculturality*
"Interculturality is not a destination; it's a lifelong journey of learning, unlearning and relearning".

[Pause 2: Think with ...]
Here is one last opportunity to think about the Resource Book with four figures who have influenced me as a thinker of interculturality. Read through these four quotes and decide if and how they summarise well the main takeaways from the book:

> In the end the Party would announce that two and two made five, and you would have to believe it. It was inevitable that they should make that claim sooner or later: the logic of their position demanded it. Not merely the validity of experience, but the very existence of external reality, was tacitly denied by their philosophy. The heresy of heresies was common sense. And what was terrifying was not that they would kill you for thinking otherwise, but that they might be right. For, after all, how do we know that two and two make four? Or that the force of gravity works? Or that the past is unchangeable? If both the past and the external world exist only in the mind, and if the mind itself is controllable – what then?
>
> *Orwell, (2009: 37)*

> "Capitalism," I'll argue here, better designates something larger: a societal order that empowers a profit-driven economy to prey on the extra-economic

supports it needs to function – wealth expropriated from nature and subject peoples; multiple forms of carework, chronically undervalued when not wholly disavowed; public goods and public powers, which capital both requires and tries to curtail; the energy and creativity of working people. Although they do not appear on corporate balance sheets, these forms of wealth are essential preconditions for the profits and gains that do.
Fraser (2022: xiv)

Writing is the passageway, the entrance, the exit, the dwelling place of the other in me.
Cixous (1993: 21)

Whether one calls oneself conservative or revolutionary, whether one composes in a conventional or progressive manner, whether one tries to imitate old styles or is destined to express new ideas – whether one is a good composer or not – one must be convinced of the infallibility of one's own fantasy and one must believe in one's own inspiration.
Schönberg (1984: 218)

As I write the last words of this Resource Book, I hope that you will take away a deeper understanding of interculturality and strategies to grasp and circumvent some aspects of indoctrination, intellectual inertia, and language indifference in your work (as much as you can!). I encourage you/us to see the concepts and activities from the book as tools to help you/us remain vigilant and reflective in ICER. I believe that, through continuous learning and self-improvement, we can better understand and address the challenges posed by interculturality in research and education. Working on this Resource Book has left me with a profound sense of responsibility too. Students, educators and scholars also have a duty to foster environments where interculturality can flourish, free *a minima* from the constraints of indoctrination and other foes that are currently 'trashing' our worlds.

We must strive to create curricula, pedagogical perspectives and research agendas that are ideologically and emotionally inclusive, diverse and open to scrutiny. *We must be willing to un-listen, to un-learn and to change*, recognising that our own growth and development are inextricably linked to that of our students, colleagues … and any other being on this suffocating earth …

Preludi (Prelude)
会 While polishing the pages of this Resource Book before handing it in to my Publisher, I tuned in to a radio program. The airwaves carried the poignant tunes of Dmitri Shostakovich (1906–1975), a composer whose life was as complex as e.g. the symphonies he wrote. The program delved into his intricate existence, set against the backdrop of the Soviet Union's oppressive regime in the 20th century. Listening to the broadcast, I was transported to a time of fear and censorship, where

every note could be a political statement and every silence a scream of protest. Shostakovich's music, with its layers of sorrow and defiance, spoke volumes about resilience in the face of adversity. The program's narration painted a vivid picture of a man torn between his artistic integrity and the demands of totalitarianism. It detailed how his works were both celebrated and condemned, how he was lauded as a genius one day and denounced as a an 'intellectual enemy of the people' the next (e.g. Volkov, 2004). The emotional weight of this constant push and pull was palpable in every story shared. As the program unfolded, I found myself deeply moved by the depth of Shostakovich's struggles. His music, a testament to his unwavering spirit, resonated with me on a profound level. The raw emotion in his compositions, the coded (hidden) messages of dissent and the quiet moments of hope amidst despair, all spoke to the indomitable nature of our contradictory condition as interculturalists. The radio host's voice was filled with reverence as they described the composer's courage in the face of state-enforced conformity. Shostakovich's life was a testament to the power of art to transcend political and ideological boundaries and to communicate what I consider to be the deepest human emotions. The radio program was a reminder that even in the darkest of times – and in frightening intercultural times like ours in 2024 – the light of creativity can shine through, illuminating the path for those of us who dare to rebel in our own ways, dream and (re-)create …

仝 Huzaifa's eyes held an innocence and a naivety that symbolised both his charm and his challenge. He was a man of profound empathy – a heart that sought to understand the world and its people, even when they were less than kind. Huzaifa met Mu Chen, whose presence was often captivating. But she was a complex character, woven with threads of self-interest and manipulation. She saw Huzaifa's kindness as a vulnerability to exploit and she did so without hesitation. Huzaifa, however, was oblivious to her intentions. He was drawn to her, his heart swelling with a sense of camaraderie that was both genuine and blind. He offered her his trust, his time and his support, only to be met with deceit and disregard. Mu Chen played her games and Huzaifa was but a piece in her grand scheme. She took advantage of his goodwill and his generosity, leaving him feeling used and isolated. Yet, even in the face of such betrayal, Huzaifa could not find it in himself to harbour resentment. One day, news reached him that Mu Chen had suffered a fall, her arm now bound in a cast. Huzaifa heard the cry of a soul in need. His heart believed that this was an opportunity to extend a hand of friendship. He thus penned a text message, a simple note of solace: "Dearest Mu Chen, I've heard of your misfortune. I cannot help but feel for you. May your arm heal swiftly, and may your heart find peace". *The message was sent.* Days passed, and Mu Chen's silence was deafening. Huzaifa's wife and friends chided him for his foolishness but he only smiled – *a smile that held no bitterness.* "I sent the message not for her but for myself", he would say. "To remind myself that even in the darkest of times, there is always room for light". His story was that of friendship, in the sense of a love for humanity, a love that could not be extinguished, no matter how many times it was tested …

References

Berliner, D., Lambek, M., Shweder, R., Irvine, R. & Piette, A. (2016). Anthropology and the study of Contradictions. *Hau: Journal of Ethnographic Theory 6*(1), 1–27. http://dx.doi.org/10.14318/hau6.1.002

Chiang, Y.-L. (2022). *Study Gods: How the New Chinese Elite Prepare for Global Competition*. Princeton University Press.

Cioran, E. (1987). *Aveux et Anathèmes*. Arcades Gallimard.

Cixous, H. (1993). *Three Steps on the Ladder of Writing*. Columbia University Press.

Dervin, F. (2022). *Interculturality in Fragments. A Reflexive Approach*. Springer.

Fraser, N. (2022). *Cannibal Capitalism: How our System is Devouring Democracy, Care, and the Planet – and What We Can Do*. Verso.

Hansen, V. (1990). *Changing Gods in Medieval China, 1127–1276*. Princeton University Press.

Harvey, D. (2014). *Seventeen Contradictions and the End of Capitalism*. Profile Books.

Orwell, G. (2009). *1984*. Infobase Holdings, Inc.

R'boul, H. & Dervin, F. (2023). *Flexing Interculturality: Further Critiques, Hesitations, and Intuitions*. Routledge.

Schönberg, A. (1984). *Style and Idea. Selected Writings of A. Schönberg*. University of California Press.

Steiner, F. (1978). A history of the first complete recording of the Schoenberg string quartets. *Journal of the Arnold Schoenberg Institute 2*(2), 122–137.

Volkov, S. (2004). *Testimony: The Memoirs of Dmitri Shostakovich*. Limelight.

INDEX

absurd 2, 54, 88–9, 91
agendas 21, 34, 38, 43, 57, 101, 107, 159
alienation 20, 57
assimilation 57, 75–6, 125
authority 12, 19, 22–3, 28, 32, 34–5, 38, 54, 62, 65, 101, 119, 125, 128
automatism 3, 25–6

balancing 9, 18, 37–8, 42–3, 62–3, 72–3, 91, 123, 144–5, 152, 159
Barnum Effect (the) 71–2, 116
barriers 4, 69, 74, 80, 89, 91, 97, 107, 122–3
bias 2–3, 6, 8, 18, 23, 31, 38, 42–3, 47, 56–7, 59–60, 62–3, 69, 73, 75–6, 90, 93–5, 98, 113, 115–16, 118, 121, 130, 132, 136, 145, 150–1, 155, 157
brainstorming 131, 133, 137
brainwashing 11, 22–4

calligraphy 78, 143
capitalistic 9, 25, 46, 56, 63, 82, 116, 138, 153, 158
censor 3, 25, 28, 116, 144, 159
collaboration 7, 69, 72, 74, 83, 97, 115, 131, 137, 151–2, 156
collage 155–6
compliance 23, 33
confirmation bias 59–60, 116
confronting 4, 15, 28, 60, 103, 114, 127, 141, 149, 153
Confucianism 26, 63, 66–8, 131

continuum 4, 56, 58, 82
contradictions 22–3, 37, 42, 56, 60, 95, 114, 138, 142–3, 152–5, 158
criteria 32–3, 37, 79
criticality of criticality 3, 25, 37, 56, 137
culturalism 35, 47, 58, 81–2, 133
culturespeak 34

deception 2, 20, 42, 127
decolonising 3, 42, 45, 53, 55–6, 69, 77, 136, 138, 143
democracy 19, 22, 24–6, 33, 35, 44, 46, 121, 125–8
dialectical materialism 100, 116
différance 97
differilitudes 30
dismissal 7, 19, 60, 116, 121–2
distortion 2, 29, 39
doctrines 20, 32–4, 36–7, 48
doublethink 20, 41–2, 116
doxa 26, 28, 45, 64
dream 1–2, 77, 140, 144, 160

echo 8, 29, 38, 68–70, 78, 81, 89, 101, 116, 127
economic pragmatism 100, 116
educators 3, 5, 13, 21, 26–7, 37, 42–3, 53, 64, 68–9, 73–4, 76, 78, 92, 94–6, 98, 103, 105, 109, 121, 128, 143, 150–1, 159
emotion 28–9, 31, 33, 35, 38–9, 41, 88–9, 98–9, 114, 116, 121, 125, 127–9, 155, 159–60

empathy 47, 96, 160
encouragement 7, 19, 34, 116
enemies 79, 89, 105, 128, 147–8, 160
epistemic diversity 43, 45, 55
epistemic friction 69–70, 86, 116
epistemic pluralism 25, 149
epistemic violence 46, 73
essentialism 25, 34–5, 43, 47, 56, 58, 61, 69, 77, 81–2, 128, 133–4
ethics 6, 28, 30, 39, 45, 57, 62, 72, 87, 93, 95, 97–8, 110, 116, 125, 130, 149–50, 154
euphemism 95, 129
evaluation 28–30, 55, 63, 90
exploitation 97, 154, 160

fallacies 38, 75–6, 116, 128
fascist 9, 31, 64, 94
fear 9, 19, 24, 29, 47, 60, 67–8, 70, 81, 116, 126, 137, 159
fluid 79, 80, 98, 143
fragments 12, 21, 43, 76, 105, 137, 151, 156–8, 161

gatekeeping 3, 62, 82
global south 3, 45, 74, 77, 105–6, 138
GPS 30

heart 1, 45, 149, 160
hegemony 76, 90, 98, 101, 116
Hofstede 25, 77, 106, 141
honesty 47, 67, 79, 99, 149, 154
human rights 45–6, 126
humility 67–8

ideologeme 26–7, 30, 34, 36, 71, 94, 107, 109, 116
imagination 12, 16, 19, 21, 64, 70, 103, 120, 140
Implicit Association Test 132
inclusive 133–4, 148, 151, 152, 159
instabilities 8, 31, 37, 122, 141, 152
Institute for Propaganda Analysis (IPA) 126–7
integrity 99, 110, 150, 160
intellectual liberation 13, 15
intention 27, 29–35, 38, 43–4, 46, 54, 74, 77, 100, 116, 126, 141, 160
inter-indoctrinate 46
interculturologies 35, 64
interdisciplinarity 11–12, 63, 124, 130, 135, 148

jargon 90–1, 101, 116
je ne sais quoi 139

kaleidoscope 156

legitimate 7, 19, 34, 116
lie-proof 140
linguanoia 94
logoclasm 100, 116

manipulate 2, 19–20, 25, 29–31, 33–5, 38, 42, 46, 56, 66, 99, 107, 116, 125, 127, 149, 157, 160
marginalisation 3, 43, 64, 70, 90, 94–5, 97–8, 101, 110
mimic 34, 78
mind seepage 42–3, 116
modesty 1, 28, 47, 143
money 9, 35, 46, 48, 76–7, 79, 106
monolith 3, 81, 121
motivation 7, 40, 54–5, 63, 75, 116, 134, 137
myths 15, 64, 119–20, 145

nuances 8, 44, 61, 81, 94, 96–7, 109, 114–16, 121, 131, 158
nudge 39–41, 116

order (ideology) 21, 38, 125, 141, 158

Panglossian reasoning 72–3, 116
peer pressure 29, 35, 116
persuasion 22, 32, 54, 125–7
philosophical 26, 61, 99, 151
polysemy 2, 47, 81, 93, 106, 118, 121
power relations 3, 28, 33, 78, 80, 96, 107, 115
predatory 76
propaganda 2, 20–5, 38, 116, 124–8, 134
prospect theory 73–4, 116
protect 2, 4, 23, 28, 75, 124, 138, 141

reflexivity 2, 14, 47–8, 53, 61, 65, 116, 118, 129–31, 150–1
reification 21, 98
reject 19, 21, 36, 43, 61, 114, 123, 129, 141, 145
repetition 20, 29, 34–5, 55, 82, 89, 116, 129, 138
resistance 13–14, 24, 29–30, 35, 39, 41, 53–5, 59–62, 68–70, 76, 82, 98, 116–17, 127, 133, 149–51

sensitivity 61, 87, 109, 113, 122, 130–1, 133, 150, 152
silos 3, 63
sleepwalk 7, 93–4, 116

slogan 9, 20, 27, 29, 35, 42, 44–5, 79, 91, 101–2, 116–17
social justice 26, 45, 115, 145
social media 69, 93, 128–30, 139, 144, 156
specialization 63, 90–1, 101, 116, 130–1
status quo 7, 43, 54–6, 59–60, 62, 65, 74–6, 82, 97, 116, 150, 154
straitjacket 47
strategies 14, 18, 23, 28–9, 34–5, 46, 73–4, 87, 98, 109, 113, 128–9, 133, 137, 149–50, 159
sunk-cost fallacy 75–6, 116
supra-national institutions 21, 34, 37, 44, 48, 78, 125
system justification theory 74–5, 116

taken-for-granted 34, 48
threats 18, 60, 105, 127, 142
token 25, 42, 44, 56, 77, 117, 128

totalitarianism 19, 125–6, 149, 160
tradition 12, 54, 59–63, 66, 78, 82, 91–2, 98, 100, 104, 106, 116, 129, 140, 148
translation 22, 37, 64, 66, 94–6, 102–3, 109, 129–31, 145, 150
truth 8, 19, 27–8, 32, 42, 48, 61, 67, 79–80, 99, 121, 125, 142, 144

uncertainty 6, 37, 59–60, 74, 79, 110, 116, 140–1, 152
unrethink 7, 15, 55, 98, 116, 124, 136–7, 141–3, 150, 152

violence 4–5, 23, 25, 33, 46, 55–6, 73, 105, 139
vital impetus 65
voice 3, 5, 20, 28, 38, 43, 47, 56, 70, 77, 81, 88, 92, 97–9, 103, 105–6, 110, 115, 121–2, 129, 143–4, 149, 160

www.ingramcontent.com/pod-product-compliance
Ingram Content Group UK Ltd.
Pitfield, Milton Keynes, MK11 3LW, UK
UKHW020046230225
455432UK00021B/288